Kinship and Social Organization in Irian Jaya

A Glimpse of Seven Systems

**Summer Institute of Linguistics and
International Museum of Cultures**

Publication 32

Barbara Jean Moore
Series Editor

Kinship and Social Organization in Irian Jaya

A Glimpse of Seven Systems

Marilyn Gregerson and Joyce Sterner
Editors

A Publication of
Cenderawasih University
Jayapura, Irian Jaya
and
Summer Institute of Linguistics
Dallas, Texas
1997

Copies of this and other publications of the Summer Institute of Linguistics may be obtained from:

> International Academic Bookstore
> Summer Institute of Linguistics
> 7500 West Camp Wisdom Road
> Dallas, Texas 75236
>
> Voice: 972-708-7404
> Fax: 972-708-7433
> E-mail: academic_books@sil.org
> Internet: http://www.sil.org

Contents

Foreword

This publication is the result of a workshop at Cenderawasih University in October and November of 1989, conducted by Marilyn Gregerson and Kenneth Gregerson as part of a cooperative program between Cenderawasih University (UNCEN) and the Summer Institute of Linguistics. It is the third major publication to result from this cooperative program that focuses upon a variety of anthropological studies of the people and cultures of Irian Jaya.

Cenderawasih University sees special publications such as this volume as extremely important at this time in the development of the country of Indonesia, and specifically Irian Jaya. Many changes are taking place at an accelerated rate. It is crucial that the people of Irian Jaya know where they have come from and with this undertanding plan appropriately for the future. As the university plans for the future, this information will help guide us in offering help to our people as they seek to adjust to the changes that will happen as our country, Indonesia, looks toward the future.

Through this publication we also hope to generate, as well as disseminate, relevant information to concerned public and private agencies regarding the cultural context within which developmental activities must somehow be made to operate effectively in the province.

I would like to take this opportunity to express my appreciation to all those who worked long and hard to make this anthropological volume possible. I am especially indebted for the anthropological consultancy and editorial assistance of Marilyn Gregerson, Kenneth Gregerson, and Joyce Sterner. Thanks also are due to the governor of Irian Jaya and his staff.

August Kafiar
Rector, Cenderawasih University

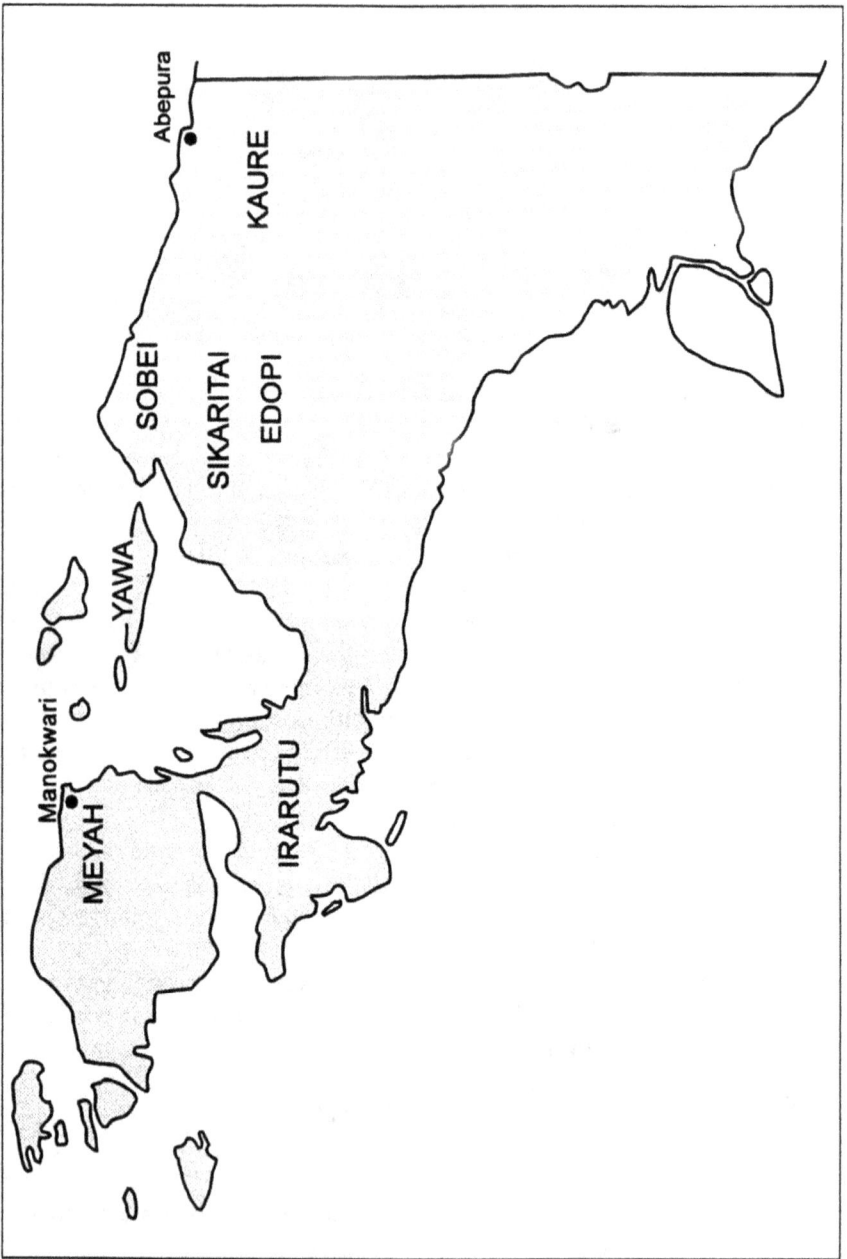

The province of Irian Jaya, Republic of Indonesia.
Ethnic groups described in this volume

Sobei Social Organization: Independence, Competition, and Rivalry

Joyce K. Sterner

People from the Sobei language group have a strong sense of identity and personal worth. Their kinship structure and social organization are subordinate to their central values of independence and personal rights. This configuration creates an atmosphere conducive to clan competition and sibling rivalry. One's position in life is established through lineal relationships but one must struggle to achieve any status among one's siblings on the horizontal or generational level. Although cooperation within the clan does occur in some garden work, house building, hosting social gatherings and feasts, and in the allocation of children, competition characterizes the clan, lineage, and even sibling relationships as they try to establish their clan's primacy of original residency, control the power of nature, preempt resources, and appear superior to others. None of these efforts, however, include manual labor any more than absolutely necessary. Wits and manipulation are the means commonly used to try to get ahead, leaving a residue of bitterness and resentment, which then leads to more competition.

Sobei kinship taxonomy encompasses nine generations. Utmost simplicity characterizes terminology for the top three and bottom three generations. Ego's generation and one generation ascending and descending (the middle three generations) are in some aspects Hawaiian but reveal Iroquois cousin

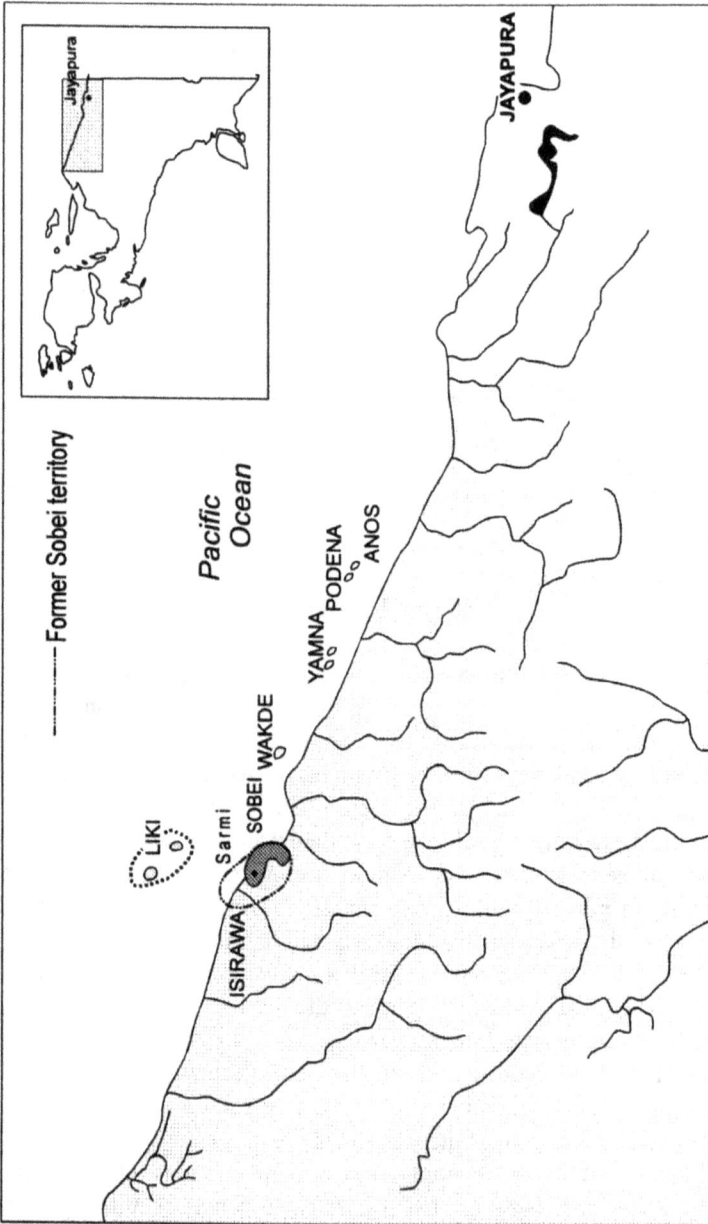

Fig. 1. Language groups on the north coast of Irian Jaya

terminology and relative age discrimination extending through two degrees of collaterality. Terms may reflect ego's sex, the relative age of the linking grandkinsmen, the relative sex of siblings in the upper two generations, and whether alter is a matrilateral or a patrilateral kinsman.

Sobei Language Group

On the north coast of Irian Jaya, Indonesia, approximately two hundred kilometers west of Jayapura, there is a town and government center named Sarmi (see figure 1). The original coastal dwellers there were the Sobei language group, who prefer to be known by the names of their three villages (i.e., a Sawar person, Bagaiserwar person, or Sarmi person). About 2000 in number, these people are related by both language and kinship to those on the islands off the coast, Likiliki, Wakde, Yamna, Anos, and Podena. Grace (1972) classified them as being on the western border of the Oceanic sub-group of Austronesian languages and this has been borne out by subsequent research (Sterner 1987).[1]

The people of Sawar take pride in being the "most superior" of the three villages and in their heritage as the original "ocean people" in the area. They have provided land for the government seat at Sarmi, as well as for the nearby Isirawa village of Mararena, and shared their fresh water supply with Sarmi and Mararena. Sago palms provide the staple food, with each family having its own sago groves as well as land used for gardens. Some also fish

---

[1]This study has been done under the auspices of the Cooperative Work Program between the Summer Institute of Linguistics and Universitas Cenderawasih between the years of 1973 and 1989. My husband, three children, and I lived in the village of Sawar off and on during those years and were adopted into the Ambani-Zeifan clan (Sterner 1981). Even though we moved to the city of Jayapura, we have kept in close touch with the people of Sawar and keep current on events in the village.

I am grateful to Bapak Derek Zeifan and his patient family for answering all my questions about their relationships. Another debt of gratitude I owe is to Marilyn Gregerson who has been my advisor on this paper.

For this study the entire population (about 600 in 1984) of the village of Sawar and all the previous generations they could remember, which totaled five to six generations for each lineage of each clan, were used. Complete family and lineage trees were made, all of the inter- and intraclan adoptions were recorded, as were all the marriages, which totaled 457. An attempt was made to get the *nama tanah* 'earth name' for each resident, although there were a few families excepted. In Sawar when ego is not sure what to call alter, he/she deduces the appropriate term by knowing what his/her father called the other person's parents.

and hunt, although hunting is less and less of an option with the decrease in wild animals due to increasing settlement of the area.

Sawar is a long narrow village, bordered on the north by the ocean, on the south by a cliff fronting a ridge, on the east by the village of Bagaiserwar, and on the west by their cemetery and gardens (see figures 2 and 3) which extend to the Orei river.

There were originally eight patrilineal, exogamous clans which at some point became grouped into three fairly exogamous phratries. Each clan is made up of one to five lineages. In cases where a clan has more than one extant lineage the lineages are ranked for seniority according to the imputed relative ages of the apical ancestors. The actual relationships of the apical ancestors are no longer known, but they are assumed to be brothers. Therefore the eldest member of each lineage calls the eldest members of the other lineages older or younger brother based on the relative ages of their apical ancestors. This older and younger sibling terminology between members of these lineages is continued down through each descending generation, except when there is a closer link between ego and alter.

Sawar traditional religion was animistic with such typical New Guinean features as men's ceremonial houses, sacred triton shells, initiation rites, and sacred flutes. Dutch missionaries arrived in the early 1900s and the Sobei accepted Christianity without hesitation, destroying the men's ceremonial houses and stopping initiations. All Sobei language speakers now consider themselves Christians and members of the denomination which was originally associated with the Dutch Reformed Church, although there are still some animistic beliefs and practices in evidence.

Political organization in Sawar takes place in three different, but somewhat overlapping, spheres. Traditional leadership is provided by the clan elders, the *ondowafi* 'traditional chief', and the *tokoh masyarakat* 'tradition leader'. These positions are held for life and belong to individual clans. Church leadership consists of the church elders, who can be both men and women. Governmental leadership within the village of Sawar is elected by the residents and then approved by the *camat* (top official in the subdistrict) in

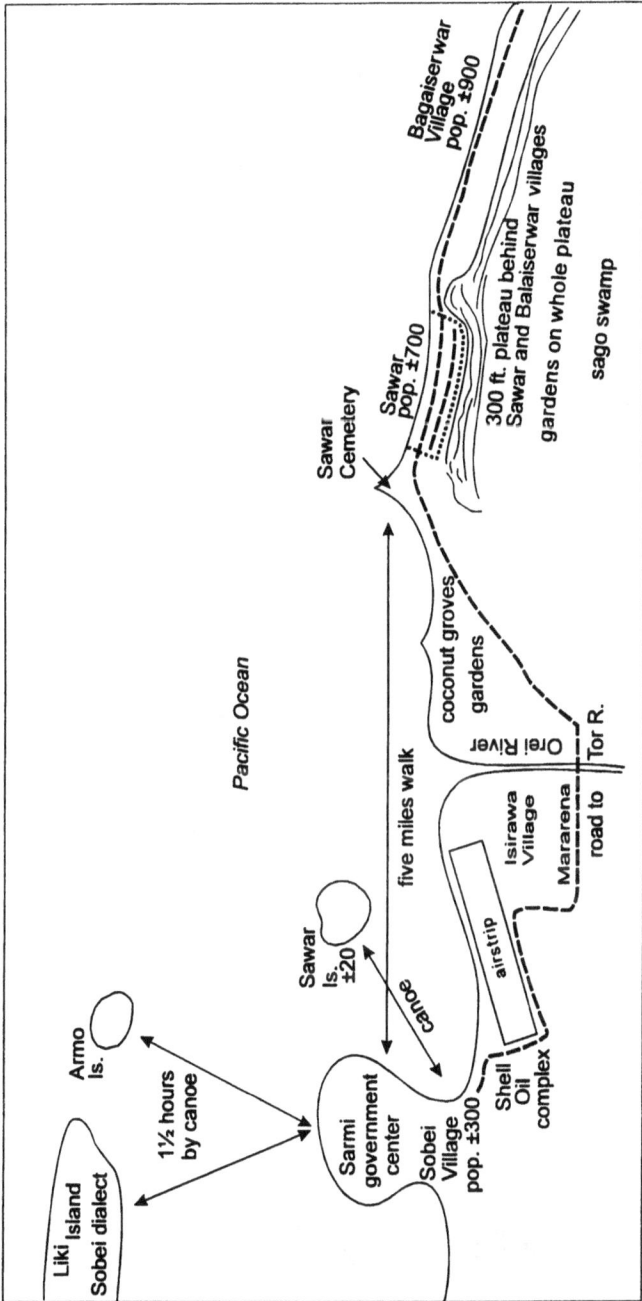

Fig. 2. The Sarmi area

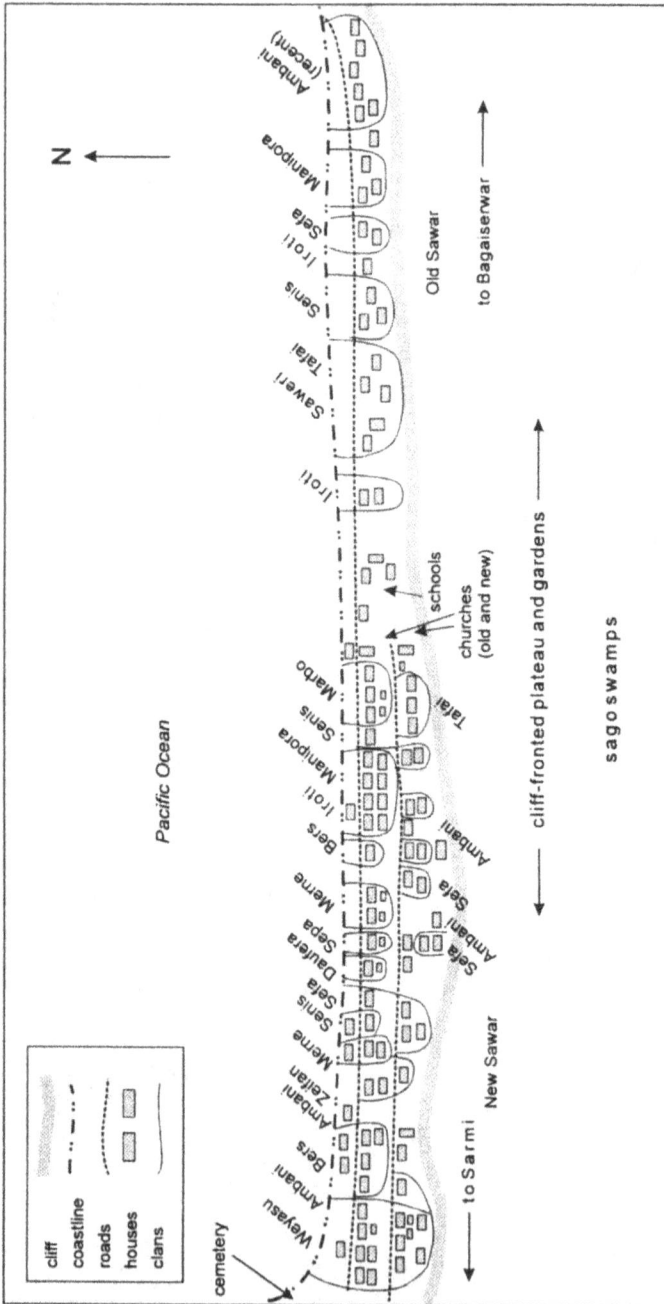

Fig. 3. Map of Sawar village—1984

Sarmi. It consists of a *kepala desa* 'village government head', a village safety officer, a secretary, and a messenger, all of whom are men, and in 1989, were from the Merne,[2] Weyasu, Sefa, and Ambani clans, respectively.

Clans and Competition

Origins

The generally accepted account of the origin of the people of Sawar is as follows.

In the beginning there were only Senis and Iroti[3] at Sawar. (That much is agreed upon by everyone except Zeifan, who says now that he was there too, but the others did not see him.[4]) Weyasu came from the west[5] at Ferkami and claims that he brought sago, river clams, tobacco, vegetables, and a bamboo and flint to make fire. (Iroti and Merne also claim to have brought fire.) Someone else (maybe Bers) came from the sea in sailing canoes and brought the sacred triton shells and other goods. Merne originally came from Arbais, further west, and brought sacred fire which had power to kill people and then raise them up again, which he taught to Senis and Iroti. They all built houses at Sawar and made foraging trips to the islands to kill people.

Weyasu brought them the knowledge that sago could only be produced by having sexual intercourse while making it. Accompanying that knowledge

---

[2]At some point in the past the Merne clan split and is now called variously Merne or Marbo. There seems to be no rhyme nor reason for which name is used other than personal preference of the speaker. Throughout the remainder of this paper the clan will be referred to as Merne/Marbo, the use of slash between the names indicating that they are used interchangeably.

[3]These names are both the current Sawar clan names and the names used for the founders of the clans. Sawar people say that at that time those men only had the one name, or if they had other names they have been lost through time.

[4]There is some controversy regarding the status of Zeifan. At the time of this study, Zeifan was apparently in the process of emerging as a separate clan but was not yet recognized as such by the Ambani, who see Zeifan as a lineage of the Ambani clan. For the purposes of this paper the clan as a whole will be referred to as Ambani-Zeifan, the use of hyphen between the names indicating this unresolved controversy. Any reference to Ambani or Zeifan individually will be to focus on either the original clan founder or the specific family group.

[5]There are people with the family names Merne and Weyasu among the Isirawa and Kwerba language groups from the western interior Sarmi area.

were the taboos that only married couples or brothers and sisters could harvest and process sago together and that men cannot eat sago prepared by their daughters-in-law. Merne brought the clan ancestors together, finding Bers along by the sea, and bringing Sefa from Yamna. Ambani came from the west at Waim, Masip, and from the Orei river.

Merne helped the ancestors start the first men's ceremonial house and taught them singing, the sacred flutes, and other things of power. Only the youngest child (when between the ages of nine and twelve years old) of each family was allowed to be taught in the men's ceremonial house and only the men were allowed to see the sacred flutes, as is typical for New Guinean societies (Oosterval 1961).

Later Manipora came from the south, over the ridge, while Daufera, Tafai, and Saweri came from Bagaiserwar, to the east.

Powers

Each clan has powers over certain realms of nature. The secret words of power are jealously kept by each clan elder, and then passed to the person of his choice, usually his eldest son, when he is near death.

The Merne/Marbo clan continued to be responsible for religious affairs and Merne is also the name of the original creator culture hero. His name is used in a modern Sobei hymn used in the Reformed church, although he is not considered a god. Merne had power over the sun and the people of the Merne/Marbo clan today still claim they can bring about continuous daylight for three consecutive days, or can prolong daylight through the night hours.[6]

In 1989 two Merne/Marbo men were teachers in Sawar and another was the *kepala desa* 'village government head'. One of the teachers was the head of the Merne/Marbo clan, who alone knew the many Merne secret words of power.

The phratry composed of the Ambani-Zeifan and Weyasu clans is descended from the union between a crocodile and a human, and has the power to control crocodiles and snakes. As is customary for totems, they are not allowed to eat crocodiles, snakes, or sailfish. In 1979, the Isirawa people living along the Ferkami River were frequently being attacked by crocodiles in the river, and three to four people a year were being eaten. The military in Sarmi intended to bomb out the crocodiles, but Derek Zeifan told them he could handle the problem without bombs. Together with Abner Weyasu (clan

---

[6]Piethein Zeifan, Derek's son, says he has personally witnessed this delay of nightfall.

elder) and Harius Zeifan (Derek's younger brother), he went up to the Ferkami River and said the words of power over the crocodiles there to stop them from eating any more people. No one has subsequently been eaten at that river.[7] When a crocodile appeared in the Orei River close to Sawar, Derek's son, Isai, attacked it and killed it with a knife in a wrestling match, an unusual event considered highly significant in light of his clan heritage.

The Iroti clan can control fire and certain fish. The Bers clan can control the ocean spirits and thus the ocean floor. If a Bers boat has a problem, they call on these spirits which then make the ocean floor rise up so they can get out of their boat and fix it right there. Anyone else would drown if they got out of the boat. The Sefa clan can control the growth of sago trees, making them grow either quickly or slowly. They used to bury people near sago trees to speed up the growth. The Manipora clan can control any pigs, calling them for slaughter or for penning. They can also summon people by mind control from great distances and they will arrive within a day.[8] The Senis clan has control over all social affairs and one of their elders is always the *ondowafi*, 'traditional chief', a position held for life.

Status

Each original clan has a relative ranking in the village which corresponds closely to the history and powers listed above. In descending order they are: Merne/Marbo, Weyasu, Iroti, Senis, Ambani-Zeifan, Bers, Sefa, and Manipora.

Locations

The location of the clans' lands within and around the village of Sawar correlates with the directions of their original arrival (see figures 3 and 4). The Ambani-Zeifan and Weyasu clans are at the west end of the village,

---

[7]One of our coworkers told us that, to her knowledge, the military had come and bombed and that was the reason the crocodiles were no longer taking people. No one in Bapak Derek's family has mentioned this event and we do not know for sure what really happened as that co-worker was not present at the time.

[8]Derek Zeifan, although an Ambani and not a Manipora clan member, also claimed to use this mind control on one occasion when he was booked to fly to the village on a certain date but wanted to go two days earlier. He said he caused the flight to be rescheduled by mind control and went on the desired date. Presumably he had this power because of his position as *tokoh masyarakat* 'tradition leader' of Sawar.

Family Name	Original Clan	Origin	Sawar Location	Total Lineages	Extant Lineages
Ambani	x	slightly west	west end	5	4
Zeifan		Ambani	west end	1	1
Weyasu	x	interior Sarmi/west	west end	12	4
Bers	x	ocean	west/ocean side	3	1
Daufera		villages east	eastern end	2	1
Manipora	x	south	central	4	2
Sefa	x	?	both east and west but toward center	4	3
Iroti	x	original	central	6	3
Merne	x	west/Arbais	central	2	2
Marbo		Merne	central	1	1
Senis	x	original	east/central	4	3
Tafai		east/ Bagaiserwar	east/central	1	1
Sarem		east/central	central	1	1
Saweri		east/ Bagaiserwar	east	2	1
Kantoli		married into Bers	west/ocean Bers land	1	1

Fig. 4. Clan origins, locations, and lineages

having arrived from the west. Merne/Marbo, Iroti, and Senis, as the earliest residents, are scattered around the central part of the village together with Manipora, who arrived from the south. Bers is located near the waterfront toward the west end of the village and also on the small Sawar island in Sarmi Bay. Saweri, Tafai, Daufera, and Manipora are scattered but live mostly near the eastern end of the village, toward the village of Bagaiserwar. Sefa houses are in the central part next to Merne/Marbo houses. But, as will be explained below in the section on residence, house locations can be dictated more by population pressures at a given time than by traditional ideals.

Phratries

Though the clans have long been grouped into relatively exogamous phratries, no one knows how this arrangement came about. The number of
phratries has remained constant, but the number of clans within the phratries
has increased over time. Three clans have subdivided and outsiders have
moved in from various places to add other family names. There are now
fifteen clan or family names in Sawar. In an attempt to simplify the situation,
the government has declared that the phratries should be considered as single
clans and should use one clan name each. To date no move is being made
to follow this edict.

At present the three phratries are composed of the following clan groupings:

1. Ambani-Zeifan, Weyasu
2. Bers, Daufera, Manipora, Sefa
3. Iroti, Merne/Marbo, Senis, Tafai, Saweri

Kantoli and Sarem have moved in, becoming integrated into the Sawar
community, but are not yet included in any of the three phratries, although
Sarem is considered a subdivision of the Tafai clan by some people.

Some Sawar people say that the Saweri clan were part of the Senis clan
until after World War II when they split off. Ambani and Zeifan split when
Sarama Ambani changed his name from Ambani to Zeifan, around 1917.
This division resulted possibly because he married Teb'oya Ambani from his
own clan and wanted to legitimize the action. This possibility is not denied
by anyone, and is supported by the fact that only his own children have kept
the name change and there is still much substitution of the Ambani name
among the Zeifan people. Just before Sarama's son, Derek, died in 1987, he
told his sons the above-mentioned story for the first time, that Zeifan was in
Sawar originally with Iroti and Senis, but that they did not see him. This
story seems to be both an attempt to justify the clan split and also to gain
status above Ambani, who would then have been a later arrival in Sawar. It
does not explain why Zeifan "pretended" to be an Ambani for so long and
will certainly do nothing to smooth already poor relationships between the
Ambani and Zeifan families.

The Merne/Marbo split is not remembered by those living now, but they
all say they were originally Merne, and some who should be Marbo by
lineage call themselves Merne by choice.

Although Iroti and Merne/Marbo are said to be grouped with the clans following them, the figures in table 1 show that fifteen of the forty-six Iroti men (nearly 33 percent) took wives from the other four clans, as did nine of the thirty-four Merne/Marbo men (more than 26 percent) . Therefore Iroti and Merne/Marbo appear to stand alone more as clans since they do not follow the customary rule of phratry exogamy. For this reason they are separated on the chart.

Sawar people do say that, although the clans and phratries should be exogamous, the nearness of the relationship within the clan is the more important criterion for determining whether marriage is permissable. However, it is clear from the chart that exogamy is an important consideration. Sawar people may not marry their siblings or their cross-cousins, nor anyone with their parents' clan names. There are some more distant cousins they may marry, but which degrees of collaterality are legal and which are not is unclear and apparently no rules are strictly followed. The rule of individual independence and rights dominates the marriage patterns. One marriage recorded was between half-siblings and another was between cross-cousins, with no apparent shame resulting, although both had the camouflage of adoption into different clans. In these cases the sociological reckoning would appear to have priority over biological reckoning.

Ignoring the Iroti and Merne/Marbo marriage statistics, there are seventeen marriages within the phratries which appear to depart from the rule of phratry exogamy and nine of them occurred within the phratry composed of Ambani-Zeifan and Weyasu. Of those nine only three had possible extenuating circumstances, such as being adopted from another clan or from outside. The other eight exceptions to the exogamous groupings were from the phratry which includes Daufera, Manipora, Bers, and Sefa, and six of those eight had adoption or outside lineage "excuses." Adopted children are allowed to choose their ultimate clan allegiance for themselves whenever they wish.

It is clear from the table that there are no real preferential marriage patterns followed among the clans or phratries, which confirms what the people say.

HUSBANDS' CLAN	WIVES' CLAN													
	Ambani	Zeian	Weyasu	Bers	Daufera	Manipora	Sefa	Iroti	Merne/ Marbo	Senis	Tafai	Saweri	outside	total
Ambani	–	–	4	5	1	–	7	9	2	4	1	6	7	46
Zeifan	1	–	2	4	–	1	5	3	3	1	1	1	4	26
Weyasu	–	2	–	6	1	3	8	6	5	6	6	1	7	51
Bers	2	–	9	–	1	–	–	4	5	4	1	–	1	27
Daufera	–	–	2	–	–	–	–	3	–	–	–	–	1	6
Manipora	2	–	3	–	2	–	4	6	1	2	4	2	5	31
Sefa	9	–	10	1	–	–	–	6	5	3	4	2	2	42
Iroti	7	3	4	4	3	2	6	–	3	5	6	1	2	46
Merne/ Marbo	3	–	8	3	–	3	4	6	–	2	–	1	4	34
Senis	2	1	8	3	–	3	9	3	3	–	–	–	6	38
Tafai	2	1	–	1	–	1	1	5	2	–	–	–	3	16
Saweri	3	–	3	3	1	3	1	2	–	–	–	–	4	20
outside	4	10	11	6	1	6	1	9	15	6	2	3	–	74
total	35	17	64	36	10	22	46	62	44	33	25	17	46	457

Table 1. Clan marriage patterns

Social Traits

Each clan has traits which give insights into the Sawar culture and the changes which are taking place. For example, more than one-fourth of the marriages documented in this study were between Sawar people and outsiders. No stigma is attached to marrying outsiders, nor is it particularly desirable to marry within Sawar clans. In fact, Sawar people are proud of marrying outsiders, and while there is some regret at gradually losing their own language and culture, no one expresses the opinion that this could be changed if people would only marry within the village. But it is interesting to note which clans most frequently marry outside the Sawar clan system.

The value that Sawar people hold most dear is personal independence. They do not work together well, neither as a community nor as phratries, clans, or lineages. One's own needs and desires are usually given the highest priority. Having said that, it is still instructive to consider the ethos of each of the clans.

The Merne/Marbo clan is the most "progressive" clan. More of their people have higher education than any other clan and they hold more wage-earning jobs than any other clan. This idea is consistent with their position as the most powerful clan and their having been responsible for both religious and secular education in previous years. They also have a relatively high proportion, fifteen out of forty-four or about 34 percent, of women who have married outside men (see table 1) and four of their thirty-four men, about 12 percent, have married outside women. Although the figures for outside marriage are not the highest of all the clans, they are quite near the top, which further illustrates their progressive outlook.

Ambani-Zeifan is the next most outward oriented. They have had the most men marry outside women and have adopted the most assorted outsiders as family members (see table 2). They have also given the most children away to siblings who had no children. This clan seems to flout the Sawar societal norms more than any other clan. They have the only recorded intraclan marriage and the most unexplained intraphratry marriages. Polygyny is allowed but is considered to cause economic difficulties and conflicts between the wives. The only two cases in recent history are in Ambani-Zeifan. One of these is an Ambani man who has two separate households and lives with the second wife. Isai Zeifan, who knifed the crocodile, married two women from other language groups and had them both in one household, then divorced the one who could not have children and has since taken another second wife, again from another language group. Derek Zeifan, Isai's father, and his wife, a Merne/Marbo woman, flouted the norms in another way. She refused to have any woman attend her in childbirth, so her husband alone helped her in each of her fourteen deliveries.

The elders of the Ambani and Zeifan lineages demonstrate a great deal of animosity and bitterness toward each other, complaining of ill treatment at each other's hands and avoiding associating with each other. Since Derek (the head of the Zeifan lineage) died, the leaders of the other lineages have been taking his land away from his children. The children attribute this action to jealousy because, they say, Zeifan ancestors were diligent in planting gardens, sago, and coconuts whereas Ambani ancestors did nothing and now they have nothing.

Family Name	Marriages Documented (Males only)	Relatives Adopted into Clan	Children Given from Clan	Outside Adoptions into Clan
Ambani	46	8	10	2
Zeifan	26	6	5	1
Weyasu	51	4	2	2
Bers	27	3	5	0
Daufera	6	1	2	0
Manipora	31	7	3	1
Sefa	42	6	3	1
Iroti	46	12	7	5
Merne/ Marbo	34	4	5	1
Senis	38	2	6	1
Tafai	13	1	1	0
Saweri	20	0	2	0
Sarem	3	0	0	0
outsiders	74	0	3	0
total	457	54	54	14

Table 2. Clan propensities to adopt

The *tokoh masyarakat* 'traditional head' was Derek Zeifan, and the village messenger was an Ambani man. Another Ambani was the driver for the oil company that was based in Sarmi. Although the position of 'traditional head' is "inherited," this position was not given to Derek's son after his death but to an Ambani leader. These men are powerful but do not get along with each other.

One Iroti lineage ancestor had no children of his own and adopted a boy from the Yamna language group as well as a whole family of Isirawa orphan children who eventually all became valued Iroti clan members. (One or two Sawar people have married Isirawa people, but generally the Isirawa are considered to be inferior people.) Iroti has also given more children to other more distant relatives within their clan and to other clans than any clan except Ambani-Zeifan (see table 2). The Iroti clan is rather quiet and unobtrusive, not concerned in village leadership or with conflicts, even though they were one of the original clans.

Bers only has one extant lineage. They are the least educated in the village, with almost none of their children attending school. They have more fishermen than other clans, as befits their origins and powers.

Tafai is a small clan which still has many ties with Bagaiserwar people as do Saweri, Daufera, Manipora, and Sarem. None of these "immigrant" clans have the status that the original Sawar clans have, but the Tafai clan has intermarried with higher status clans and so gained in respect. One of the most notorious sorcerers is a Tafai, and another is a Saweri, which is worth noting, since sorcery is normally attributed to other language groups and these two clans are considered "immigrants."

The Weyasu clan has suffered the most attrition in terms of lineages. The oldest Weyasu man is the Sawar safety officer. There is another Weyasu man who is a *mantri* 'village health official', and another who is a school teacher. They are the second highest clan in status and do have power in the village.

Relationships and Rivalry

Positioning by Lineal Relationships

A Sawar person's identity, position, and status is largely determined by the clan and lineage into which he is born. Subsequent adoptive heritage may determine inheritance, name, and residence, but birth heritage determines his life status and dictates his position in the various clan and lineage quarrels.

Ancestors and Descendants. Ancestors provide a Sawar person with roots and origin status in the community, and establish his relationships to the other clans and lineages, but the individual identity of these distant ancestors is not important. Future descendants are even less important to Sawar people, who live emphatically in the present. Although some Sawar people are foresighted enough to plant trees for posterity, others are not. Some Sawar people have sold their family land to gain cash, although others do recognize the folly of this action.

Parents. Kinsmen of the parental generation are all considered caretakers in various degrees for ego, including collateral kin to the second degree. However, behavioral distinctions are made among those called "father" and "mother." The biological parents are expected to provide food, shelter, clothing, training, and discipline for their children. Others carrying the parental classification may help in time of need, give small items on request, take over when children are orphaned, and give gifts and shelter at times, but do not carry basic responsibility for the child, nor can they punish by beating. In Sawar, personal preference and temperament do more to determine relationships than societal norms, and mother's brothers, while ideally caretakers and helpers, have been known to defraud and steal from their sister's children.

Caretaking in Lineal Relationships

It is a pattern of life that older people take care of younger ones until they themselves become of such advanced age that the younger ones must start caring for them. In Sawar society as in many others, degrees of relationship also indicate degrees of caretaking responsibility.

Children. Children are a valued resource to Sawar people. They serve as helpers in the home, sago processors, comforters, hedges against loneliness, and old-age social security. The parent-child relationship is the least stressful relationship in Sawar culture. There is no competition and little observable conflict. If the children do not obey while small, they may be physically forced to comply, but later on very few repercussions follow disobedience. Beatings are rare and if the child can escape, other relatives will help shield him from the angry parent. Parents make compensation sadly but willingly for their children's misdemeanors or crimes if they have the wherewithal to do so, but children often disregard parental advice as to marriage, divorce, and problems.

If children go away to work, they are expected to bring back money for their parents. If they do not, verbal disapproval and shame are the only consequences, and they do not appear to make much difference to the erring children, even though shame in this type of culture is normally a powerful force. It is expected that young people will sow some wild oats, and many do. However, once there are children from a union, most settle down and conform to the normal expectations for adults in the society.

Grandchildren. Grandchildren are valued highly by the grandparents and are a comfort and a real resource of help and provision for them. Sawar grandparents indulge their grandchildren but also play a secondary training role for them. As the grandparents get older, one or more of their grandchildren will live with them to help with errands, food procurement and preparation, and other jobs. This assistance also takes caretaking responsibility off the children's parents who must work to provide for their own families. Widows and widowers often live with their children, who may build them a separate house nearby.

Special Lineal Functions

Inheritance. Inheritance of garden land, sago plots, house land, and sometimes stands of coconut trees, is patrilineal and equally divided among all the sons. They are part of clan land, passed down in lineages and families. However, if daughters marry outsiders and stay in the village, they may also receive an equal portion.

If there are no male heirs, or no heirs at all, the last member of a lineage may designate someone from another lineage to inherit his land. This practice is inevitably a source of conflict with others who want the land, particularly if they feel they have more right than the one who was chosen. The topographical limitations of Sawar leave very little room for expansion, and this causes much competition over land allocation and many adjustments in living patterns.

Adopted outsiders may also be given garden land and a place for a house of their own. For example, Piter Ambani had been adopted from another language group and married a Weyasu woman. In his old age, with no male heirs, he selected Derek Zeifan to be his heir. Derek named his fourth son to inherit Piter's property. However, Piter's Sawar land had been loaned to him by the Weyasu clan upon his marriage, so Derek's son's inheritance was in Piter's village of birth; Piter's Sawar land reverted to the Weyasu clan upon his death.

Derek Zeifan (1919–1987) had five living sons and four daughters. It is instructive to see how he, an ambitious but very tradition-minded man, allocated his property and tasks among his children. His first son received the clan words of power. He also now has the same church responsibilities Derek had, although that is more by inclination than inheritance. Derek arranged the second son's marriage in a very atypical autocratic fashion and probably had a hand in the son's joining the provincial navy and living away from home. The third son Derek gave to his childless sister and her Muslim husband. The fourth son received the Ambani inheritance as mentioned above and was told to continue Derek's work of teaching us the language and culture. The fifth son took over Derek's house land and dwelling, although this action was not due to any known tendency to ultimogeniture, but rather to family circumstances. Derek's daughters all married outsiders and those choosing to live permanently in Sawar received some of his village land, garden land, sago plots, and coconut tree stands.

Exigencies due to the number of family members resident in Sawar have a great deal to do with land allocation within families. Little, if any, is reserved for the person who moves to another location, but their portion is used by their near kinsmen, who have the right to do so. Anyone using even one sago tree without right or permission is provoking a serious quarrel. Most Sawar disputes are over land, food resources, spouses, or children.

Adoptions. In the pattern of Sawar adoptions, children are given or loaned to parental relatives who need them, sometimes with a letter of permission from the unrelated parent, though often not. Children can even be loaned to outsiders who want them or who need help in their families, although this action signifies special friendship and obligation. Sawar people distinguish verbally at times between children who are loaned to help and those who are truly given, but often it is difficult to formally define the situation.

Among the five generations of Sawar people studied there were more than fifty adoptions within Sawar clans. Fourteen people were adopted from outside locations and lived in Sawar, took Sawar names, and married Sawar people according to traditional clan marriage patterns. These outside adoptions were all from the earliest generations recorded. More recent adoptees from outside have not married into Sawar clans, nor have they changed their family names to that of the adoptive clan.

Within Sawar, adoptions are frequent but appear to be decreasing. Children have been given to others for the following reasons: death of a parent, divorce or remarriage of a parent, in lieu of the bride price, because the parents had too many children, or because the parents felt sorry for someone with no children, no sons, or no daughters (see table 3). Most of those given out of pity were given to blood siblings, but some were also given to cousins, parents' siblings, parents themselves, or by parents to their childless children. Upon the death of the adopted person, the birth family should pay compensation to the adoptive family for their care and nurturing of the adoptee.

The adoptive child is at liberty to take the name of his real parents or his adoptive parents. Those adopted as older children usually keep their birth name unless they are particularly fond of their second parents and want to please them. In cases where several siblings have been adopted out due to the death of a parent, some have taken one family name and some another. But Sawar people remember both biological and adoptive parents and relationships can be maintained in both lineages, if different. As mentioned above, some of the marriages which seem "illegal" in terms of birth into exogamous phratries are "legal" by adoptive lines, and vice versa.

The totals given for table 3 are not consistent with the total number of adoptions analyzed because there is considerable overlap in the reasons given for adoptions. For example, parents who are dying tend to give their children to relatives with no children, or when the levirate is followed a man may marry his deceased brother's wife so that the children follow their mother to the second husband. Thus one adoption may be entered under more than one row. The columns indicate which category of relative received the child, and the rows give the reasons for the child's move to the new family. These reasons may be clarified as follows: (1) from pity for a family with no children, (2) death of one or both parent(s), (3) divorce of parents, (4) given in lieu of bride price payment, or (5) unknown causes. These figures do not include outsiders who were adopted into Sawar clans,

Reason for adoption	True Sibling	Collateral Sibling	Parental Relative	Subsequent Spouse	Unknown	total
No children	15	3	4		2	24
Death	10	3	1	14		28
Divorce	2		3			5
Brideprice	1		2			3
Unknown	3		1		3	7
total	31	6	11	14	2	67

Table 3. Analysis of Sawar adoptions

as those seem to be motivated by other considerations, except for the one
Iroti man who had no children.

Naming. As is typical for much of Irian Jaya, Sawar people have three
types of names: their clan name, Christian name, and *nama tanah* 'earth
name' or 'traditional name'. The oldest two generations studied had only
traditional names. The next two generations had both Christian and traditional names. Some of the newest generation are being given two Christian
names as well as their traditional and clan names. A person may have a
number of traditional names, several Sawar people have three. Traditional
names are of three varieties: (1) names of ancestors; (2) names of places,
animals, things, or spirits significant to the parents; and (3) names which
have no special significance. A number of people have traditional names
with phonetic similarities to their Christian names (e.g., *Fitoria, Fitou*).

Without extensive tabulations, it appears that no more than three people
have the same traditional name and those names which are repeated are of
ancestors, not places or things. People who have the same name call each
other *naneton,* which has no other meaning. Those who have an ancestral
traditional name are descendants of the ancestor named with a slight majority
of names taken from the paternal side. Outside people adopted into Sawar
families are given traditional names, usually names belonging to ancestors or
other family members.[9] It is often the grandparents of a child who give the
traditional names while the parents select the Christian names, which are
then officially given at the child's baptism into the Christian Reformed
Church.

Traditional names are for use within the household or nuclear family, and
are basically a parental or sibling prerogative. It is a sign of the distance in the
marriage bond that husbands and wives do not use traditional names for each
other, but only Christian names. As soon as a person marries, his family
begins to use teknonymic terms instead of personal names. A child's spouse

---

[9]Our own family members were given traditional names by Bapak Derek and his wife.
My husband was given two names, one of which was the same as Derek's younger
brother, Harius, and the other a name of an Ambani ancestor, Derek's grandfather's older
brother. I was given the name of one of their daughters, which was the name of a spirit
that Derek's wife saw one day on the beach. Our first son was given three names: the
first one belonging to a very close friend who was related to both Derek and his wife;
another name meaning a type of leaf; and another having no particular meaning. Our
second son was given the name of another of Derek's sons. Our daughter was given the
name of a different leaf. We were frequently called by these names within the family.

is called "so-and-so's spouse," and as soon as a child is born both parents become "so-and-so's mother (or father)," frequently even to their own parents and siblings. However, other terms of address may also be used, as described in the sandwich filling subsection of the Sandwich Kinship Structure section.

The kin term selected for use is often keyed to the reason for addressing the person. For example, if a person wants something from a relative he will use the descriptive term which most specifically delineates rights and obligations, whereas if he merely wants the attention of the other person he will more likely use teknonymic or generational terms.

Avoidance Relationships

Avoidance customs characterize the relationships of ego to his spouse's parents and to his children's spouses. It is forbidden to pronounce their names or even say a word which is homophonous with the name, although some modern Sawar people will say the name if no other Sawar person can hear them. The traditional penalty for breaking this taboo is not known, but it is definitely considered rude to say their names. The term of reference for those relationships is *dawon* 'taboo relationship', but the terms of address for spouse's parents are *teman* 'father' and *tinan* 'mother' or a teknonymic term. Children's spouses are addressed with teknonymic terms. Daughters-in-law may not serve any food or water to their parents-in-law. Sons-in-law must serve their parents-in-law until the bride price is paid. There are no joking relationships.

These in-law taboos make it easier for the individual nuclear families within one household to eat separately from each other, usually sequentially. However, this may lead to problems over food sharing. One sibling may get the sago, another the vegetables and another the protein, but there may not be enough of everything to go around to all the families.[10]

Paramount Generational Relationships

In ego's generation, siblingship and marriage provide the closest ties and obligations, and also the most stress and competition. The sibling tie is the

---

[10]We observed that the head of the household received the best food (usually the protein) and if there was enough then it was shared with the others. Derek Zeifan's household contained twenty-one people in 1984, making food supply for everyone difficult.

next closest after parent-child, and the brother-brother dyad is the closest sibling tie. The children of two brothers are considered to be "from the same womb," but these same brothers may be continually jockeying with each other for position and status. Nevertheless, Sawar siblingship and lineage structural dynamics would appear to be consonant with Kelly's analysis of the Etoro social structure in spite of the sibling competition and rivalry, which he did not find (Kelly 1974). Marriage is usually based on mutual attraction between age-mates but also has the potential to be an arena for conflict between spouses and also affines.

Sibling Rivalry. Sawar siblings, particularly brothers, express rivalry primarily in terms of authority and status. Younger brothers try to prove that they have more authority over their siblings than do their elder brothers. Elder brothers disparage their younger siblings as irresponsible and flighty. Both male and female siblings are quick to point out any discrepancies between ideal behavior and any sibling's actual behavior. They are equally quick to rationalize and excuse their own behavior, asserting their independence and right to make decisions which may go against the wishes of parents and older siblings. Siblings may share possessions, but usually do so with reluctance, and sometimes steal from each other or use up resources left with them for safekeeping. They tend to act as if "What's mine is mine, and what's yours is mine, too." Few repercussions attend such affairs except for hard feelings, which lead to more of the same behavior later.[11]

When a married sibling (usually a brother) is presumed upon overly much for shelter and food, putting a financial burden on his family, his spouse will make scenes, even to throwing out the visitors with a great show of bad temper. This action does not improve relationships and gives the spouse a bad reputation, but it serves to protect the surface sibling relationship while also saving the family finances. Derek Zeifan's son admitted that he had used this strategy on a number of occasions.

Sibling Cooperation. Siblings do cooperate in two main areas: food procurement and preparation, and the sharing of children. Brothers and sisters, or husbands and wives, will go to process sago together, the men chopping

---

[11]This competition and rivalry has not been noted in other descriptions of New Guinean cultures as far as I know. Oosterval mentioned this type of competition on the Tor River, but only between villages and language groups (1961:190). Even in Dobuan society, where sorcery was prevalent (Fortune 1963), people felt safest with their consanguineal kin.

down the tree and pounding, while the women do the washing and kneading. If a sago tree is already chopped and split open, sisters may go together to get sago. Siblings will also, however reluctantly, share tobacco, betel nut, food, and money with each other if asked.

If someone does not have any children, a sibling of either the wife or husband will likely give them a child, sometimes more than one or one from each side. Children also move casually from one of their parents' siblings to another for residence depending on events, school needs, or lack of room at home.

Marriage

The marriage relationship takes third place in precedence and emotional closeness, following the parent-child bond and the sibling bond. It is a relationship usually chosen by the participants, but one which is focused primarily on procreation. Both spouses help to care for and train the children. Even though the children are linked irrevocably to the father's lineage, they are given away just as frequently to the mother's side as to the father's, showing the strength of the generational sibling bond in opposition to the lineal bond.

In the three oldest Sawar generations studied, there was some evidence of marriage patterns which, if norms at one time, have totally disappeared in current Sawar generations. One of them is sister exchange, which is still common in the Sarmi area among the Berik, Kwerba, and Isirawa language groups (Oosterval 1961; Erickson 1976). There are eleven clear cases of sister exchange (some collateral) and two others possible. There are also three cases where two brothers married two sisters. Moreover, there is some evidence for a former levirate/sororate tendency as eleven men married their brother's wife after his death and three men married their wife's sister, also sequentially as far as can be determined.

Marriage Preparations. Marriages are initiated either by the parents or the young people themselves, and negotiations are entered into by the parents with patrilineal clan elders acting as intermediaries. The meetings to make the arrangements are quite formal and are arranged in advance. Each party hosts one meeting and provides food for it. In one case where the bride's parents were not truly in favor of the match, they did not come to the prearranged meeting at the groom's parents' home, even though they had hosted their meeting already. This absence signified that the arrangement was off.

The two rites of passage payments due at the time of the wedding, the "milk price" and the bride price, must be decided upon and enough collected by the groom and his lineage to pay at least the milk price (see Rites of Passage Payments below).

Sexual relations normally precede the wedding ceremony, and although promiscuity is frowned upon, having several relationships is not necessarily considered promiscuous. Marriage relationships may be entered into and left quite easily as long as there are no children. The milk price can be returned if it has already been paid at the wedding ceremony.

If the young people want to marry but the parents are not willing, they may run off together and sanction will be granted after the first child is born. If parents try to force an unwanted marriage on their child, there may be initial obedience with a divorce later. In one case the daughter went through with the ceremony but ran away three days later and refused to live with the man. She later married another man and has stayed with him. Derek Zeifan and his wife arranged a marriage for their absent second son with a girl from Bagaiserwar. Without telling him, they took the girl into their home, announced to everyone that she was his wife, and after several weeks sent her alone (highly unusual) on a boat to the town where the son was living with a letter telling him of their wishes. He took her in, but after a few weeks sent her back to the village saying he did not want her. However, she was already pregnant and after the baby was born, he accepted her and the child and they have continued as man and wife.

Marriage Ceremony. Weddings are not usually held in the church due to the fact that the Dutch missionaries who evangelized Sawar taught that marriages in the church were irrevocable. In order to have a way out, the people marry almost entirely with traditional betel nut exchange ceremonies in their homes. The groom and his friends go to the bride's home and get her, taking her to the groom's house for the ceremony with a whole procession of the bride's family, friends, and honored guests, as is typical for other coastal groups in Irian Jaya (Merrifield et al. 1983:237, 266).

The ceremony includes addresses by various clan elders, family members, and village authorities as to the meaning of marriage and responsibilities involved in it. The amounts and items in the milk price and bride price (if paid) are publicly announced and sometimes displayed. Then the couple feed each other betel nut with lime, which comprises the actual wedding ceremony.

Guests bring money gifts which are put in a special plate under a napkin. Following the ceremony a meal is served to all the guests, usually plates of rice topped by meat and noodles. Currently, this is often followed by the drinking of beer or liquor, sometimes excessively. This ritual is also becoming a common practice among coastal Irian groups (Merrifield et al. 1983:238, 266).

Marriage Residence. Residence of a newly married couple is ideally patrilocal, unless the bride price has not been paid. In that case the couple will live with the bride's family and the groom will serve them in any way they ask until the bride price has been paid or the first child has been given to them. At that time they may move out and start their own home. But house room, land availability, needs of aging relatives, and compatibility all have higher priority than the ideal in determining residence, and any sequence of residence is possible.

Marriage Roles. Roles in marriage are clear-cut, but not ironclad. Women prepare food, collect vegetables, get firewood, pound and carry sago, carry water, assist in childbirth, take care of the children most of the time, and fish along the beach.

Men work with wood—making canoes, building houses, or logging. They also fish from canoes, hunt, dig, chop, pound sago, climb coconut trees, gather house materials, and deal with authorities.

Both men and women can be elders in the church, although women plan the social events and men plan new church construction, etc. Only men are village leaders in any secular capacity. Men are the ones who hold the secret words of power in their possession and now are the ones who do most of the sorcery. There is no evidence of the hostility or opposition between men and women that seems prevalent in some New Guinea cultures (Kelly 1974; Brown and Buchbinder 1976).

Marriage Relationship. The marriage relationship imitates the society as a whole. The husband is boss and heads up the household, keeping his wife in line with beatings if necessary. He may also be kind, however, helping his wife with the children and even with cooking and washing if she is ill. This type of helpfulness is generally admired by the community.

Usually women attend each other during childbirth, although a more trained woman usually comes to cut the cord after delivery. Husbands do not normally attend births. However, as mentioned earlier, Derek Zeifan attended his wife alone, by her choice, when she delivered their children.

Wife beating is permissible unless the wife is sick or pregnant, in which case others will intervene. This oversight is particularly the responsibility of the village safety officer who may then beat the offending husband.

If women are extremely angry at their husbands during a fight, they may strip off their clothes to humiliate him in front of the onlookers. Intervention only occurs in husband-wife fights if personal injury is imminent. Spouses will more often attack the house and knock down walls, etc., thus symbolically injuring each other. Marital fights may be caused by incompatibility with the parents-in-law, by lack of the husband's ability to provide well for his wife, by either one's slighting of the children such as not giving them food, or by unfaithfulness, real or imagined.

Marriage/Divorce. Most divorce occurs among young couples with no children and is caused by incompatibility (frequent fights and beatings) or unfaithfulness. Children from a divorced marriage are usually given away, either to the wife's parents or siblings. Men generally do not want to care for children other than their own, although in one case of unfaithfulness where the husband still wanted the wife, he claimed the baby. When a child is expected to be born out of wedlock, the girl's father will investigate the identity of the baby's father. If the baby's father refuses to marry the girl or claim the baby, then another family is looked for to claim the baby. Once claimed, the baby is no longer considered illegitimate. Two unmarried Sawar girls chose to keep their babies and those babies were considered illegitimate until the girls later married.

Rites of Passage

Payments. There are four rites of passage payments in Sawar. First, the *sisorani weyan* 'milk price' is paid at the time of the wedding by the husband and his family (on behalf of the wife) to the bride's parents' cross-siblings and their children. If they are generous they may divide it among other relatives as well. This payment is obligatory at the wedding, and as its name suggests, is to compensate the bride's parents' cross-siblings' clans for the loss of her nurturing ability. The payment usually consists of a combination of money, cloth, and dishes, but the amount is voluntary. There has been no intimation that bargaining or negotiating takes place in regard to the amount of these payments, but we have often heard complaints about stinginess in making payments or sharing of payments received.

A second payment, also ideally (but seldom actually) made at the time of the wedding, is the *mesne* 'bride price'. It is also paid by the husband and his family, but to the bride's father and brothers, presumably to compensate for the loss of the daughter's progeny and work in the home. If the groom cannot afford this payment he is in virtual bondage to his parents-in-law until it is paid. A possible alternative, which is still being taken today, is to give the first child to the bride's parents in lieu of the bride price. This practice is further evidence that the bride price is compensation for the loss of the children.

The third and fourth payments are made in relation to death. After a death, the coffin must be made and the grave dug by the deceased's cross-cousins or their oldest descendents. Some time (ranging from months to years) after the burial, the *dabu sa'a weyan* 'head price' is paid by the dead person's children and family to the ones who made the coffin and dug the grave. The amount of this payment is voluntary but is usually directly related to the quantity and quality of materials and time used in making the coffin and grave. When Derek Zeifan died, none of those who should have made the coffin were willing or able to do so, therefore no head price will be paid. The fourth payment is the one mentioned earlier in the section on adoptions in which a deceased adopted person's adoptive family is compensated by his birth family for their care and nurturing of him. In the case of an older person such as Derek Zeifan, this payment is accompanied by a ceremony called *etran itoti* 'burning the stick', and the person's cane is burned in a special fire. This custom refers to the resolving of the debt incurred by the family whose child was cared for by someone else. It is believed that if this is not done, none of the deceased person's children will have success in life.

Celebrations. Rites of passage celebrations other than those involved in the payments listed above are related to birthdays and menopause. At a child's first birthday, or at any birthday the parents wish to commemorate, they will give a celebration. This celebration involves inviting both patrilateral and matrilateral kinsmen to their house on a designated evening and having one of the church elders hold a church service there. Then a meal is served, after which hymns are sung for part or all of the night. If the singing lasts until dawn, a second meal is served around 2:00 or 3:00 a.m. Tobacco and betel nut are supplied freely throughout the celebration, even during the church service. The invited guests bring gifts for the child which are usually food items, bead jewelry, handmade decorations, or money.

At menopause, or whenever a woman's family is sure she will not give birth again, her husband's clan may hold a traditional dance party (interestingly called *meryou samo* 'late afternoon time') which can last for several days or as long as food supplies hold out. The woman's children are formally counted by her husband and his close male kin. (In former times they were numbered with dog teeth on a string.) During this celebration the husband's clan feeds and gives presents to the wife's birth clan in direct proportion to the number of children she bore, to compensate them for the loss of those children. However, this action is not called a "payment" with the terminology of the other rites of passage payments listed above and it is optional. Such parties are usually held only for those women who have borne large families and are from clans with enough prestige and resources to be able to host such an event. Two such parties were held in December, 1988, one of the few times in recent memory.

Obligations

A person is obligated to give whatever is asked by one's closest relatives if one is able to do so. In order of priority these relatives are: parents and uterine siblings, then mother's brothers, sister's sons, and all cross-cousins. From these relatives, food, betel nut, tobacco, and other small items may be requested or even taken without asking, although money must always be asked for. Larger items such as stereo tape players can be requested but may be refused. Other parental siblings, *soni,* are not obligated to give to ego. Affines of this close degree (sibling and parental) are, however, obligated to give what is asked if it is in their power to do so, although they often complain bitterly at the time and later.

The entire clan and phratry are expected to share expenses and cooperate in hosting large social gatherings or feasts held for a variety of reasons. Lists of items needed from each family are made up and sent around. Affines of ego's generation are expected to help in giving small parties or in building gardens.

Social Interaction

Sawar people do not visit each other unless they have a specific purpose or are of the same clan or the clan of their mother. When a visit to relatives is made, the relationship is emphasized in the opening greetings. Only women of the same clan or who have married into that clan go fishing along the beach together.

Prior to the 1980s all washing of clothes and dishes, and most bathing was done at the fresh water springs along the beach. But women of different clans did noticeably little talking and socializing. Then the government put in three wells in different parts of Sawar. When women of different clans or lineages had to share the same well, those who owned the land where the well was located humiliated the others until they refused to go back. The other women then got their husbands or brothers to dig their own wells, even though there was considerable apprehension that so many wells would dry up the underground stream supplying the fresh water.

There has been great difficulty in getting the different clans to cooperate on anything for the village as a whole. Materials collected for the new church kept disappearing, as did any accumulated money. The church elders decided to allot each clan a certain amount of materials to contribute toward the new church, but even that was unsuccessful as different lineages refused to cooperate. Village workdays are very poorly attended.

Sandwich Kinship Structure

The term "sandwich kinship structure" was chosen to describe Sawar kinship taxonomy because if the nine generations are viewed as horizontal lines on a page, the top three lines are identical to the bottom three lines but in reverse order, while the middle three lines or generations are varied, and differ from each other in terminology patterns. The middle three generations form the filling of the sandwich and the outer six generations are the "bread" that holds the filling in place (see figures 5 and 6). Most of the terms of reference are inalienably possessed, and in this paper they are all given in the third person singular form.

Sawar kinship structure is a classificatory and partly generational system extending to two degrees of collaterality (Schusky 1972). Sawar terms of address tend to be generational, whereas terms of reference include Iroquois cousin terminology along with some elements of bifurcate merging terminology complicated by reckoning relative age of kinsmen.

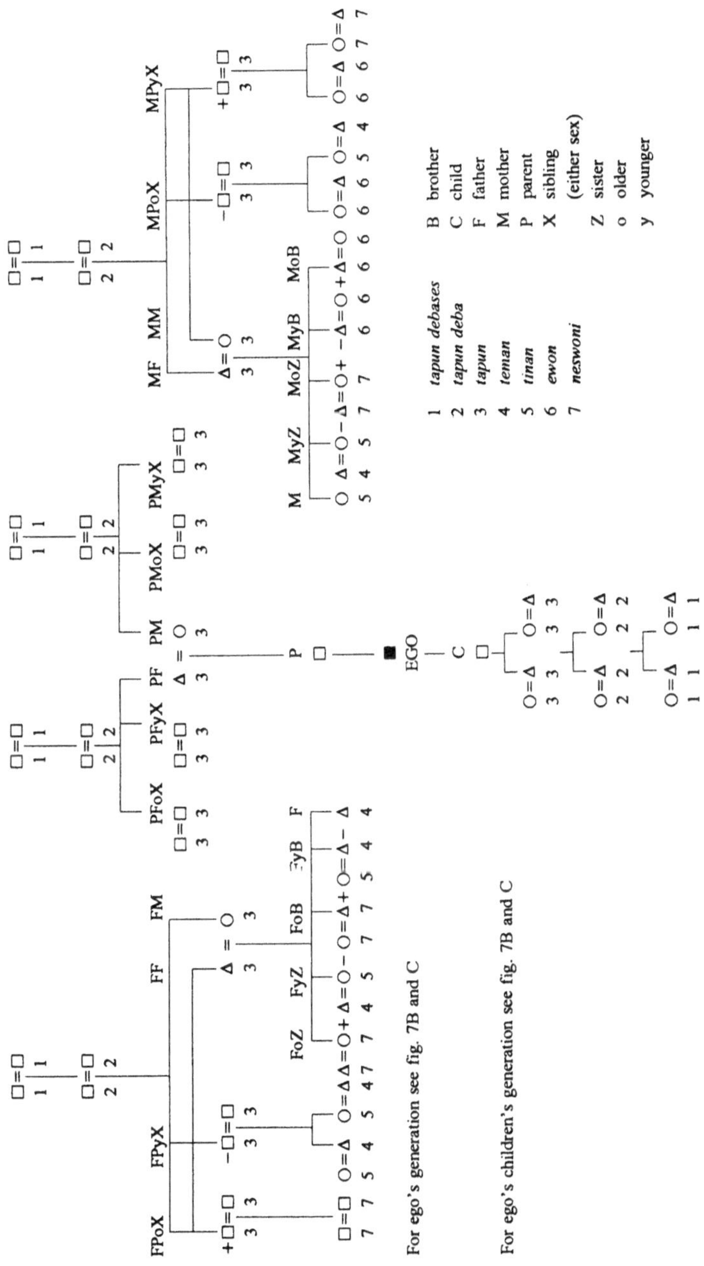

Fig. 5. Six "outer layer" generations

A. Parent's generation

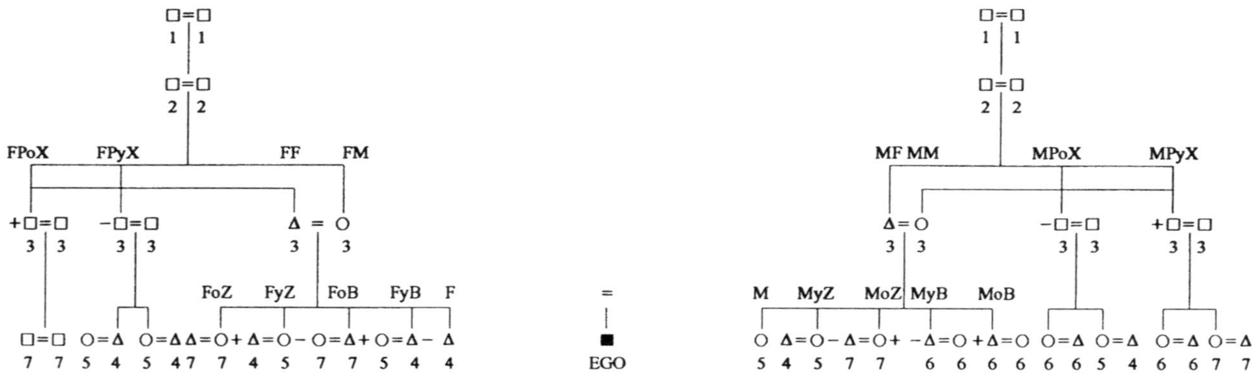

For ego's generation see fig. 7B and C

3 *tapun*
4 *teman*
5 *tinan*
6 *ewon*
7 *neswoni*

B brother
F father
M mother
P parent

X sibling
Z sister
o older
y younger

Fig. 6. Three "sandwich filling" generations (1 of 5)

B. Male ego's generation and first descending generation

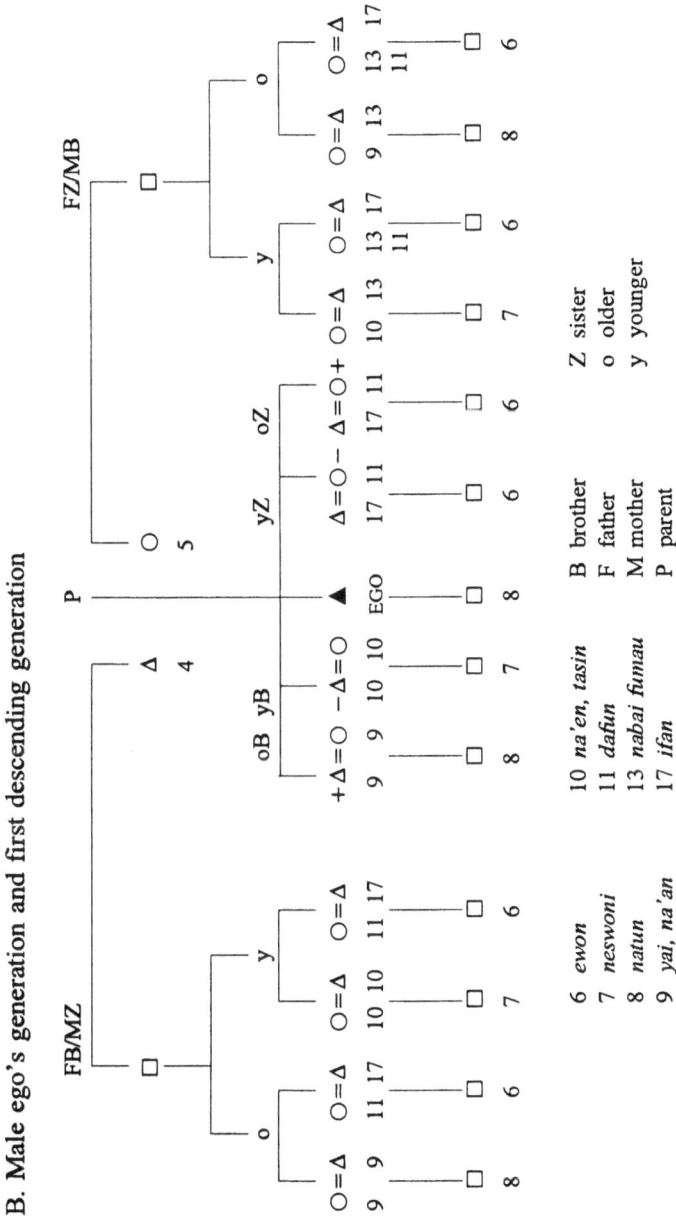

Fig. 6. Three "sandwich filling" generations (2 of 5)

6 *ewon*
7 *neswoni*
8 *natun*
9 *yai, na'an*
10 *na'en, tasin*
11 *dafun*
13 *nabai fumau*
17 *ifan*

B brother
F father
M mother
P parent

Z sister
o older
y younger

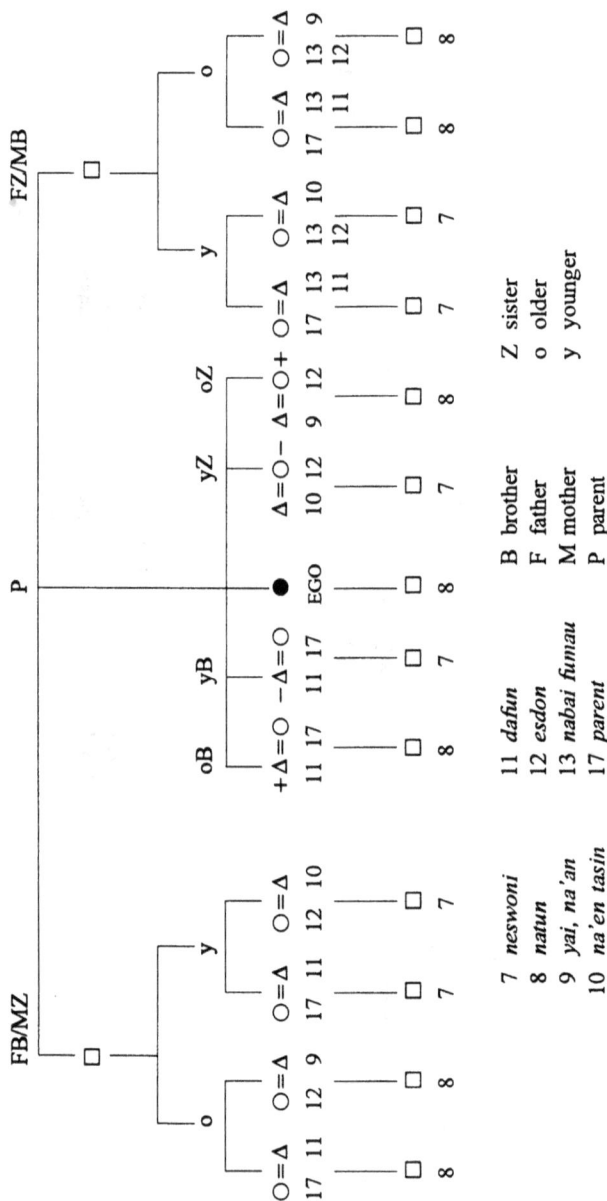

C. Female ego's generation and first descending generation

Fig. 6. Three "sandwich filling" generations (3 of 5)

7   neswoni
8   natun
9   yai, na'an
10 na'en tasin

11 dafun
12 esdon
13 nabai fumau
17 parent

B   brother
F   father
M   mother
P   parent

Z   sister
o   older
y   younger

D. Male ego's cousins to the second degree of collaterality

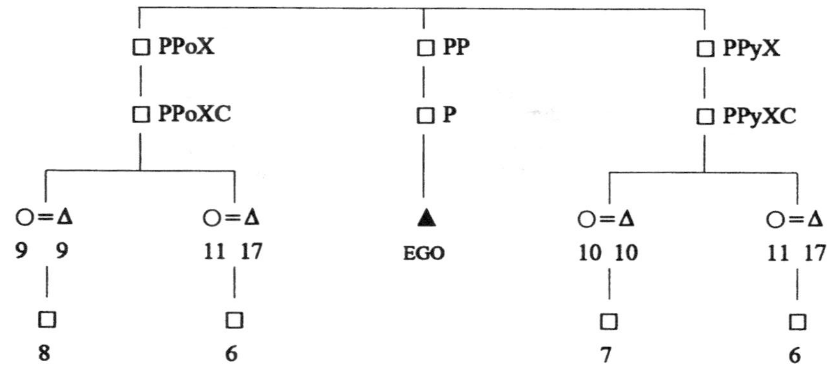

Fig. 6. Three "sandwich filling" generations (4 of 5)

6 *ewon*
7 *neswoni*
8 *natun*
9 *yai, na'an*
10 *na'en, tasin*
11 *dafun*
17 *iifan*

C child
P parent
X sibling (either sex)
o older
y younger

E. Female ego's cousins to the second degree of collaterality

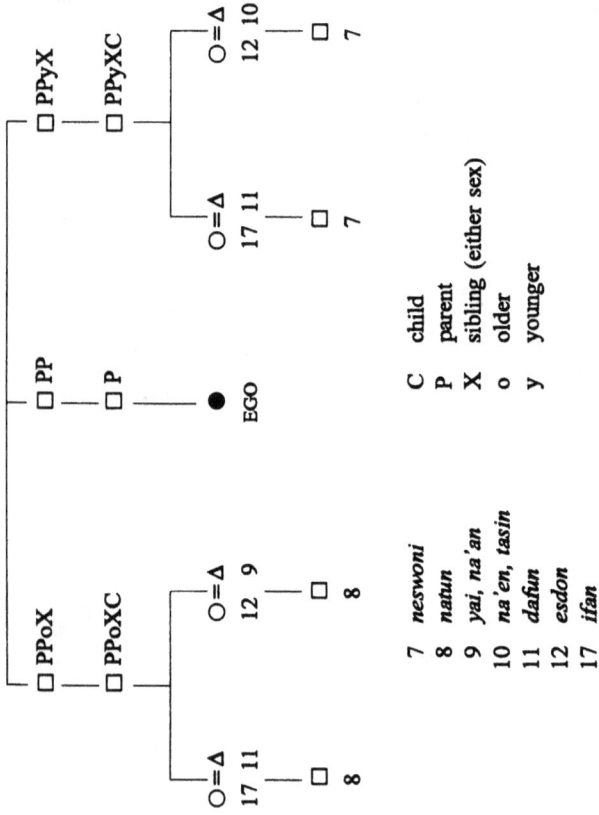

Fig. 6. Three "sandwich filling" generations (5 of 5)

7   *neswoni*
8   *natun*
9   *yai, na'an*
10 *na'en, tasin*
11 *dafun*
12 *esdon*
17 *ifan*

C   child
P   parent
X   sibling (either sex)
o   older
y   younger

Outer Layers

The outer six generations of Sobei kinship, following the sandwich analogy, are completely classificatory and generational. There is one referential kin term, *tapun debases,* for all kinsmen four generations removed from ego. Similarly, all kinsmen three generations removed from ego are referred to as *tapun deba,* and all grandkinsmen are referred to as *tapun.* But a single term of address, *tapun,* serves for all six of those generations. Modifiers indicating *temto* 'male', or *mefne* 'female', can be added if desired to any sex-neutral term, such as for grandkinsmen.

Sandwich Filling

The "sandwich filling" consists of three generations, here designated as parental, ego's, and children's, which have rather more complex terminology.

Again, a speaker may choose to use terms of address which are generational, as in a Hawaiian system, though in the middle three generations there are a number of alternate terms which may be used. The same two terms of address (*mam* 'father', and *nen* 'mother') may be used for all those in the parental generation including affines, and two terms of address (*yai* 'older sibling' and *na'en* 'younger sibling') may also suffice for all of ego's generation including affines. However, other terms of address are not only possible but frequently used. In the children's generation individual given names are used most commonly for address or reference, but a single term, *natun,* usually used as a term of reference, can be used for all members of the first descending generation.

Parental Generation. Kinship terminology for ego's parents' generation consists of four terms used in a system which is partially bifurcate merging extending to two degrees of collaterality bilaterally. Two of the four terms are reciprocal and have different forms for reference and address, some of which are inalienably possessed (see figure 7). In descending generations males and females use the terms differently because of the mother's brother distinction.

neswoni (addressed as *soni,* or as *mam* 'father' and *nen* 'mother') are parents' older siblings and their spouses, and the children of grandparents' older siblings, except for mother's brothers and their spouses.

	Reference Term Inalienably Possessed (3p sing.)	Reference Term Neutral	Approx. English Gloss	Term of Address
1.		*tapun debases*	great-great-grandkinsman (reciprocal)	*tapun*
2.		*tapun deba*	great-grandkinsman (reciprocal)	*tapun*
3.		*tapun*	grandkinsman (reciprocal)	*tapun*
4.	*teman*		father	*mam*
5.	*tinan*		mother	*nen, nenwai*
6.	*ewon*		mother's brother and spouse; sister's child (male ego only)	*wawa, mam, nen;* child's name, *teknonymy*
7.	*neswoni*	*soni*	father's older siblings, mother's older sister; niece, nephew	*soni, mam, nen, soni,* child's name, *teknonymy*
8.	*natun*		child	child's name, *teknonymy*
9.	*yai, na'an*		older sibling	*yai*
10.	*tasin*	*na'en*	younger sibling	*na'en*
11.	*dafun*		cross-sex sibling (reciprocal)	*dafun*
12.	*esdon*		sister (female) (reciprocal)	*sedon*
13.	*nabai fumau*		cross-cousin (reciprocal)	*nabai, yai, na'en*

Fig. 7. Sobei kinship terms (1 of 2)

Reference Term Inalienably Possessed (3p sing.)	Reference Term Neutral	Approx. English Gloss	Term of Address
14.	*nabai*		type of cousin	*nabai*
(not on	*nemen'ato*		(reciprocal)	
charts)	*nabai seba*		matrilateral cross-cousin	*nabai*
	nabai manitiwo		head price cousin	*nabai*
15.	*eson*		spouse	Christian name, *teknonymy*
16.	*dawon*		parent-in-law; child-in-law (reciprocal)	*mam, nen;* *teknonymy*
17.	*ifan*		sibling-in-law of the same sex (reciprocal)	*yai, na'en*
18.	*kweisu*		wife's younger brother & wife	*kweisu, na'en*
19.	*fumwan*		wife's sister's husband	*fumwan, yai, na'en*
20. (not on charts)	*penabi*		children's spouses' parent	*penabi*

Fig. 7. Sobei kinship terms (2 of 2)

teman and *tinan* are the terms of reference for father and mother, respectively, and for all their younger siblings and cousins and their spouses, again except for mother's brothers and their spouses. Spouse's parents, although in a taboo relationship and referred to as *dawon*, may also be addressed as *mam* and *nen*, the terms of address for father and mother. These terms of address may be applied to stepparents, but the referential terms are not. Stepfathers are referred to as *teman eyafse* 'caretaking father', and stepmothers as *tinan eyafse* 'caretaking mother'.

ewon are mother's brothers and male cousins and their spouses. The specific term of address for *ewon* is *wawa*, but as stated above, the terms for father and mother are more commonly used.

Siblings. There are three different, but somewhat overlapping systems of nomenclature for siblings and cousins: Hawaiian terms of address, Iroquois cousin terminology, and a relative age differentiation.

The most common forms of address and reference in ego's generation are the age-distinctive terms, *yai* 'older sibling' and *na'en* 'younger sibling'. This importance of the age distinction is shown by the fact that these are the only relationships with two terms of reference each. *na'an* and *tasin*, respectively, are additional terms for these siblings, as shown in figure 7. Parallel cousins are called by these older or younger terms according to the relative ages of the linking parents. All cousins in the second degree of collaterality may be referred to or addressed by these terms and the relative age of alter is determined by the ages of the linking grandparents. These older/younger terms may also be used for all affines of ego's generation and may be further extended to anyone in ego's generation from other lineages as described earlier. Due to the small size of the language group and the high degree of interrelatedness, it is safe to say that everyone in ego's generation could be included under one of these two terms.

The second most common way of differentiating siblings is with terms of relative sexual identity. As has been previously stated, the brother-brother bond is the closest sibling relationship and, significantly, it is the only dyad which uses only age reference terms. Cross-siblings use the special term *dafun* both as reference and address, and their relationship is basic to the mother's brother-sister's son bond which pervades New Guinean kinship (Kelly 1974; Brown and Buchbinder 1976; Oosterval 1961). Sisters have a special word for their relationship, using *esdon* as reference and *sedon* as address.

In Sobei cousin terminology, as in the Iroquois pattern, cross-cousins are called *nabai fumau* and older/younger sibling terms are used for parallel cousins. *nabai fumau* are considered the closest nonuterine relatives of the same generation. When Sawar people say that someone is their *nabai fumau* they do it with special emphasis and indicate the strength of the bond. We have seen no evidence of rivalry or competition in this relationship. For these reasons I have given this term individual ranking. There is no evidence that the term *nabai fumau* is extended collaterally.[12]

nabai is the term of address for all those ego calls 'cousin', including *nabai fumau*. But the other *nabai* terms, that is, *nabai* with or without any of its other modifiers, are hard to define.

nabai nemen'ato is a term which is used inconsistently for parallel cousins, cross-cousins of the second degree of collaterality, those of mother's clan, and for the grandchildren of both parallel and cross-cousins. The term *nemen'ato* derives from a term for younger sibling.

nabai seba has been described as referring to all those of ego's generation in the clans belonging to mother's phratry. The term *seba* has reference to "mother's group." This term is very seldom used and just came to light after years of gathering and checking Sawar kinship data at sporadic intervals. It is uncertain whether it refers to the clans in mother's maternal or paternal phratries.

One last *nabai* term is *manitiwo*. It has reference to all the *nabai* who are entitled to share in the head price after ego's death. *nabai fumau* have first rights and may divide the head price with their children or with *nabai nemen'ato* if they feel so inclined. Many do not share the head price with others, putting their own interests first (see Rites of Passage, above).

Some Sawar people say that the term *nabai* without modifiers can be extended to refer to anyone having the name of either father's or mother's clan if specific definition of their status is uncertain. For example, this term could be used of people from other villages and language groups with the same clan name, because it is assumed that they are relatives. With this much ambiguity in *nabai* 'cousin' taxonomy, perhaps it is sufficient to note

---

[12]Despite repeated and varied attempts to determine precisely what relationships are included in the *nabai* set of terms, the results are still contradictory and confusing. According to a few people there are collateral *nabai fumau*, but no evidence could be found for it in attested relationships. Three blood brothers named three different sets of people as their *nabai nemen'ato*. One source insisted that *nabai nemen'ato* were those from the mother's father's side, but since Sobei kin terms are reciprocal and balanced that seems unlikely.

The difficulties in eliciting these terms are caused partly by people being related to each other in several ways and partly by the fact that they are descriptive distinctions which seem to be falling into disuse, particularly among the young people, while the generational terms appear to be increasingly used. Further study would need to be done among the very old people to determine the traditional use of these terms.

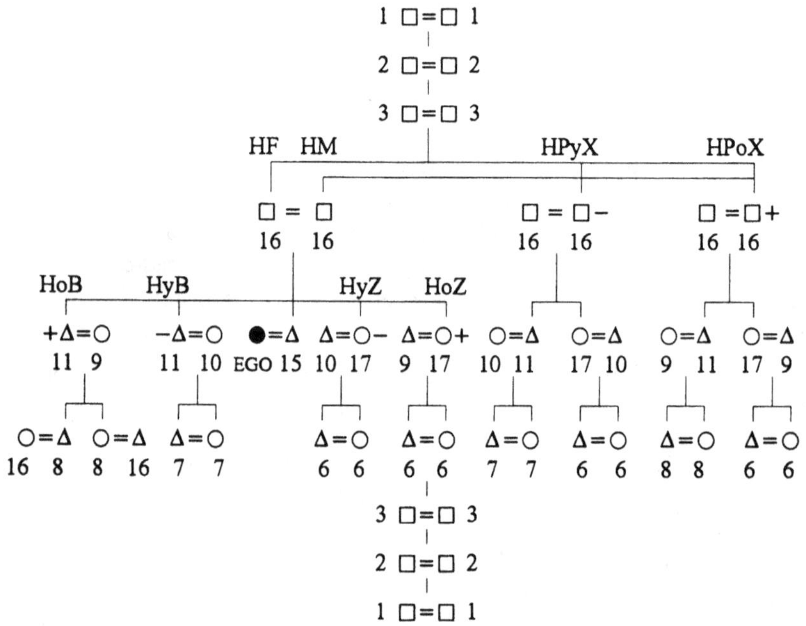

1 □=□ 1

2 □=□ 2

3 □=□ 3

HF   HM   HPyX   HPoX

□ = □   □ = □-   □ =□+
16   16   16   16   16 16

HoB   HyB   HyZ   HoZ

+Δ=O   −Δ=O   ●=Δ   Δ=O-   Δ=O+   O=Δ   O=Δ   O=Δ   O=Δ
11 9   11 10 EGO 15 10 17   9 17   10 11 17 10 9 11 17 9

O=Δ   O=Δ   Δ=O   Δ=O   Δ=O   Δ=O   Δ=O   Δ=O   Δ=O
16 8 8 16 7 7   6 6   6 6   7 7   6 6   8 8   6 6

3 □=□ 3

2 □=□ 2

1 □=□ 1

1 *tapun debases*	6 *ewon*	9 *yai, na'an*	15 *eson*
2 *tapun deba*	7 *neswoni*	10 *na'en, tasin*	16 *dawon*
3 *tapun*	8 *natun*	11 *dafun*	17 *ifan*

B brother	M mother	X sibling	o older
F father	P parent	(either sex)	y younger
H husband		Z sister	

Female Ego

Fig. 8. Affinal kinship chart (1 of 2)

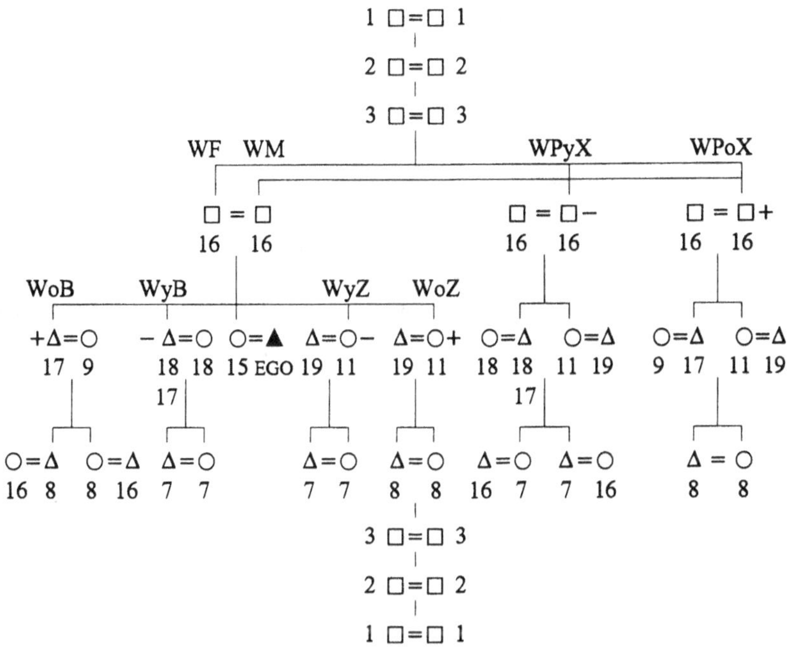

Fig. 8. Affinal kinship chart (2 of 2)

1	*tapun debases*	7	*neswoni*	11	*dafun*	17	*ifan*
2	*tapun deba*	8	*natun*	15	*eson*	18	*kweisu*
3	*tapun*	9	*yai, na'an*	16	*dawon*	19	*fumwan*

B	brother	P	parent	X	sibling	o	older
F	father	W	wife		(either sex)	y	younger
M	mother			Z	sister		

Male Ego

that these terms seem to be related to the rites of passage payments and their recipients.

Affines. All affines of two or more generations removed from ego are called by consanguineal terms (see figures 7 and 8).

Affines of the first ascending generation are all called *dawon* 'taboo relationship'. Affines in the first descending generation are referred to by the same terms as spouse uses for that person.

Affines of ego's generation may be distinguished in additional but restricted ways. The older/younger sibling terms are used for one's spouse's siblings of the same sex as spouse (e.g., wife's sister, husband's brother) depending on the relative age of ego's spouse to alter. Affines of the same sex as ego (e.g., husband's sister, wife's brother, sister's husband, brother's wife) may be referred to as *ifan,* except that a man may also call his wife's sisters' husbands *fumwan* and his wife's younger brother and his spouse *kweisu.* This last term appears to be only known and used by the older generation. Children's spouses' parents are referred to and addressed as *penabi.* Ideally co-parents have a warm, sharing relationship, but in reality it is often full of strife and competition.

Children's Generation. All of the first descending generation may be referred to by ego generationally as *natun* 'child'. If a descriptive term is desired, female egos still refer to the children of their older siblings and older collateral siblings as *natun.* But the children of their younger siblings and younger cousins are called *soni.* Males may refer to the children of female siblings *(dafun)* as *ewon,* children of older male siblings as *natun* and children of younger male siblings as *soni.* Terms of address for the children's generation are simply their names until they have had children, and then teknonyms are used.

Summary of Sobei Kinship Terms. The following kinship terms and their referents, described in prose as well as by standard abbreviation, have been discussed:

1. *tapun debases* All kinsmen of ascending and descending generations four generations removed from ego, both affinal and consanguineal.

2. *tapun deba* All kinsmen of ascending and descending generations three generations removed from ego, both affinal and consanguineal.

3. *tapun* All kinsmen of ascending and descending generations two generations removed from ego, both affinal and consanguineal.

4. *teman* Father and father's younger male siblings and parents' younger sisters' husbands to the first degree of collaterality. This term is the same for male or female ego.

   F   FyB   PyZH   FPyXS   PPyXDH

5. *tinan* Mother and the spouses of any man called *teman* 'father' as listed above. Parents' younger siblings and collateral younger siblings are all called 'father' and 'mother' except for mother's brothers and male cousins. 'Father' and 'mother' are the reciprocals for 'child'.

   M   PyZ   FyBW   PPyXD   FPyXSW

6. *ewon* Both male and female egos use *ewon* as listed below and it is reciprocal.

   MB   MBW   MPXS   MPXSW

   Males only additionally use this term for all offspring of female siblings and female cousins (or everyone they call *dafun*) *ewon*, and it is reciprocal. (Ego's wife also calls these *ewon*, e.g., HZC, HPXDC.)

   ZC   PXDC   PPXCDC

   Note: The term of address for *ewon* is *wawa*, but also all *ewon* may be addressed as 'father' and 'mother' if older, or as 'child' if in a younger generation.

7. *neswoni* This term, when referring to kin in ascending generations, is the same for male and female egos and it is reciprocal. It is used for parents' older siblings and their spouses, (except for mother's older brother) and for grandparents' older siblings' children and their spouses (except for mother's male cousins and their spouses). The term of address for this is *soni*.

   FoX   FoBW   PPoXD   PPoXDH   MoZ   PoZH   FPoXS   FPoXSW

Females call the children of all younger siblings and cousins by this term.

yXC   PyXCC   PPyXCCC   HyBC   HPyXSC

Males call the children of all younger brothers and cousins by this term.

yBC   PyXSC   PPyXCSC   WyXC   WPyXCC

8. *natun* Female ego's own child and all children of older siblings or cousins to the second degree.

C   oXC   PoXCC   PPoXCCC   HoBC   HPoXSC

Male ego's own child and all children of older male siblings or cousins' siblings to the second degree of collaterality.

C   oBC   PoXSC   PPoXCSC   WoXC   WPoXCC

9. *yai, na'an* Older siblings and cousins to the second degree of collaterality and their spouses. Older affinal siblings and their spouses also to the second degree.

male ego   oB oBW FoBS MoZS PoXSW PPoXCS
                   PPoXCSW WoBW WPoXSW

female ego   oZH PoXDH PPoXCDH HoBW HoZH
                   HPoXSW HPoXDH

Note: *yai* is the most common term of address for these relatives.

10. *na'en, tasin* All younger siblings and cousins to the second degree and their spouses. Affinal younger siblings and their spouses, to the second degree, for female ego only.

male ego   yB yBW FyBS MyZS PyXSW PPyXCS
                   PPyXCSW

female ego   yZH PyXDH PPyXCDH HyBW HyZH
                    HPyXSW HPyXDH

Note: *na'en* is the most common term of address for these relatives.

11. *dafun* Any cross-sex sibling or cousin to the second degree.

    male ego   Z FBD MZD PPXCD WZ WPXD

    female ego   B FBS MZS PPXCS HB HPXS

12. *esdon* Used only by females for female siblings and cousins to the
    second degree of collaterality.

    Z   FBD   MZD   PPXCD

13. *nabai fumau* Cross-cousins; male and female egos.

    FZC   MBC

Note: This is a term of reference. The term of address for this and all
other *nabai* terms is *nabai* if distinction is made, otherwise the
older/younger sibling terms are used.

14. *nabai* *(nemen'ato)*   At least MFBCC; male and female egos.

       (seba)   Persons of ego's generation whose family
                         name is from mother's phratry

       (manitiwo)   All nabai having the right to share in the head
                         price, i.e., *nabai fumau, nabai nemen'ato* of
                         the deceased. (These terms are not on figures
                         6 and 7.)

15. *eson* Spouse   H   W

16. *dawon* Spouse's parents and all their siblings and their spouses. Children's and all classificatory children's spouses; taboo relationship (both male and female ego).

> HP HPX HPBW HPZH WP WPX WPBW WPZH SW DH

17. *ifan* Spouse's cross-sex siblings and their collateral equivalent to the second degree.

> male ego   ZH PXDH PPXCDH WB WPXS
>
> female ego   BW PXSW PPXCSW HZ HPXD

18. *kweisu* Wife's younger brothers and their wives.

> WyB WyBW WPyXS WPyXSW

19. *fumwan* Wife's sisters' husbands. WZH WPXDH

20. *penabi* (not on charts) Children's spouses' parents.

> SWP DHP

Key:

B	brother	F	father	P	Parent	X	sibling	o	older
C	child	H	husband	S	son		(either sex)	y	younger
D	daughter	M	mother	W	wife	Z	sister		

Conclusion

Sawar kinship can best be characterized as paradoxical. It is both simple and complex, in some aspects following Hawaiian and in other aspects Iroquoian with added age complexities. The closest kin bond is brother-brother, yet it is also the greatest arena of rivalry. This primarily brother-brother sibling rivalry permeates the society from the sibling apical ancestors of the lineages down through to the smallest set of siblings. Additionally, the clans compete with each other for status, for primacy of original residence, for rank, for land, and for authority.

Sawar people have great independence of spirit, while being tied irrevocably to their kin. Sawar people cannot achieve full identity alone, but they certainly try. If two brothers are identified so closely that their children are considered to be of the same womb, and yet brother-brother rivalry is a dominating motif, then perhaps Sawar society typifies Walt Kelly's Pogo's famous expression, "We have found the enemy, and he is us."

References

Brown, Paula and Georgeda Buchbinder, eds. 1976. Man and woman in the New Guinea highlands. Washington, DC: American Anthropological Association.

Erickson, Carol. 1976. Isirawa kinship and exchange marriage. Bulletin of Irian Jaya 5(1):22–44.

Fortune, D. F. 1963. Sorcerers of Dobu. New York: E. P. Dutton & Co.

Grace, George W. 1972. Notes of the phonological history of the Austronesian languages of the Sarmi coast. Bulletin of West Irian Development 1(3):21–54.

Kelly, Raymond. 1974. Etoro social structure. Ann Arbor, Mich.: The University of Michigan Press.

Merrifield, William R., Marilyn Gregerson, and Daniel C. Ajamiseba, eds. 1983. Gods, heroes, kinsmen: Ethnographic studies from Irian Jaya, Indonesia. International Museum of Cultures Publication 17. Dallas: Cenderawasih University and The International Museum of Cultures.

Oosterval, George. 1961. People of the Tor. Amsterdam: Royal Van Gorcum.

Schusky, Ernest L. 1972. Manual for kinship analysis. 2nd ed. New York: Holt, Rinehart and Winston.

Sterner, Joyce K. 1981. Adoption into a Sobei clan. Bulletin of Irian Jaya 9(1):1–8.

―――. 1987. Sobei verb morphology reanalyzed to reflect POC studies. Oceanic Linguistics 26(1 and 2):30–54.

Yawa Marriage and Kinship:
A Two-Section Iroquois System

Linda K. Jones

Iroquois and Dravidian kinship terminologies are alike in distinguishing cross- from parallel kinsmen but differ in the way cross- and parallel relationships are distinguished among more distant kinsmen, particularly with respect to ego's parents' cross-cousins, ego's second (and more distant) cross-cousins (Keesing 1975:108), and the children of ego's cross-cousins (Scheffler 1971:238–239). Iroquois systems are widespread and are associated with a variety of marriage patterns, while Dravidian systems have been especially associated with what has been described as "two-section" or sometimes "alliance" systems (Dumont 1971; Keesing 1975:108). Keesing (1975:107) says "the Dravidian subtype is commonly (but not always) associated with a requirement that a male ego marry a woman who falls in the cross-cousin category" and that (1975:111) "there are apparently some Iroquois terminologies where the equivalences are made between consanguineals and in-laws that are supposed to be a concomitant of Dravidian alliance systems," although he does not list specific examples.

This paper describes a society, the Yawa of Irian Jaya, Indonesia, which has a kinship terminology with precisely this combination of Iroquois and Dravidian features. The "two-section" system of the Yawa is not a moiety system, but rather the "two sections" are egocentric and related to a pattern of obligatory cross-cousin marriage, so that one section is "my kind of people" and the second section is "the other kind of people, with whom we marry"

(Keesing 1975:108). The dual organization in Yawa is expressed in kinship terminology through the distinction between parallel and cross-relatives. The terminology is Iroquois in type, yet there are terminological equivalences between consanguineal and affinal kinsmen.

Ethnographic Setting

The Yawa people,[1] numbering about 6000, occupy the center of Yapen, a long mountainous island lying off the north coast of Irian Jaya, Indonesia[2] (see figure 1). Originally they resided mostly in tiny hamlets in the interior of the island, but at the behest of the government during the Dutch administration in the early decades of this century, they were gathered in villages, most of which are located along either the north coast or the south coast of the island, but with one very large village and one smaller one in the interior. Despite the rugged mountainous terrain and lack of roads, there is considerable traffic between the mountain villages and the coastal villages and between neighboring coastal villages.

There are multiple clans among the Yawa, which are patrilineal and exogamous. Men marry their distant cross-cousins and then reside patrilocally, first with the man's parents and later independently in their own house. Traditional political structure is no longer extant, having been replaced by Indonesian provincial and district infrastructure.

The Yawa subsist by slash-and-burn agriculture and by hunting game in the rain forest. They market surplus garden produce in one of the nearby

---

[1]My husband Larry and I studied the Yawa language and culture from 1983 to 1992 under the auspices of the Program Kerjasama Universitas Cenderawasih dan Summer Institute of Linguistics (the UNCEN-SIL Cooperative Program). We have visited virtually all the Yawa villages and lived for extensive periods of time in two of them—Rosbori on the north coast of Yapen and Sarawandori on the south coast.

While many of my Yawa friends have helped in my understanding of the kinship system, those who contributed most significantly were: Yubelina Baba, Dominggus Kapanai, Efraim Karubaba, Borden Paai, Kornelius Paai, Neli Paai, Zet Paai, Oktofina Rawai, Betuel Rumansara, and Kornelia Rumansara. I wish to thank Marilyn Gregerson for her helpful comments. I am grateful for the forbearance of my husband and two young sons during the writing of this paper. Finally, I am also thankful for my baby daughter, Charis, who kept me reminded of my own kinship obligations at home.

[2]Speakers of the Yawa language reside in the following districts: Kecamatan Yapen-Barat, Kecamatan Yapen-Selatan, and Kecamatan Yapen-Timur, all in Kabupaten Yapen-Waropen.

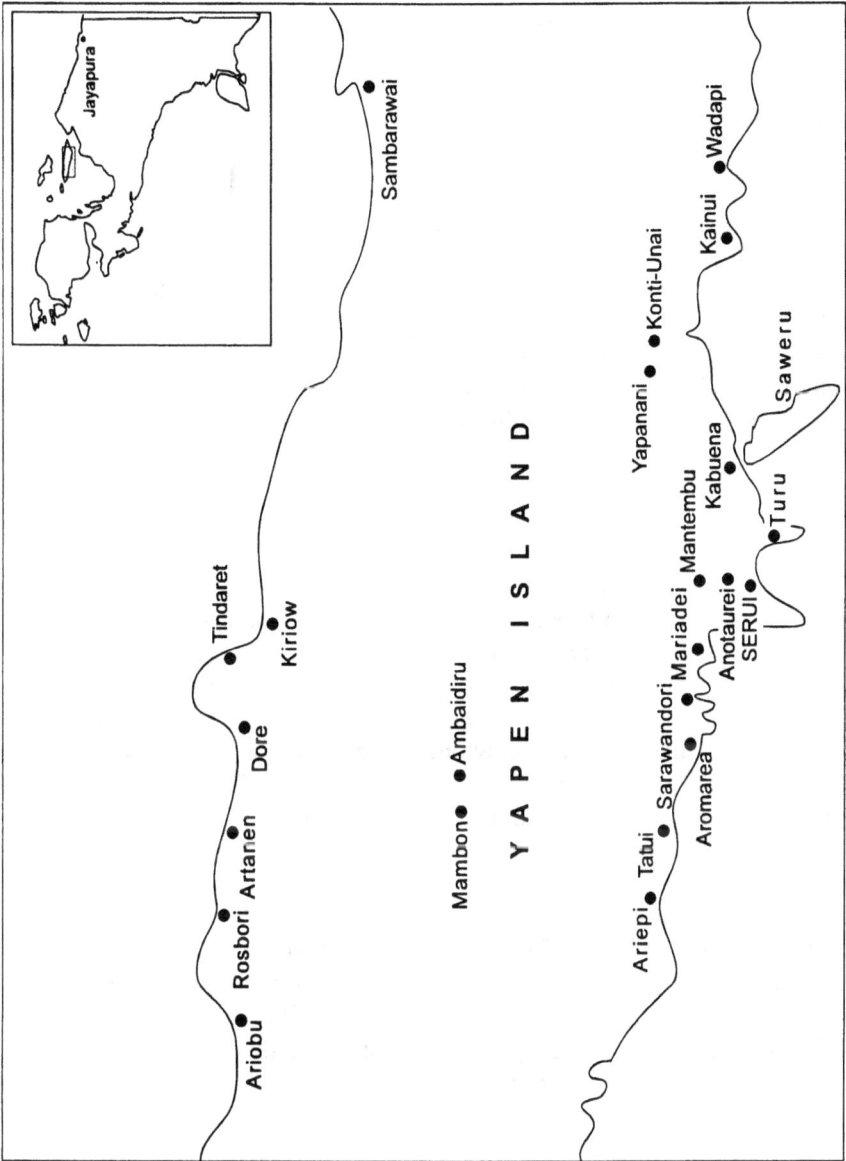

Fig. 1. Map of Yapen Island, Irian Jaya

towns, but by far the greatest source of cash for the coastal people is the sale of the sago that they process. For the mountain people, coffee is the primary cash crop.

The Yawa speak a Papuan language,[3] but they are surrounded by Austronesian-speaking peoples on all sides. There has been considerable intermarriage between the Yawa and their neighbors and indeed, some family names are found all over the island. Because of the high degree of contact between these different language groups, their cultures have become quite homogeneous. Furthermore, there has been a long history of sporadic contact with other peoples, such as the Chinese many centuries ago, followed by the Sultanate of Tidore, later the Dutch, and most recently western Indonesians. Although the Yawa were formerly animistic in their beliefs, Christianity was introduced about 50 years ago, and today the Yawa claim to be 100% Christian. There are two principal denominations, both Protestant.

Clan Organization

A Yawa's social identity is his *keret,* his 'family name'. Family names in six Yawa villages[4] are listed in figure 2. It can be seen that family names are not localized; for instance, the names Maniambo and Paai occur in four of the villages, while Karubaba and Rumansara are found in three.

The number of family names per village is not reflective of village size; some family names represent only one family, others many. Village sizes are approximately: Ariobu/Insari 100, Rosbori 125, Artaneng 300, Tindaret/Kiriowi 450, Ambaidiru 600, and Mambon 100.

Yawa family names do not correspond neatly with any anthropological category; they are not always clan names and they are never just lineage names (there are no named lineages). Actually, all Yawa have two *keret* names, a *kereto akoe* 'big family name' and a *kereto mamaun* 'small family name'. However, the particular *keret* that an individual identifies with in everyday usage may be either one of these. It is not, however, the individual's choice; rather he goes by whichever of the family names is used by the larger group to which he belongs.

---

[3]The Yawa language has been classed by Voorhoeve (1975) as a stock-level isolate in the Geelvink Bay Phylum.
[4]Since this list covers only six Yawa villages out of a total twenty-five, it is far from a complete list of all the Yawa family names.

Ariobu/Insari	Rosbori	Artaneng
Anderi	Ayeri	Kuwei
Baba	Imbiri	Maniambo
Imbiri	Karubaba	Rawai
Kapanai	Paai	Rumansara
Maniambo	Rumansara	Sembai
Moman	Wanggori	
Paai		

Tindaret/Kiriowi	Ambaidiru	Mambon
Aba	Atewa	Karubaba
Andit	Karubaba	Paai
Maniambo	Maniambo	Rumansara
Merani	Mora	
Paai	Paai	
Rawai	Rawai	
Turunat	Sembai	
Varian		
Yawandare		

Fig. 2. Family names in six Yawa villages

The largest social grouping among the Yawa corresponds to *kereto akoe* 'big family name', which I will call 'clan'. Each clan is a nonoverlapping grouping of two or more subclans, the latter term corresponding to *kereto mamaun* 'small family name'. Figure 3 shows some of the clans and the subclans comprising them. By comparing these with the family names in figure 2, which are those used in daily life, it is evident that sometimes the everyday family name is the clan name and other times it is the subclan name. In one case, the Paai clan, all member subclans except one (Yawandare) go by the clan name. In other clans, such as Sembai, the situation is more split, with some of the member subclans going by their subclan names, while other member subclans are only identified by the clan name. And in yet other cases, all the subclans within the clan go only by their subclan name (e.g., the subclans in the Mindim clan). The conventions regarding which name is used, whether clan or subclan, have apparently existed for some time, since people of one clan do not usually know the subclan names of another clan if the latter people only use their clan name.

Paai	Rumansara	Mindim	Sembai
Kapitarau	Aenbuga	Anderi	Kapanai
Mambo	Karotut	Baba	Maniambo
Pajuri	Kuwei	Imbiri	
Radivun			
Tantanisy			
Wanawivatan			
Yawandare			

Fig. 3. Four Yawa clans and their included subclans

Clans figure significantly in Yawa social structure because of the rule of clan exogamy and also because of the bonds which commit clan members to one another. The significance of the clan in the economic structure is principally as a land-owning group. Individuals or families do not own any land, whether in the village or in the forest. The land all belongs to the clans. Just as the clan endures, regardless of whether particular clan members die, so the land tenure continues. (There are sometimes, however, disputes over land claims.) Land is not divided up to clan members, it is not inherited, and it may not be sold. Clan members merely use the land for gardening and hunting. However, it is also common for families to make gardens on land belonging to a clan other than their own. As long as relationships between the parties concerned are cordial, permission is not even needed.

Village Structure

While clans and subclans are organized along kinship lines, villages are not. Clan distinctions are not represented spatially in the villages. Segments of each clan may, in fact, be scattered over a number of villages, and conversely, in every village there are several different clans represented (see figure 2). Furthermore, within a village, there is no particular clustering of the households of one clan or even of one subclan.[5] As houses deteriorate, new ones are constructed in some unoccupied space, not necessarily nearby, and thus the physical layout of the village is constantly changing.

---

[5]While this dispersion is true in the majority of Yawa villages, in at least one large village, Ambaidiru in the interior, there is a tendency for some clustering of households of the same clan.

The only significant factor in the spatial organization of a village is a religious one. Where there is more than one church denomination in a village, there has historically been a split of the village into two sections, with many of the converts to the newer church separating themselves into a new section of the village by a substantial physical space, reflective of the religious separation they felt. In recent years, however, as hostility between the two churches has subsided, the physical separations have become less rigid.

Since the time when the people began gathering together in villages at the government's request, the village has become an important political unit. The government supervises the election of the political leaders, who are chosen from each village. Besides its political function, the village has, of course, other important functions for the residents. When there is a major work project, such as erecting fences in the village, cutting the grass in nearby fields, or putting a new roof on someone's house, the men of the village band together to do these tasks. Many small parties, such as a house dedication party, as well as an occasion like a funeral, are times when the villagers gather together. During childbirth, most of the village women visit the laboring woman, lending emotional solidarity and physical assistance. When a young man is collecting the bride price for his wife, his fellow villagers contribute, regardless of whether there are kin ties. Conversely, when a woman marries, some of the bride price that is received will be distributed among the people of her home village.

Within a village, the basic unit is the household. The nucleus of the household is generally a man, his wife, and his unmarried sons and daughters. If a man has more than one wife (still true of some older men), his wives and their children all live with him under one roof. Since the Yawa are patrilocal and a man brings his new wife to live in his parents' home, there may also be one or more married sons and their families in the household. The new couple occupies their own room in the parental home generally until several children have been born, at which time spatial pressures push the young family out on their own.

Besides the male head of household, his spouse, and descendants, there are often other relatives who also live (temporarily or permanently) in the household. Perhaps there is a child or two of some near kinsmen who have temporarily come to reside with the family. Children of brothers are especially apt to be traded back and forth like this, and a man's younger unmarried brother often comes to live with him. This fostering may lead to a long term arrangement. There is often a widow in the household as well.

She is usually related to the male head of household, either his mother or the widow of a brother, since widows are supposed to be taken care of by their deceased husband's clan. Only rarely is the widow a sister or a daughter of the head of household.

A widow may also be head of household. Especially in cases in which she has older children at the time of her husband's death, a widow may continue living in the same home rather than move in with her husband's close kin. It is rare that a widow would return to live permanently in her home village or remarry into a clan other than her deceased husband's, because if she does, her children must remain in her husband's village with her husband's close kin. Her children belong to their father's clan, not to her. Consequently, a widow head of household is not uncommon, and sometimes two widows whose husbands were brothers live together.

Statistics from one village surveyed (Artaneng) will illustrate these typical household patterns. There are twenty-three households (excluding outsiders such as school teachers), seventeen of which are headed by a married man and one by a widower. The remaining five households are headed by women: one by a divorcee and four by widows. One of the latter households consists of a widow and her five children, two are headed by a pair of women who are the widows of brothers, and one has three women who are the widows of three brothers. Besides these widows, there are nine other widows in this village, all of whom are living with relatives. Six of these are living with a married son, one with her deceased husband's parents, one with her deceased husband's brother, and one with her own brother. (This latter case was considered temporary because her deceased husband's brother's present house was too small.) The data regarding the widows make it clear that the rule of patrilocal residence is strong, since each of the sixteen widows is residing in the village of her deceased husband. Even in the case of the widow living with her own brother, she is able to reside with him because her family happens to be from the same village as her deceased husband.

Completing the statistical account of households in this village, besides the nuclear families and the widows, other residents include one handicapped woman who never married and who lives with her brother, one adolescent boy living with his married older brother, and several "foster" children, that is, children temporarily residing with their relatives.

Consanguineal kin

Terminology

Consanguineal kin in Yawa society are classified disjunctively as *taundave* 'close' kin [lit. 'very own'],[6] or *randani* 'distant' kin. Not all Yawa set the boundary between *taundave* and *randani* kin in the same relative place. As a minimum, however, everyone would agree that *taundave* refers to those kin who belong to the two descent groups defined by a person's two sets of grandparents and all their descendants. That is, all those persons descended from ego's paternal grandparents, as well as those descended from ego's maternal grandparents, are ego's *taundave* kin. On the other hand, ego's *randani* kin are related more distantly; they are the collateral lineages of second ascending or higher generations. They include kin on both mother's and father's sides.

However, some Yawa classify at least some of the kinsmen of the second degree of collaterality as *taundave*. It appears that in such cases, the criterion is not a matter of lesser or greater genealogical distance, but rather, whether or not the links connecting a particular kinsman to ego are known. If all the links are known, then some Yawa insist that the kinsman is *taundave*, regardless of the genealogical distance; if the links are not all known, the kinsman must be *randani*. However, I have found no Yawa who knows the names of all his or her great-grandparents and none who knows the identities of all his or her grandparents' siblings. Knowledge of these kinsmen is either partial or lacking altogether. Consequently, the extension of the *taundave* classification into the second degree of collaterality is never more than partial. Perhaps this lack of knowledge may be explained by the fact that it is not in one's self interest to know the links since admission of such knowledge would limit marriage choices.

The significance of the distinction between *taundave* kin and *randani* kin lies in the marriage rules. That is, a person should never marry a *taundave* kinsman, including a cross-cousin who is *taundave*.

The Yawa begin reckoning their kinship with their patrilineal clan affiliation. The system is classificatory and bifurcate merging, distinguishing cross- from parallel relatives in each of the middle three generations ($+1$, 0, -1 generations), what Keesing (1975:105) has called the Dravidian-Iroquois

---

[6]Actually, the word *taundave* is an adjective which simply means 'very own'. However, in the context of kinship terminology it means 'close kin' (e.g., mother's brother would be *awani taundave*).

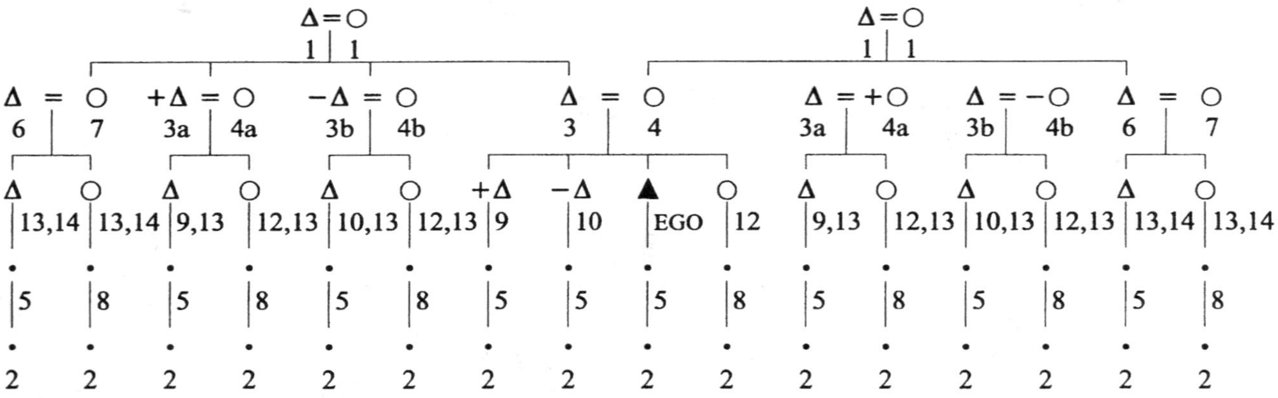

Term	Core Meaning	Term	Core Meaning
1. anena	grandkinsman	6. awateap, awani, kamoki	uncle
2. ajavi, anena	grandchild	7. andam, ara	aunt
3. ajap	father	8. augai, aivaki, kamoki	nephew/niece
3a. ajayo anuija	older father	9. anuija	older sibling (same sex)
3b. ajayo rijata	younger father	10. rijata	younger sibling (same sex)
4. akoyam	mother	11. anakavo	woman's brother
4a. akoyo anuija	older mother	12. anamam	man's sister
4b. akoyo rijata	younger mother	13. arakova	sibling
5. kavo, arikainy	child	14. aetaka	cross cousin

Fig. 4. Close consanguineal kin (Reciprocal terms are boxed together)

type. The terminology for *taundave* kin[7] is shown in figure 4, and for *randani* kin in figure 5. Figure 5 shows all the kin of the second degree of collaterality for father's father and mother's father, which represent the two descent groups that include the cross-cousins most important in Yawa marriages. (Terminology for the kin of father's mother and mother's mother is similarly reckoned.) For each distinct term in the kinship charts, the closest relationship that ego has with a kinsman designated by that term is taken to be the core meaning of the term, which then is given in the nearest English translation. Thus, while there are a number of kinsmen that ego refers to as his *awani,* the closest one is his mother's brother, which in English would be translated as 'uncle'. Hence, the core meaning of *awani* is listed as 'uncle'. Extensions of the terms to other kinsmen can be seen in figures 4 and 5, and are also spelled out in the appendix. There are alternate terms in some cases, which appear to have exactly the same denotata. These alternate terms may be due to dialectal differences or to borrowing from other languages. Symbols used in the figures are explained in the list of abbreviations at the end of the paper.

Only FF and MF kinship charts are included. The chart for FM is not given because it is exactly the same as for FF with the sole exception that ego's true grandparent is female in the FM chart but male in the FF chart. In every other category, the FM chart is identical to the FF chart. Similarly, the kinship chart for MM is not included since it is identical to the chart for MF except for the sex of ego's true grandparent. Numbers refer to the terms listed in figure 4.

As mentioned previously, in the middle three generations parallel kinsmen are designated by different terminology from cross-kinsmen. In the first descending generation, this yields two basic categories, roughly glossed as 'child' and 'nephew' or 'niece'. There are two terms for the former category[8] and three apparently alternate terms for the latter category, only one of which distinguishes sex, and that distinction is strictly optional. By the addition of a

---

[7]The terms are generally given in the fullest nonpossessed form. In everyday speech, shortened forms are more usual. For example, the suffix which specifies sex (*-p* 'masculine' and *-m* 'feminine') is usually dropped, unless needed for clarification. In usage, these terms are always preceded by a possession marker. Only two terms, those for 'father' and 'mother', take bound prefixes, indicating inalienable possession. For first person singular, these forms become *injaya* and *ingkoa.* All other terms take a separate possessive word.

[8]Only one of these terms is, strictly speaking, a kinship term. That is *kavo,* which must be preceded by a possessive, while *arikainy* is simply a generic term for 'child'. In the sentence, "I saw a small child," where kinship is not asserted, only the word *arikainy* may be used. But "he is my child" could use either word.

Father's Father Kinship Chart

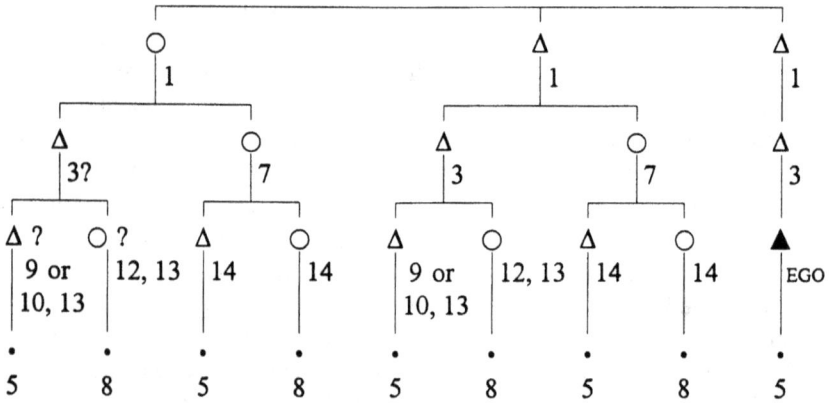

Mother's Father Kinship Chart

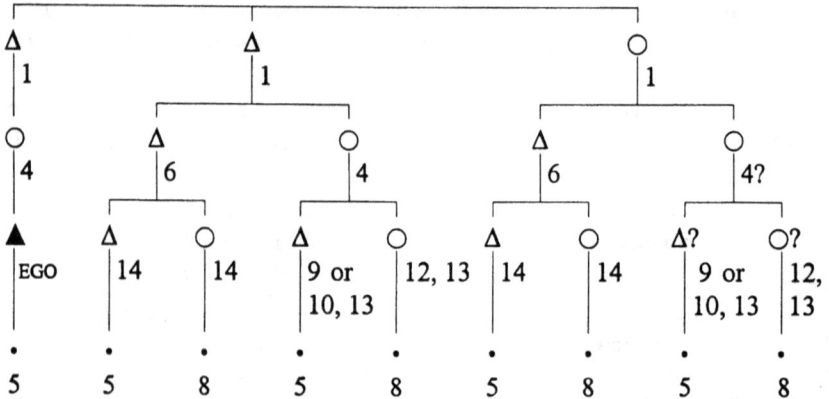

Fig. 5. Distant consanguineal kin

suffix, -p 'masculine' or -m 'feminine', sex may be specified with the term *augai*. (These suffixes are optionally added to certain other kinship terms as well.) In the first ascending generation, the sex of the kinsman is obligatorily factored in, which yields a set of four terms with core meanings of 'father', 'mother', 'uncle', and 'aunt'. The kinsmen to which all these terms are extended may be seen in figures 4 and 5.

In ego's generation, there is an additional dimension besides sex and the parallel versus cross-relationships. As is common throughout Indonesia, siblings are categorized by their relative age with respect to ego. *anuija* means 'older' while *rijata* means 'younger'. Used alone, these terms refer to siblings of the same sex as ego. Thus, when a woman speaks of her *anuija* she means an older sister, but when a man speaks of his *anuija* he means an older brother. For an opposite-sex sibling, there are special nonreciprocal terms; a woman refers to her brother as *anakavo,* while a man uses *anamam* for his sister.

In addition, the terms *anuija* 'older' and *rijata* 'younger' may be added as adjectives to other kinship terms. Thus, for clarification, a girl might speak of her *anakavo anuija* 'older brother'. The 'older' or 'younger' descriptions are almost always added to 'father' and 'mother' terms when ego is referring to someone other than his or her biological parent (e.g., *ajayo rijata* is taken to mean 'father's younger brother' or 'mother's younger sister's husband'). In fact, there is another term *yasyin* 'middle', which is used to refer to the second of three or more siblings of the same sex. For example, if one's father has three brothers, the middle one would be called *ajayo yasyin* 'middle father'. To refer unambiguously to one's biological father, a descriptive term *pinavaki* 'who bore me' is added to the term for father.

Only among true siblings do the 'older' or 'younger' terms accurately reflect actual chronological seniority. For other parallel kinsmen of the same generation, what is crucial is the birth order of the two linking kinsmen. Thus, ego calls his same sex cousin *anuija* 'older' or *rijata* 'younger' depending on the birth order of the ancestral siblings that constitute the link between them. For example, if the two linking kinsmen were their fathers who were brothers, then the children of the older brother would all be referred to by the 'older' terminology, regardless of which are older in an absolute sense. There is a special term, *mambe netaive,* which refers to the 'older' or 'younger' relationship that two parallel kinsmen of the same sex and same generation have.[9] A *mambe netaive* relationship is considered special, particularly between males.

Cousin terminology is also bifurcate merging in that terminology for parallel cousins is the same as for siblings, but distinct from cross-cousin terminology. Because of Yawa marriage patterns, cross-cousin is a very important category. There is a single term *aetaka* which applies to cross-cousins of either sex and is used irrespective of relative seniority. The term always refers to a same-generation kinsman whose linking parent is of the opposite sex to ego's linking parent. Consequently, with respect to the classification of second and more distant cousins, the system is like Iroquois because, as Lounsbury (1964:1079) carefully notes, "the sexes of intervening links, when present, are irrelevant to the reckoning"; only the sexes of the first and last link are relevant. (This irrelevance contrasts with Dravidian-type terminology where the sex of all known intervening links is critical in affecting the classification. This distinction between Iroquois and Dravidian kinship types was first pointed out in Lounsbury's paper.)

Having said this, however, it must be added that all cross-cousins may also be referred to by sibling terminology, and in everyday usage, such terminology often predominates. To make the categorization precise, the Yawa frequently compound sibling and cousin terms into one descriptive phrase (e.g., *sya anamo sya aetak* 'my cross-cousin sister').[10] The closer the kinsman, the more likely that only sibling terms will be used. As one language assistant explained to me, among close kin sibling terms are *makoeve* 'big' (i.e., 'important'), while cousin terms are *mamaun* 'small' (i.e., 'unimportant'). Since Yawa prescribe cross-cousin marriage, but only between *randani* 'distant' cross-cousins, the regular use of sibling terms instead of the cross-cousin term for *taundave* 'close' cross-cousins can be understood as functioning to underscore the status of such kinsmen as unmarriageable by ego.

---

[9]This distinction is similar to that found in the Wandamen word *netavava* 'same sex elder sibling' (Flaming 1983:248). Although Wandamen is not linguistically related at all to Yawa and is geographically quite distant, being in the "Bird's Neck" area of Irian Jaya, it is closely related linguistically to the Austronesian languages of Yapen which surround the Yawa. Furthermore, the Wandamen kinship system, as described by Flaming, appears to be in many respects similar to the Yawa system, indicating some cultural links.

[10]The linguistic structure marks the noun *aetak* as modifying the noun *anamo*, which is why I have glossed it as 'my cross-cousin sister'.

There is one category of kinsman that is a problem in the analysis. This is the category of ego's parent's same sex cross-cousin. By Iroquois-type reckoning, this kinsman would be predicted to be 'parent' (that is, 'father' or 'mother', depending on the sex). Indeed, many of the genealogies I collected did categorize this kinsman according to the prediction. However, there were some cases in otherwise reliable genealogies where the kinsman in question was instead termed 'uncle' or 'aunt', and where this classification did not appear to result from a different, but closer, genealogical path. Perhaps one source of confusion is that, because of residence patterns after marriage, kinsmen of this category usually reside in some other, perhaps distant, village, so that ego very possibly has had no contact with that person and thus had no need to calculate a kinship term for him or her until I requested it in the genealogy.

Furthermore, I have recorded several marriages between offspring of same sex cross-cousins. Since these marriages were deemed totally proper, it must be the case that the linking parents were conceptualized as cross-related and therefore the offspring were, too. Thus, the way in which ego categorizes parent's same sex cross-cousin has automatic consequences in the categorization of that kinsman's offspring. The problematical categorization of these collateral kinsmen is indicated by question marks in figure 5.

Only the middle three generations ($+1$, 0, and -1 generations) distinguish among kinsmen. In higher or lower generations, there is only a single term. All kinsmen of higher generations ($+2$ or higher) are lumped together as *anena*, which refers ambiguously to grandparents, great-grandparents, and so forth, and also means 'ancestor'. Actually, it is a rare Yawa who knows any names of kinsmen beyond his grandparents, or even the names of his grandparents' siblings. The term *anena* may be used reciprocally for kin of the second descending generation, that is, a grandparent and his grandchild refer to each other as *anena*. There is also a special term *ajavi* which is not reciprocal and refers only to the grandchild (or great-grandchild, etc.).

The terms discussed above and those given in figures 4 and 5 are all terms of reference. Terms of direct address may be formed from most of these terms simply by suffixing *-e* or suppleting the final vowel with this suffix (e.g., *anene* 'grandkinsman [direct address]'). Possessive markers are not used with direct address, except for the bound markers which occur with the words for 'father' and 'mother'. Neither are descriptive adjectives such as *anuija* 'older' used in direct address. For example, father's older brother is addressed simply as 'my father' rather than 'my older father' which is a translation of the usual term of reference. Kinsmen of the first and second ascending generations are always addressed by their kin term modified into the direct address form in the way just described.

On the other hand, a close kinsman of ego's generation is generally addressed simply by his (or her) given name until he marries and bears his first child, after which he is addressed by *teknonymy* (i.e., 'father of so-and-so', using the name of his firstborn child). This is the pattern between spouses as well; they use given names until the first child is born, after which they use *teknonymy* in addressing each other. For distant kinsmen of the same generation, the address form is *arakove*. (Actually, while this term has 'sibling' as its core meaning, it may be extended to any person of the same generation where the genealogical relationship is either unknown, such as a Yawa from a distant village, or is assumed to be nonexistent, such as an outsider.) Kinsmen of the first descending generation are generally addressed by their given names if they are unmarried, otherwise by *teknonymy* as described above. With nieces and nephews, however, kin terms are occasionally used. Grandchildren are called either *anene* or by their given names.

Kinship Behavior

The bonds of kinship are strongest to one's *taundave* kin and involve mutual support, material reciprocity, and assistance in crises. Adults have asymmetrical ties of "succorance-dependence" (Keesing 1980) with their kinsmen who are still children. However, the ties are symmetrical ones of reciprocal support between adult kinsmen. Support may be given in small ways, such as splitting a sago log with a kinsman or offering hospitality to a visiting kinsman, or it may be offered on major projects, such as helping a kinsman fell trees in a new garden or assisting him in putting on a new roof.[11]

taundave kinsmen are a guarantee of social security, whether it be by providing foster care to a child or providing long-term care for the handicapped, a widow or widower, or elderly parents. When it is simply a child that needs to be watched for a few hours, an older close kinsman is called upon. In times of crisis, such as a serious illness or a death, close kin rally around.

Material reciprocity both expresses and forges close ties between kinsmen. The most common material items are food gifts, especially surplus garden produce, fish, or wild pork. But other kinds of material goods are also given to a close kinsman. A woman might weave a bag or roofing thatch for her

---

[11]All examples of kin behavior in these next few paragraphs were by personal observation or were reported to me by language assistants.

brother, while a man might bring firewood to his sister. A woman might give her sister a new dress, and a man might carve a canoe for his brother. A man might take a bambooful of palm wine to his cousin, or make a bow and arrow set for his sister's son. A niece gets medicinal leaves to place on the aching limbs of her mother's brother. A grandparent gives a sago tree to his newly married grandson. A young man sends a bottle of homemade coconut oil to his father's brother. In cases of financial strain, a sister lends money to a needy brother, and a brother gives money for school expenses to his younger brother. The greatest financial strain is, of course, the bride price, and all adult *taundave* kinsmen, both patrilateral and matrilateral, are expected to contribute to the bride price. Conversely, when a bride price is received, it is distributed to these same close kin. (Besides tapping close kinsmen for the bride price, the groom's family solicits contributions from all their fellow villagers, as mentioned above.)

Formerly, the mother's brother-sister's child relationship was quite important, but it is less so today. For example, formerly, when the sister's child died, the child's mother's brother took some or all of the deceased's belongings. This practice does not occur nowadays. However, among some Yawa, there is still a special ceremony that the mother's brother performs for his sister's daughter when she "comes of age." There is a big party, with feasting, singing, and dancing. The climax of the party occurs when the girl's ears are pierced by her mother's brother, and he presents her with her first earrings.

Of the various paired relationships among *taundave* kin, the most significant is the brother-brother relationship. As mentioned above, there is a special term for such a relationship: *mambe netaive.* For the Yawa, the brother-brother relationship is the "dominant dyad" (Hsu 1971) among consanguineal kin. Its dominance has already been glimpsed in the previous discussion regarding widows. When a man dies, the expectation is that his widow will be cared for by one of his brothers. If her children are older, she may choose to live in her own residence, but nonetheless one of her deceased husband's brothers will be the guardian for her children, and also their primary benefactor. If the deceased man had an unmarried brother (or even a classificatory brother of his patriclan) of suitable age, it is likely that that brother will marry the widow. On the other hand, if the widow chooses to remarry into a different clan, she forfeits the raising of her children to her deceased husband's clan, which in practical terms, usually means the children go to one of the brothers of the deceased man.

While they are alive, older brothers look after their younger brothers. If a younger brother goes for further education, he can count on financial help from his older brother. When their parents die, a younger brother who has not yet married can count on living in his older brother's home. When the brothers are all grown men, they look to each other for assistance in major projects, such as felling trees in a garden or building a house. If one brother has a special skill, such as making canoes, his brothers expect to benefit from that skill.

Affinal Kin

Affinal kin terminology in Yawa presents a curious blend of terminology which is unique to affines with terminology which is not at all unique to affines, but in fact is the same terminology which is used for consanguineal kin. Thus, it would appear that in some way, the Yawa perceive some of their affines as being related to them analogously as their own consanguineal kin. Indeed, in many instances affines who are referred to by consanguineal termi- nology are not blood-related, or at least not related in any way that the people can actually trace. How is it that these affines are classified as consanguineal kin? An explanation is offered later in the section on The Social Logic of Yawa Kinship Terminology. First, this section lays the groundwork by dis- cussing the terminology of affines. The overall system is detailed in figure 6.

The set of terms which are unique to affines is actually quite small. There are terms for 'husband' and 'wife'[12] and two sets of terms relating these individuals to their parents-in-law. One set of terms, based on the morpheme *anu*, is used between the husband and his parents-in-law, and a different set of terms, based on the morpheme *ajama*, is used between the wife and her parents-in-law. In other words, these morphemes are the basis for reciprocat- ing terms between a child-in-law and his or her parents-in-law. To the basic morphemes *anu* and *ajama* may be added suffixes which specify the sex of the referent. Thus, *-p* 'masculine', suffixed to *anu*, gives *anup*, which may refer to either of the masculine members of this son-in-law/parents-in-law threesome. Since the mother-in-law is the only female in this threesome, the feminine form *anumam* refers unambiguously to her. The situation is reversed with *ajama* which denotes a daughter-in-law and her parents-in-law. In this three- some there are two females, the daughter-in-law and mother-in-law, both of which are referred to by the feminine form *ajamam*, while the masculine form

---

[12]In everyday parlance, a man's wife is also called his *wanya* 'woman' and she calls him her *anya* 'man'.

ajamap refers unambiguously to the father-in-law. However, the daughter-in-law and mother-in-law terms may be disambiguated by the addition, interestingly enough, of the adjective *kove* 'living' or *kakai* 'dead', respectively.[13]

Affinal Kin Terminology for Male Ego

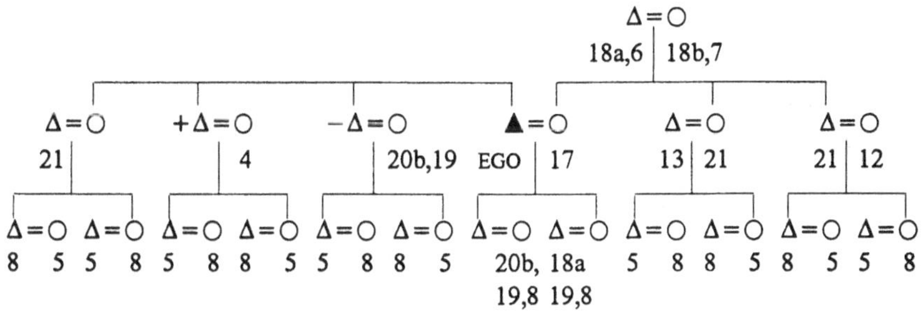

Terminology for Female Ego (where different)

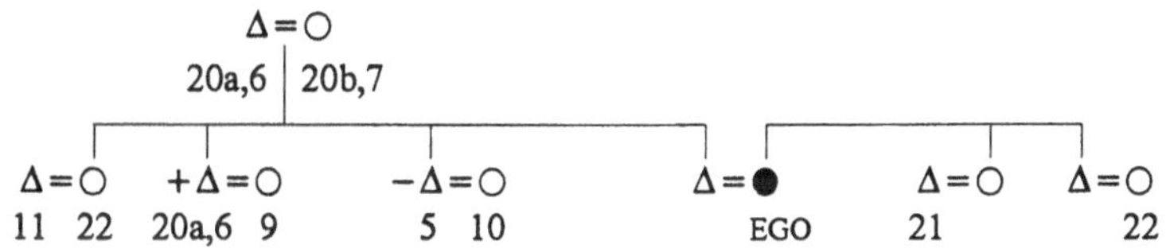

Fig. 6. Affinal kin (1 of 2)
(Reciprocal terms are boxed together)

---

[13]It was explained to me that the mother-in-law is called 'dead' because it is presumed that she, being older, will die first.

Affinal Terms	
Term	**Core Meaning**
15. *vainy*	coparents-in-law
16. *anap*	husband
17. *anamu*	wife
18. *anu*	man and his parent's-in-law
a. *anup*	son-in-law, man's father-in-law
b. *anumam*	man's mother-in-law
19. *tamaisya*	child-in-law
19. *tamaisya*	child-in-law
20. *ajama*	woman and her parents-in-law
a. *ajamap*	woman's father-in-law
b. *ajamam*	daughter-in-law, woman's mother-in-law
21. *amai, araki*	sibling-in-law
22. *arema*	woman's sister-in-law
Consanguineal Terms Used For Affines	
Term	**Core Meaning**
4. *akoyam*	mother
5. *kavo, arikainy*	child
6. *awateap, awani, kamoki*	uncle
7. *andam, ara*	aunt
8. *augai, aivaki, kamoki*	nephew/niece
9. *anuija*	older sibling (same sex)
10. *rijata*	younger sibling (same sex)
11. *anakavo*	woman's brother
12. *anamam*	man's sister
13. *arakova*	sibling

Fig. 6. Affinal kin (2 of 2)
(Reciprocal terms are boxed together)

In addition, there is a nonreciprocal term *tamaisya,* which means only 'child-in-law' (that is, either 'daughter-in-law' or 'son-in-law'). Also there is a special term *vainy* which the two sets of parents of the married couple use to refer to each other.[14]

For siblings-in-law, there are only three terms in Yawa that are strictly affinal, and not consanguineal, terms. These are *amai, araki,* and *arema.* The first two denote various affines, such as 'wife's sister', 'wife's brother', and 'sister's husband'. Both *amai* and *araki* are reciprocating terms, but they may be made specific for sex by the addition of a gender suffix. The term *arema* is a reciprocating term which is used only between two women who are related to each other as husband's sister or brother's wife.

In summary, there are nine terms that are unique to affines, three of these for sibling-in-law relationships, three for child-in-law/parents-in-law relationships, two for the husband/wife relationship, and one for the relationship between the two sets of parents of the couple.

By contrast to the relatively small set of terms unique to affines, sixteen terms used for affines are basically consanguineal terms (lower portion of figure 6). In fact, the only consanguineal terms that are not also used for affines are just these three: *ajap* 'father', *anena* 'grandkinsman', and *aetaka* 'cross-cousin'. Furthermore, if we consider that the spouse of a Yawa is normally his or her cross-cousin, we see that only two consanguineal kin terms are not relevant to affinal relationships. The pervasive use of consanguineal kin terms for affines can be partly explained with respect to social function, as we see in the following section.

Marriage

Marriage Patterns

This section examines more closely the marriage patterns among the Yawa. There are three basic rules: clan exogamy, cross-cousin marriage, and no marriage among *taundave* kinsmen. These are essentially summed up by the Yawa stating that they must marry their *aetako randani* 'distant cross-cousin'. (Although this phrase does not exclude fellow clanspersons, clan

---

[14]This term has apparent cognates over a widespread area in Irian Jaya and has evidently been borrowed by other unrelated languages. For example, in Wandamen the term is *bai* (Flaming 1983:253), in Kaure it is *payan* (Dommel, this volume), and in Orya it is *bayan* (Phil Fields, p.c.). the Indonesian word is *besan.*

exogamy goes without saying for the Yawa.) The marriage system is "prescriptive" in Maybury-Lewis' sense (1971:201) as one "in which there is a rule of marriage with a prescribed category of relative."[15] The Yawa prescribe marriage with a cross-cousin (who is appropriately distantly related).

There are, of course, marriages that do not conform to the marriage rules. Most common is the case in which a Yawa has taken a spouse that is a *vatano maran* 'outsider', that is, someone from a distant area such as Waropen, Manokwari, or Jayapura. Such a spouse is outside the kinship network and so could not be a cross-cousin, but such a marriage is socially acceptable. However, other marriages that violate the marriage rules, such as one between a man and a woman of the same clan, or between a woman and her classificatory uncle, or between cross-cousins who are first cousins, are considered *koveramu* 'no good' or *tatugadi* 'bad'. Such couples are accepted into the community, but the people cluck disapprovingly when referring to the marriage and are not surprised if the couple has some misfortune, such as being barren or one of them dying prematurely. Even so, almost every genealogy I recorded had at least one such 'bad' marriage.

Before Christian influence, polygyny used to be common, but now is found only among older men. One man told me his grandfather had at one time been married to five wives. In cases of multiple wives, each one was supposed to be from a different clan, although this was not always the fact. As already mentioned, levirate marriages are common. There are also marriages which involve exchanges of sisters.

Formerly, all (first) marriages were arranged by the parents or, if the parents were both dead, by the close elder kinsman who was the guardian. Many marriages were arranged when the prospective mates were very young children, or sometimes not yet born. Nowadays parents still arrange many of the marriages (the term for which is *vainye rave*), but it is more usual to wait until the girl has reached puberty. The two sets of parents seal the agreement by sharing a meal *(anaisyo vainye)* together and shaking hands. This establishes a special relationship between them and they henceforth refer to each other by the special kinship term *vainy* 'coparent-in-law'. When parents have promised their children to each other in this way, such engagements are not lightly broken. However, nowadays young people are not forced to marry

---

[15]Maybury-Lewis is at great pains to be precise in the definition of prescriptive marriages. At this point, I am not defining the Yawa rule of marriage so carefully. However, it will become clear, especially in the section entitled The Social Logic of Yawa Kinship Terminology, that the Yawa marriage system is indeed 'prescriptive', even in Maybury-Lewis' careful sense.

against their will, and so sometimes the engagements are broken *(vainye raotar)*. When it happens, there is supposed to be compensation paid by the party who breaks the engagement. Since engagement periods are often lengthy, a bride price may not be negotiated until the marriage is near. Women are typically in their late teens and men in their twenties when they marry.

In recent years more and more young people have arranged their own marriages.[16] The usual method is for a young man to write a letter proposing marriage which he sends secretly to the young lady of his choice (who should be a distant cross-cousin). Before she responds, the girl may seek someone's advice, most likely a brother. If she replies affirmatively, the couple then exchanges letters negotiating when and how the marriage will take place. Sometimes they even go so far as to inform the political leader of the village of their plans, but not their parents.

Yawa marriages are not celebrated by any special ceremony. In both types of marriage—those arranged by the parents and those arranged secretly by the couple—the man and woman simply begin living together. There is no wedding party, no ritual, no marking of the occasion in any way. A date is simply agreed upon, and then the man brings the woman to live in his parents' home. If the couple had secretly agreed to the marriage, the parents may simply wake up the next morning to find the new bride in their home. The reaction by the parents is sometimes disappointment or anger, but the marriage is nonetheless accepted. "What else can you do?" the people say. It seems that if the couple has already had sexual intercourse, the union is considered irrevocable.

All marriages, regardless of who arranges them, involve a bride price *(romane)*. If the couple "elopes" by living together without the parents' prior agreement, then after the fact a bride price will have to be negotiated. All the groom's matrilateral and patrilateral *taundave* kin, plus all the people from the groom's village (whether or not kinsmen), are expected to contribute so that he can *wanya ramavun* 'buy a wife'. Kin who reside in distant villages are not expected to contribute. Usual bride price items are dishes, clothing, cloth (ordinary *kain,* not old or traditional pieces), and money. Formerly, very old Chinese porcelain dishes were included, but these have become scarce. Sometimes one of the bride's kinsman makes a special request, such as for a radio or a pressure lamp, and these items are ordered

---

[16]In these cases, the two sets of parents will not establish the special *vainye* relationship.

in the bride price negotiation. The lowest bride prices, calculated as the total value of all the items including money, run about 200,000 to 400,000 rupiah (approximately \$112 to \$225 U.S. dollars in 1989 prices). The highest bride prices run double this amount and usually involve marriage to a person who is not from Yapen Island. The bride price is not paid at the time of the marriage, although a food gift is usually given by the groom's family to the bride's at that time. Indeed the bride price is seldom paid before several children have been born to the couple; if there are no children, the groom's family may refuse to pay the bride price. When the bride price is finally ready, a date is set when the groom's kinsmen and fellow villagers gather to bring their contributions to the bride price, the groom's family throws a party, and hands are shaken all around. At some later time the groom's father (or an appropriate substitute) delivers the bride price to the bride's brother, who divides everything up as evenly as possible to the bride's kinsmen. This distribution is informal, and not marked by any special occasion.

Marriage and Kinship Terminology

It is in the patterns of residence upon marriage that we can see the social functions of some of the terminology for affines. The Yawa are strongly patrilocal, and furthermore, a newly married couple almost always lives with the groom's parents, usually for a period of several years.[17] The new bride becomes an important part of the labor force and is expected to do the sorts of tasks that an older daughter would do.

In this regard, an important question is how the bride addresses the members of her new household and how they address her. In the previous section, I listed *ajamap* and *ajamam* as the terms for 'father-in-law' and 'mother-in-law'. However, in everyday speech, the new bride addresses them as *awate* 'uncle' and *anda* (or *ara*) 'aunt'. As the parents of her *aetaka,* these are the terms she called them even before marriage. The parents-in-law may reciprocate with 'niece' terminology.

There is an important caring relationship that the new bride has with her husband's brothers, which is a natural extension of the caring relationship that is usual between brothers. Throughout childhood, the older brother had been looking out for his younger brother, and this practice continues when the older one marries and brings his new wife to live in the family home.

---

[17]If the groom's parents are already deceased, the newlyweds usually reside with whomever had become the groom's guardian.

The older brother, now an adult, is almost like a father to the younger brother, and the older brother's wife is like the boy's mother. These roles are reflected in the affinal terms used. The boy calls his older brother's wife *akoyam* 'mother' and she calls him *kavo* or *arikainy,* both meaning 'child'. When the boy ultimately marries and brings his new wife into the home, for the older brother it is as if his son got married, and he calls the new bride his *ajamam* or *tamaisya* 'daughter-in-law'. She reciprocates with the terms for 'father-in-law'.[18]

Consider another relationship the new bride in the home has, namely, with her husband's older brother's wife. If both women are living in the same house (because the older brother has not yet moved out), then the women often form a bond. They help take care of each other's children, they share food, they may share their tasks. They are married to two brothers and thus their futures are intertwined. If both their husbands die, they may live together as widows. Not surprisingly, then, they refer to each other as sisters (even though it is exceedingly rare that they actually are). The older brother's wife calls the younger one's wife *rijata* 'younger sister' and in turn is called *anuija* 'older sister'.

Thus, many of the consanguineal terms that are used for affines relate to the new relationships created by a man bringing his new wife to live in his parents' home. Living in this home are the husband's parents, his brothers and their wives, and his sisters. The sisters will eventually marry and leave. But the other members of the husband's family remain there, if not always in the same house, at least nearby. With these "permanent" members of her husband's family, the woman uses the closer consanguineal terms, which symbolically represent the closer social ties.

The Social Logic of Yawa Kinship Terminology

The Yawa Two-Section System

As we have just seen, social function can explain the use of consanguineal terms for affines in some categories of relationship. However, there remains a residue of consanguineal terms used for affines that are not so easily explained. The residue includes the sibling terms which are used for relationships

---

[18]Flaming (1983:251) analyzes the corresponding Wandamen affinal terminology similarly in terms of their social function.

such as *anakavo* 'husband's sister's husband', *arakova* 'wife's sister's husband', and *anama* 'wife's brother's wife'. Also in the residue are the consanguineal terms which are used for the spouse of a classificatory child or a classificatory nephew or niece.

To explain this terminology, we must first look at the married couples involved in each case. These are arranged in figure 7 with one couple listed per line. Using genealogical notation relative to ego, the member of the couple whom ego calls by the "closer" term is listed on the left, the other member is listed on the right. By "closer" term, it is meant that if ego refers to one member of the couple by a consanguineal term and the other by an affinal term, then the consanguineal term is considered "closer." If ego refers to both members of the couple by consanguineal terms, then the parallel term is considered "closer" than the cross term.

Terms of Reference for Male Ego

WBW	*anama* 'sister'	WB	*amai* 'sibling-in-law'
WZH	*arakova* 'brother'	WZ	*amai* 'sibling-in-law'
BS	*kavo* 'child'	BSW	*augaim* 'niece'
BD	*kavo* 'child'	BDH	*augaip* 'nephew'
Z	*anama* 'sister'	ZH	*amai* 'sibling-in-law'
ZSW	*kavo* 'child'	ZS	*augaip* 'nephew'
ZDH	*kavo* 'child'	ZD	*augaim* 'niece'

Fig. 7. Terminology for selected married couples (1 of 2)

Terms of Reference for Male Ego

MBSW, FZSW	*anama*[19] 'sister'	MBS, FZS	*aetaka* 'cousin'
yB	*rijatay* 'younger brother'	BW	*ajama* 'daughter-in-law'
SWM	*anama* 'sister'	SWF	*araki, aetaka* 'sibling-in-law','cousin'

Terms of Reference for Female Ego

HZH	*anakavo* 'brother'	HZ	*arema* 'sister-in-law'
HoBW	*anuija* 'older sister'	HoB	*ajamap, awate* 'father-in-law','uncle'
B	*anakavo* 'brother'	BW	*arema* 'sister-in-law'
BSW	*kavo* 'child'	BS	*augaip* 'nephew'
MBDH, FZDH	*anakavo* 'brother'	MBD, FZD	*aetaka* 'cousin'

Fig. 7. Terminology for selected married couples (2 of 2)

Notice that I have added to the figure a number of other married couples besides the ones whose members were mentioned at the beginning of this section as constituting a residue. That is because the terminology for the residual affines is really just a part of a larger terminological system. Examining the figure, one can see that all the terms to the left are strictly "parallel" consanguineal terms, while all the terms to the right are either

---

[19]Actually, there is no single way to classify spouses of an *aetaka*. Some Yawa call an *aetaka's* spouse by sibling terms, others by sibling-in-law terms. The difference is probably due to the dual status of MBC and FZC as both cross-cousin and also sibling. Recall that the two terms may even be compounded into one phrase (e.g., *sya anamo sya aetak* 'my cross-cousin sister'). Viewing MBC or FZC as a sibling would require the spouse to be viewed as a sibling-in-law. However, emphasizing the cross-cousin nature of the relationship would require viewing the spouse as a sibling. Hence, if MBC or FZC is categorized as 'sibling', then the spouse is categorized as 'sibling-in-law'; if MBC or FZC is categorized as 'cross-cousin', then the spouse is 'sibling'. Either way, the kinsman and his or her spouse end up in opposite categories of each other, which is what is significant.

"cross" consanguineal terms or affinal terms. What this configuration means is that the spouses of parallel kinsmen are cross-kinsmen and affines. In other words, in some sense cross-kinsmen are conceptually equivalent to affines.

This is precisely the way TWO-SECTION SYSTEMS operate (Dumont 1971). It would appear that conceptually the Yawa divide their social world into two sections: "my kind of people" and "the other kind of people, with whom we marry" (Keesing 1975:108).[20] From ego's perspective, "his kind of people" are his classificatory fathers and mothers, his classificatory siblings and their offspring, and his classificatory children. "The other kind of people" are ego's classificatory uncles and aunts, his classificatory cousins, and his classificatory nieces and nephews. Also included in "the other kind of people" are affines such as father-in-law, mother-in-law, son-in-law, daughter-in-law, and sibling-in-law. Grouping cross-kinsmen with affines is natural in a social system, such as the Yawa system, in which there is a prescriptive rule that a man marries his cross-cousin. Essentially, for the Yawa, cross-kinsmen are potential affines.

It is important to emphasize that the two-section system is not based fundamentally on genealogical distance, such that persons who are genealogically closer to ego are in one section (ego's), while in the opposing section are those persons who are genealogically more remote. That this is not the case is easily demonstrated in figure 7. Since every symbol in the genealogical notation represents one more link distant from ego, if the system were based strictly on relative genealogical proximity to ego, then for every couple it would have to be the case that the member of the couple who is in ego's section (always on the left) would be denoted by a shorter notational string than that used to denote the member of the couple who is in the other section (always on the right). However, this line of reasoning does not hold for many of the couples. For example, WBW is a longer notation than WB (reflecting the fact that WB is closer genealogically to ego than WBW is). However, in Yawa conceptualization, WBW is closer, since she is categorized as ego's 'sister', while WB is merely a 'sibling-in-law'. Another striking example is ZD and ZDH. ZD is ego's 'niece', but her husband is conceptually ego's 'child'. Hence, niece's husband is conceptually closer to ego than the niece herself. What this perspective means is that no matter who ego's niece marries, that man is

---

[20]The conceptual split into two sections is only relevant for the middle three generations (ego's, $+1$, and -1). For $+2$ and -2 generations, there is only one section—everyone is essentially "my kind of people."

classified as ego's child, even if he has no known kin relationship whatsoever to ego.

Two-section systems are sometimes associated with exogamous moieties, but there are no such moieties in the Yawa system, either named or unnamed. In fact, it can be proven quite simply that moieties could not exist by considering the marriages involving three populous clans, the Karubaba, the Rumansara, and the Paai clans. If Yawa society were divided into two exogamous moieties, then two of these three clans would have to be in the same moiety, and therefore marriage would be prohibited between those two clans. However, there are numerous marriages involving each of the possible combinations of these three clans, and all are considered proper marriages.

Dumont (1971) has interpreted the two-section systems in Dravidian societies as being "symmetrical alliances," or as Scheffler (1971:231) puts it, "mutually exclusive and intermarrying units." This perspective implies two fixed sections which have a sort of compact between them. Dumont's analysis has been disputed by others (Scheffler 1971:231) and it most certainly is not the sort of model that best fits the Yawa system. Rather, it seems that for each individual Yawa, his social world is divided into two sections, which are simply described by the phrases already used above, "my kind of people" and "the other kind of people." This division of the society is unique for every Yawa (besides true siblings) because each individual has a unique genealogical history which determines his or her two "kinds" of people. There are not two "fixed" sections of any sort in Yawa society. Rather, the Yawa two-section system is egocentric in that it is totally relative to the individual member of the society.

Marriageability as the Organizing Principle of Yawa Kinship

We may now turn to what could be called the social logic of Yawa kinship terminology. The salient organizing principle for the kinship terminology is marriageability. It is on the basis of marriageability that a Yawa categorizes the people in his or her social world into two sections.

Because a Yawa must marry an *aetaka* 'cross-cousin', it is imperative to identify who one's *aetaka* are. Having established who the persons are in the *aetaka* category, ego presumes everyone else in his or her generation to be *arakova* 'sibling'. Thus, in ego's generation, there are really only two categories: everyone may be categorized as either *aetaka* or *arakova*. Of these two categories, *aetaka* is the marked one, being reserved only for the category of potential spouses.[21] The other category, *arakova,* is unmarked, and includes everyone else of ego's generation (i.e., everyone not known to be a potential spouse).

To sum up, the two sections of a Yawa's social world are established on the basis of marriageability. Ego and all his *arakova* are in one section (nonmarriageable), while all ego's *aetaka* are in the other (marriageable) section. Further, also in ego's section are all the classificatory parents and children of ego and his *arakova,* while in the other section are all the classificatory parents and children of ego's *aetaka.*

Multiple Clans in the Yawa Two-Section System

We may ask now how this all relates to the organization of Yawa society into numerous clans. As already shown, it is not possible to divide the clans into two nonoverlapping moieties that would be exogamous. However, from the perspective of any particular Yawa individual, his social world could be said to be divided into just two clans, "his clan" and "the other clan." This is a theoretical model or construct that is helpful in explaining how ego categorizes his kin and affines.

Labeling ego's clan as Clan A and the other clan as Clan B for convenience of reference, we can examine how this model works. There are four basic rules needed at this point. (The fourth rule is elaborated below.)

(1) Patrilineal descent—when A is male, his children are A's and when B is male, his children are B's

(2) Exogamous marriage—an A must marry a B

(3) Same generation marriage—an A must marry a B of his or her generation

(4) Dual classification of a married woman of the first ascending generation—she is classified by ego as belonging to her birth clan when she is a link in a genealogical chain, but she is classified as belonging to her husband's clan when she is the end point of the chain between her and ego.

Assume, then, that ego is male and belongs to clan A. Then ego's true father and all his true siblings are also clan A. (Refer to figure 8 throughout

---

[21]Since ego calls both male and female cross-cousins *aetaka,* the category actually includes potential spouses for both ego and ego's true siblings, both male and female.

Ego's Siblings and Their Offspring

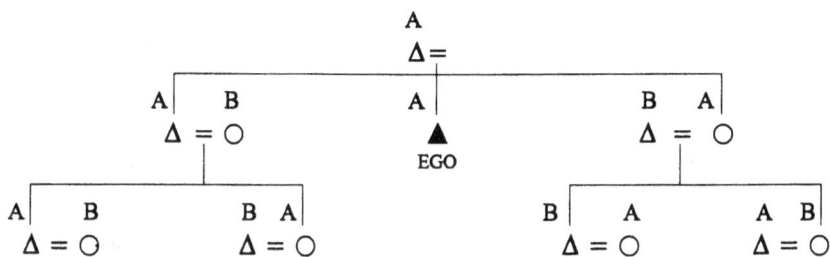

A
Δ=

A	B		A		B	A
Δ	= O		▲		Δ	= O
			EGO			

| A | B | | B | A | | B | A | | A | B |
| Δ | = O | | Δ | = O | | Δ | = O | | Δ | = O |

Ego's Parents, Aunts, and Uncles

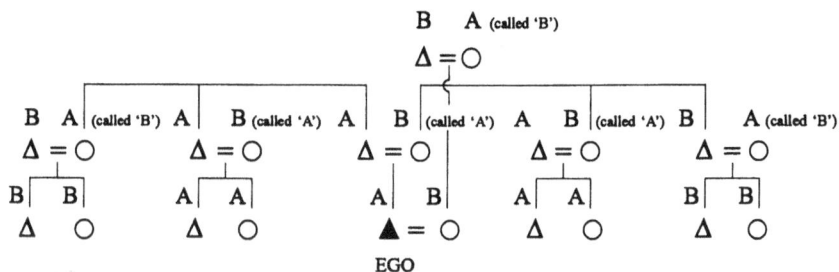

B A (called 'B')
Δ = O

B A (called 'B')	A B (called 'A')	A B (called 'A')	A B (called 'A')	B A (called 'B')
Δ = O	Δ = O	Δ = O	Δ = O	Δ = O
B B	A A	A B	A A	B B
Δ O	Δ O	▲ = O	Δ O	Δ O
		EGO		

Ego's Affines

B A
Δ = O

A B		A B		B A
▲ = O		Δ = O		Δ = O
EGO				
A B				
Δ = O				

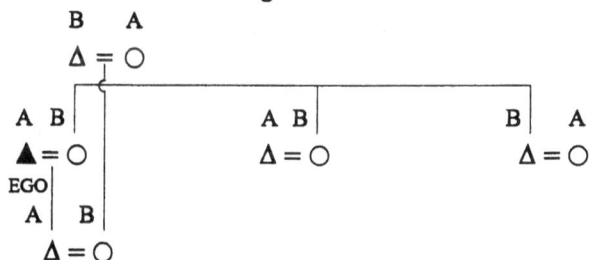

Fig. 8. Ego's kin and affines from the perspective
of a two-section (two-clan) system

this discussion.) Because of the exogamy rule, ego's father must have married a woman from clan B. Therefore, ego's mother is a B, and so then must be his maternal grandfather (because of patrilineal descent). Also mother's brother must be a B, and since he is "other kind" of the first ascending generation, ego calls him 'uncle'. Because of patrilineal descent, mother's brother's children must also be B's. This means that these children are potential spouses for ego and his sister (who must marry B's of their generation). These potential spouses ego calls his *aetaka* 'cross-cousin'. If an *aetaka* (who is a B) marries someone other than ego, that spouse would have to be an A, in other words, someone from ego's own clan. Not surprisingly, then, ego calls his *aetaka's* spouse his own sibling.[22]

When ego marries, his wife will have to come from the B clan. His wife's father must be a B also (because of patrilineal descent), so he is "other kind" of the first ascending generation, same as ego's mother's brother. Accordingly, ego extends the term for MB, 'uncle', to his father-in-law.

Now consider what ego calls his mother-in-law. Since ego's wife's mother is married to ego's wife's father (of clan B), she must be from clan A. However, from ego's perspective as a generation below, wife's mother is not functioning in her birth clan, but rather in her husband's clan. In this model, she is like a B to ego. Thus, the motivation for the fourth rule given above is that from ego's perspective, a married woman of the next ascending generation functions as a unit with her husband in the husband's clan. She belongs now to her husband's clan because she was *ramavun* 'bought' from her birth clan. Therefore, when ego refers to her, he uses the female term that corresponds to whatever term he uses for her husband.

Now we can understand the terminology ego uses for women of the first ascending generation. His own mother, although from clan B, is seen as now belonging to clan A, and so it is appropriate that ego call her 'mother'. Ego's wife's mother is viewed by ego as belonging to wife's father's clan, and so ego refers to her by the female terms that correspond to the terms he uses for wife's father. Since ego may refer to wife's father either as 'father-in-law' or 'uncle', then wife's mother may be variously 'mother-in-law' or 'aunt'. Another significant woman of the first ascending generation is father's sister. Although her birth clan is A, from ego's perspective she now functions in her husband's clan, which must be clan B. Therefore, ego calls her 'aunt', which is the female term that corresponds to the 'uncle' term he uses for her husband.

---

[22]See footnote 19.

Next consider ego's siblings-in-law on his wife's side. Ego's wife is a B and so are her sister and brother. When ego's wife's sister marries, her spouse will have to be an A. No wonder, then, that ego calls WZH his 'brother', since the two men are from the same clan. Similar reasoning explains why WBW is called 'sister'.

Next consider ego's sister. She, being an A, must marry a B. So ego calls him by a sibling-in-law term since he is "other kind." The children of this man and ego's sister will be B's, so they are the "other kind" too, hence, ego calls them 'niece' and 'nephew'. However, when ego's nephew marries, being a B, he will marry a same-generation woman from ego's own clan A (i.e., a clan A woman of the first descending generation). This woman, who is nephew's spouse, is therefore appropriately called ego's 'child'. Again, similar reasoning explains the terminology for ZD and ZDH. The reverse situation explains BS and BSW as well as BD and BDH.

Consider some rather distant relationships, such as the relationship between the two sets of parents of a couple. When ego's son (clan A) marries a woman from clan B, the woman's father is, of course, a B, but her mother must be an A (because of clan exogamy). However, ego is an A, too, so he calls his son's mother-in-law (SWM) his 'sister' (even though in reality she may be from a totally different clan from him).

In the Yawa system, sometimes seemingly remote kin or affines are categorized with terminology that is basically close consanguineal kin terminology. With the model just proposed, this practice is easily explained. If everyone is conceptualized as belonging to either Clan A or Clan B, then if a particular genealogical category happens to end up in Clan A by the way the rules work, a person in that category may be called by a close consanguineal term, even if the actual genealogical connections are either remote or unknown. In one striking piece of evidence of the validity of this analysis, one Yawa language assistant whom I asked about his son's mother-in-law could not recall the woman's given name, or even clan name, but he confidently said she was his *anama* 'sister'.

Now we are in a position to circle back to the question raised in the beginning of this section, namely, how a two-section (or two-clan) system relates to the organization of Yawa society into numerous clans. For in reality, there are not just two clans in Yawa society, but many, each with its own *keret* 'family name'. However, the two-clan model I have proposed still applies in the following way. Since the system is egocentrically defined, ego begins with his own *keret* A as identifying Clan A and his mother's birth *keret* B as identifying Clan B. He refers to persons with *keret* A by parallel kinship terminology and to persons with *keret* B by cross/affinal kinship terminology. When ego relates to someone (alter) who has a different *keret,* whether C, D, E, F, or whatever, he traces the shortest known genealogical chain between alter and a person of *keret* A or *keret* B. Depending on the links in the genealogical chain, ego is able to categorize any alter, regardless of his *keret,* as standing in an analogous relationship to himself as do either persons of *keret* A or persons of *keret* B. If the relationship is determined to be like a *keret* B relationship (the marked relationship), then cross/affinal terminology appropriate to alter's generation and sex is applied. Otherwise, parallel terminology is assumed. The net result of categorizing all persons as having a relationship to ego like *keret* A relationships or like *keret* B relationships creates two superclans, or two egocentrically defined unnamed moieties.

Marriage Preferences

Theoretically, a Yawa may marry any *aetako randani* not of his own clan. Examining figure 5, which shows the structure of ego's kinsmen of the second degree of collaterality, we see that for a male ego, four such categories are FFBDD and FFZDD (from FF's chart) and MFBSD and MFZSD (from MF's chart). If we had FM's chart, we would also get FMBDD and FMZDD and from MM's chart we would have MMBSD and MMZSD. For the second degree of collaterality, there would be eight categories of female *aetaka*. With higher degrees of collaterality, there would be additional categories, but they would not be substantially different, differing merely in how remote were the ancestral siblings that formed the original links.

Although there are eight categories of female *aetaka* who represent potential spouses for ego, in practice Yawa generally take wives from only two of these categories, FFBDD and MFBSD. It is not prohibited to take a wife from another category (and I have recorded some such marriages), but the vast majority of wives in Yawa marriages are taken from these two categories.

These two categories are actually the most obvious choices for ego's spouse. Women of the MFBSD category (as well as similar categories involving a more remote ancestral link) are essentially women who have the same clan name *(keret)* as ego's mother's birth clan name. (This relationship can be seen by tracing it out on the MF's chart in figure 5.) And in practice it is one way Yawa men decide that a woman is an *aetaka* (even though they may have no idea of how to trace the actual genealogical connection to prove it); if a woman of ego's generation bears the clan name of ego's mother's birth clan, she is assumed to be an *aetaka.* This relationship is assumed because this woman is the daughter of a man of mother's clan, whom ego's mother would therefore have considered to be a classificatory brother. This *aetaka* is then a classificatory MBD.

The other category which is an obvious choice for a spouse is FFBDD. Women in this category are also easily identifiable because they are the daughters of women whose birth clan name is the same as ego's father. The actual clan name of these *aetaka* does not matter. What is crucial is that the woman's mother belonged to father's clan, that is, she was father's classificatory sister. Hence, the daughters of father's sister clanswomen are equivalent to classificatory FZD.

To summarize, the two preferred categories for ego's wife are classificatory MBD and classificatory FZD. The Yawa marriage system is thus a PRESCRIPTIVE BILATERAL CROSS-COUSIN MARRIAGE SYSTEM (Maybury-Lewis 1971).

In practice, this system functions as follows. A Yawa man knows that a woman of his generation is an *aetaka* whom he could marry if either (1) she has the same clan name as his mother, or (2) she is the daughter of a woman with his own clan name. These two very simple rules-of-thumb identify women of the two basic preferred categories, FFBDD and MFBSD, as well as women of related preferred categories of higher degrees of collaterality. (Women in the other six categories listed above for *aetaka* of the second degree of collaterality are less simply identified: they involve a granddaughter and/or grandmother relation or else a cross-cousin relation to one of ego's parents.)[23]

---

[23]FFZDD is "granddaughter of a woman of ego's clan," or alternatively, "daughter of father's cross-cousin." FMBDD is "daughter of a woman of grandmother's clan," or alternatively, "daughter of father's cross-cousin." MFZSD is "granddaughter of a woman of mother's clan," or "daughter of mother's cross-cousin." MMBSD is "daughter of a man of grandmother's clan," or "daughter of mother's cross-cousin." MMZSD is "granddaughter of a woman of grandmother's clan." Lastly, FMZDD is "granddaughter of a woman of grandmother's clan."

I have attested marriages involving some of these six categories. I believe that in each case the spouse was identified as a marriageable *aetaka* through reckoning via granddaughter/grandmother relations rather than reckoning through cross-cousins of ego's parent. However, these definitions are not really precise enough, as they do not include qualifiers such as "maternal/paternal" before "grandmother" or "male/female" before "cross-cousin." This imprecision makes a considerable difference in a purely theoretical sense. When the qualifiers are not added, reckoning by means of the above definitions may in fact yield an incorrect categorization: a woman is reckoned to be a "cross-cousin" although in a pure Iroquois system she is a "sibling." For example, one Yawa marriage, considered proper, involved a woman of FFZSD category who, in a purely consistent Iroquois system, should be a "sibling." But since she was "granddaughter of a woman of ego's clan," the couple believed she was a "cross-cousin." Perhaps this imprecision explains why the question-marked categories in figure 5 are ambiguous to the Yawa.

A hypothetical, but realistic, example is shown in figure 9. In the figure, only persons relevant to the example are included. The women of ego's generation, being most relevant to the marriageability question, are shown with full names, but all other persons are named only by their clan name or, if the clan name is irrelevant, are left unnamed. The broken lines with dots at the grandparent generation represent that these ancestors were not necessarily true siblings, but merely belonged to the same clan. Ego is *Isak Paai* and his cross-cousins include all the women shown in ego's generation. Of these women, not all are potential spouses. For example, two are *taundave* 'close' cross-cousins—Torsina Rumansara (MBD) and Naomi Atewa (FZD). Another woman, Yubelina Paai, while technically a cross-cousin, is not a potential spouse because she is of ego's own clan. Furthermore, ego may not realize that Antonia Rawai is a cross-cousin he could marry, since she is related to ego at the level of his maternal grandmother. If ego is a typical Yawa, he probably does not know the identities of his maternal grandmother's siblings, especially her sisters, nor whatever became of them. Thus, ego's known potential spouses are Aplena Karubaba, Sopia Sembai, Dortea Wanggori (all FFBDD) and Alponsina Rumansara (MFBSD).

Conclusion

Analysis of the Yawa kinship terminology, including terms for kinsmen of the second degree of collaterality, shows that it is Iroquois in type. However, the terminology also reveals a striking two-part structure that is analogous with the two-section systems generally associated with Dravidian terminologies. I have suggested that indeed, the Yawa kinship system is best analyzed as a two-section system and, like the Dravidian two-section systems, it is associated with bilateral cross-cousin prescriptive marriage.

The Yawa two-section system operates in the context of multiple clans which are not organized into moieties. The complexity of multiple clans is handled conceptually by dividing the social world into only two "superclans," which are totally relative to ego: ego's "own superclan" and the "other superclan." The other superclan is the marked case, and consists of ego's mother's birth clan plus all those persons, regardless of their clan name, who ego reckons are related to him in an analogous way as ego's mother's clansmen. Ego's own superclan consists of ego's own birth clan plus all those persons who ego reckons are related to him analogously as his own clansmen. Also in ego's own superclan are any persons he does not

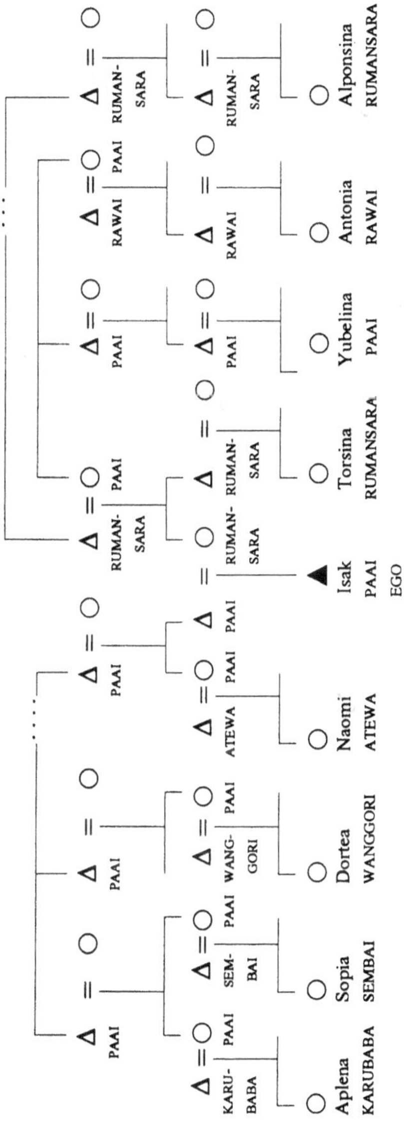

Fig. 9. Hypothetical kinship chart showing some of ego's female *aetaka* 'cross-cousins'

otherwise know how to classify. I have suggested four rules for reckoning a person's superclan relative to ego.

The Yawa two-section system is reflected in the kinship terminology. Parallel kinship terminology is used for persons in ego's own superclan, while cross-kinship terminology is reserved for persons in the other superclan. This same distinction applies to most affines as well. Rather than using special affinal terminology for affines, parallel or cross-kinship terms are generally used, depending on superclan membership. Thus, many affines are terminologically equivalent to consanguineals.

The organizing principle for the kinship terminology is marriageability. All ego's potential spouses are in the other superclan. In choosing a wife, ego usually chooses a same-generation woman from his mother's clan or the daughter of a woman from his father's clan. Superimposed on ego's two-clan world is another important division: the division of ego's kin into *taundave* 'close' kin and *randani* 'distant' kin. In choosing a wife, ego is forbidden to marry any *taundave* kin or any woman of his own clan.

List Of Abbreviations

B	brother	H	husband	S	son
C	child	M	mother	W	wife
D	daughter	m:	male ego	X	sibling
F	father	o	older	y	younger
f:	female ego	P	parent	Z	sister

Appendix: Yawa Kinship Terminology

Following is a list giving all the basic terms used by the Yawa for their consanguineal and affinal kin. Compound terms such as *ajayo anuija* 'older father' are not included, but are discussed in the paper. Also not included are *anya* 'man' or 'male' (for 'husband') and *wanya* 'woman' or 'female' (for 'wife'), which are not specifically kin terms.

The first column denotes the generation relative to ego. The second column gives the Yawa term with the nearest English translation for its primary referent. The third column lists the kin category which is presumed to be the primary referent of the Yawa term. The last two columns list the kin categories to which the Yawa term may be extended; the first of these columns is for extensions to consanguineal kin and the second is for extensions to affinal kin.

My aim in this listing is not only to be technically precise in the representation of kin categories but also to make the presentation "reader friendly" so that the general kinship structure is readily apparent. To this end I have used full genealogical notation only for the first few terms (actually just for the consanguineal kin of the first few terms, not for the affinals). Later terms are frequently listed in prose descriptions (e.g., the consanguineal extended referent of *kavo* is described as 'child of 'brother''). In all such prose descriptions, a word 'x' enclosed in single quotes is to be read as 'ego's classificatory x'. Thus, 'child of 'brother' ' is to be read as 'child of ego's classificatory brother'. I feel that these prose descriptions probably more accurately reflect the way the Yawa reckon kin categories than using full genealogical notation, in that the way a Yawa reckons how a particular person is related to him is by considering the category of that person's nearest kinsman for which he already knows the kin term. The kinship charts presented in figures 4, 5, and 6 may be consulted if full genealogical notation is desired for terms where it is not given in this appendix.

Generation	Term	Primary Referent	Extended Referents Consanguineal	Affinal
+2, +3, ..., +n	*anena* 'grandparent'	PP	PPX, PPP, PPPX, etc.	spouse of 'grandparent'
+1	*ajap* 'father'	F	FB, FPXS, FPPPXCS, FPPPXCCS, etc.	spouse of 'mother'; spouse's 'uncle'
+1	*akoyam* 'mother'	M	MZ, MPXD, MPPXCD, MPPPXCCD, etc.	spouse of 'father'; spouse's 'aunt'; m:spouse of 'older brother' (m:oBW)
+1	*awateap, awani, kamoki* 'uncle'	MB	MPXS, MPPXCS, MPPPXCCS, etc.	spouse of 'aunt'; spouse's 'father'; husband's 'older brother' (HoB)
+1	*andam, ara* 'aunt'	FZ	FPXD, FPPXCD, FPPPXCCD, etc.	spouse of 'uncle'; spouse's 'mother'
+1	*anup* 'son-in-law' or 'father-in-law'	DH, WF	—	spouse of 'daughter'; wife's 'father'
+1	*anumam* 'mother-in-law'	WM	—	wife's 'mother'

(continued)

Gener-ation	Term	Primary Referent	Extended Referents Consanguineal	Affinal
+1	*ajamap* 'father-in-law'	HF	—	husband's 'father'; husband's 'older brother'
+1	*ajamam* 'daughter-in-law' or 'mother-in-law'	SW, HM	—	spouse of 'son'; husband's 'mother'; m:spouse of 'younger brother' (m:yBW)
0	*anuija* 'older same sex sibling', e.g., 'man's older brother' or 'woman's older sister'	oB, oZ	m: FoBS, MoZS, PFoBCS, PMoZCS, PPFoBCCS, PPMoZCCS, PPPFoBCCS, etc., f: FoBD, MoZD, PFoBCD, PMoZCD, etc.	wife of husband's 'older brother' (HoBW); wife of 'older cross-cousin'
0	*rijata* 'younger same-sex sibling'	yB, yZ	m: FyBS, MyZS, PFyBCS, PMyZCS, PPFyBCCS, PPMyZCCS, PPPFyBCCS, etc., f: FyBD, MyZD, PFyBCD, PMyZCD, etc.	wife of husband's 'younger brother' (HyBW); wife of 'younger cross-cousin'
0	*anakavo* 'woman's brother'	B	son of 'father' or 'mother'; but also MBS, FZS (because of dual classif. of *aetaka* as 'cross-cousin' and 'sibling')	husband of husband's 'sister' (HZH); father of spouse of 'child' (SWF, DHF); husband of 'cross-cousin'
0	*anama* 'man's sister'	Z	daughter of 'father' or 'mother'; but also FZD, MBD (because of dual classif. of *aetaka*)	wife of wife's 'brother' (WBW); mother of spouse of 'child' (SWM, DHM); wife of 'cross-cousin'
0	*aetaka* 'cross-cousin'	MBC, FZC	child of 'uncle' or 'aunt'	m:father of spouse of 'child' (m:SWF, DHF); f:mother of spouse of 'child' (f:SWM, DHM)
0	*anap* 'husband'	H	—	—

(continued)

Gener-ation	Term	Primary Referent	Extended Referents	
			Consanguineal	Affinal
0	*anamu* 'wife'	W	—	—
0	*araki, amai* 'sibling-in-law'	ZH, WB, WZ	—	spouse of 'sister'; wife's 'brother'; wife's 'sister'; spouse of 'brother'; but also can be: spouse of 'cross-cousin' (because of dual classif. of *aetaka*)
0	*arema* 'sister-in-law'	f:BW, HZ	—	f:spouse of 'brother'; husband's 'sister'; but also can be: f:wife of 'cross-cousin' (because of dual classif. of *aetaka*)
0	*arakova* 'sibling'	B, Z	any same-generation kin not known to be *aetaka*	spouse of spouse's 'sibling', esp. WZH; spouse of 'cross-cousin'
−1	*kavo, arikainy* 'child'	C	m:child of 'brother'	spouse of 'nephew' or 'niece'; husband's 'younger brother' (HyB)
−1	*augai, aivaki, kamoki* 'nephew', 'niece'	m:ZC f:BC	m:child of 'sister' f:child of 'brother'	spouse of 'child'
−1	*tamaisya* 'child-in-law'	SW, DH	—	spouse of 'child'; m:spouse of 'younger brother' (m:yBW)
−2, −3	*anena, ajavi* 'grandchild'	CC	child of 'child'; child of 'grandchild'	spouse of 'grandchild'; spouse of 'child' of 'grandchild'

References

Dumont, Louis. 1971. The marriage alliance. In Jack Goody (ed.), Kinship, 183–98. Middlesex, England: Penguin Books.

Flaming, Rachel. 1983. Wandamen kinship terminology. In William R. Merrifield, Marilyn Gregerson, and Daniel C. Ajamiseba (eds.), Gods, heroes, kinsmen: Ethnographic studies from Irian Jaya, Indonesia, 244–53. International Museum of Cultures Publication 17. Dallas: Cenderawasih University and The International Museum of Cultures.

Hsu, Francis L. K. 1971. A hypothesis on kinship and culture. In F. L. K. Hsu (ed.), Kinship and culture, 3–29. Chicago: Aldine.

Keesing, Roger M. 1975. Kin groups and social structure. New York: Holt, Rinehart and Winston.

————. 1980. The uses of kinship: Kwaio, Solomon Islands. In Linda S. Cordell and Stephen Beckerman (eds.), The versatility of kinship, 29–43. New York: Academic Press.

Lounsbury, Floyd G. 1964. The structural analysis of kinship semantics. In Horace G. Lunt (ed.), Proceedings of the Ninth International Congress of Linguists, Cambridge, Mass., 27–31 August, 1962, 1073–93. The Hague: Mouton.

Maybury-Lewis, D. 1971. Prescriptive marriage systems. In Jack Goody (ed.), Kinship, 199–224. Middlesex, England: Penguin Books.

Scheffler, Harold. 1971. Dravidian-Iroquois: The Melanesian evidence. In L. R. Hiatt and C. Jayawardena (eds.), Anthropology in Oceania: Essays presented to Ian Hogbin, 231–254. London: Angus and Robertson.

Voorhoeve, C. L. 1975. East Bird's Head, Geelvink Bay phyla. In Stephen A. Wurm (ed.), New Guinea area languages and language study, Vol. 1: Papuan Languages and the New Guinea Linguistic Scene, 867–78. Pacific Linguistics Series C 38.

Kaure Kinship: Obligations, Restrictions, and Taboos

Peter Barbarossa Dommel

Of special interest in considering Kaure kinship are the role expectations and interpersonal behavior associated with certain kin relationships. When a parent dies, for example, his or her children are likely to be beaten by their cross-cousins for any disobedient acts toward their parent while he or she was alive. Relationships between affines are regulated by extreme avoidance behavior which is carefully delineated.

Descriptive terminology characterizes Kaure kinship, though they have the option of using classificatory terminology if they so desire. Some unusual aspects of Kaure kinship terminology are the matrilateral and patrilateral terms used for grandkinsmen, the lack of terms for certain affines, and the fact that though all cross-cousins are called *keli,* their spouses are distinguished both by sex and by age of the cross-cousin relative to ego. Another interesting feature is that the Kaure custom of sister-exchange marriage is frequently reflected in their terminology.

The Kaure

The Kaure people of the Eastern Lakes Plain area of Irian Jaya, Indonesia currently live in the three villages of Harna, Masta, and Wes around the Lereh airstrip about fifty miles southwest of Sentani, and in the recently rebuilt village of Aurina about thirty miles southeast of Lereh. All of these villages are in the Kecamatan Kaure, Kabupaten Jayapura. The total Kaure population is between 400 and 450 people, a few of whom live in Irian Jaya's capital city, Jayapura.

The traditional animistic religion was nominally replaced by Protestant Christianity beginning in the early 1960s when Dutch Reformed missionaries arrived in the area. Some Kaure converted to Seventh Day Adventism in the early 1970s through the work of American missionaries of that denomination. Now all Kaure belong to one of these two denominations, though the majority (perhaps ninety percent) adhere to the Protestant denomination, *Gereja Kristen Injil,* fostered by Dutch Reformed Protestant missionaries.

Kaure is classified by Voorhoeve (1975:45) as a non-Austronesian language of the Kaure family, Kaure stock of the Trans-New-Guinea phylum. The people of Harna and Masta speak the same dialect, which differs slightly from the one spoken at Wes and Aurina. Kaure is the only known tonal language in the area.[1]

Kaure Clans

There are eighteen patrilineal clans in the Kaure language group. Eleven of these are "double clans" since at some point in the past they were joined by another clan. Many people today are still aware of the fact that they have descended from a clan that no longer exists (see figure 1).

However, in one instance, only part of the Hirwa clan joined the Nakabi clan and, therefore, the Hirwa clan still exists separately. The same applies to the Wama clan which joined the Dalem clan, but still exists in the neighboring Sause language group. Consequently there is a restriction against marriage between the Hirwa and the Nakabi clans and also between the Dalem and the Wama.

As in the nearby Kemtuk language group (van der Wilden 1976:10), the Kaure clan names have no meanings except the following three: *Seh* 'dog', *Kasu* which is a kind of tree bark, and the former clan name *Nowen* 'hawk'. Those names which have meaning refer to the clan totems.

---

[1]Tone is not written on Kaure terms in this paper. For further information, however, see Dommel and Dommel (1991).

This research was conducted primarily with the people of Harna and Masta. My family and I have been living at the village of Harna on a semipermanent basis since we began our work in June 1985 under the Cooperative Program of the University of Cenderawasih and the Summer Institute of Linguistics.

Clan Name	Former Clan Joined to Present One	Totem
Auri	Ajadel	kangaroo
Bitaba	Tilija	species of saurian
Dalem	Wama	cuckoo
Hamun	Marti	wasp
Hirwa		wild chicken
Kasu	Kapai	
Kormasi		
Koyao		
Kwarje		
Lai (Laidel)		
Masita	Haitelo	
Nakabi	Hirwa	wild chicken
Pokoko	Nowen	hawk
Seh	Kwanholai	dog
Sita		hornbill
Wati		
Yamle	Lidel	pig, worm
Yaplik	Tapok	sago grub

Fig. 1. Kaure clans and totems
(Clans with no totem listed do not remember their totem.)

Eleven clans trace themselves back to a totem animal, bird, or insect, which cannot be eaten by members of the clan. Notice that the Yamle clan has two totem animals. Any man who takes a wife must observe not only the food taboo of his own clan but also that of his wife's clan. The wife, however, does not observe the food taboo of her husband's clan, and the couple's children only observe the food taboo of their father's clan. If such a taboo is violated, it is feared that sickness will strike the offender.

Usually the oldest man in each clan is recognized as its headman, for it is he who has the most relatives that call him "father" and honor him as such. However, there are some cases where a man's recognized expertise, knowledge, or wealth have brought him the headman position.

The dominant clan is the Auri. Its ascendancy goes back to mythological times when the Auri are said to have told all the other clans where to settle. Today they still own the most Kaure land, their people are often selected as community leaders, and their clan name is found in the surrounding language groups and among Kaure who have moved away and long since lost their language and traditions. In spite of this dominance the only large grouping of the Auri is in Harna village, as shown in figure 2.

The Kaure residence pattern is patrilocal, and a household normally consists of a nuclear family and occasionally an additional widowed mother or father. This practice is similar to the neighboring Nimboran (May 1981:3).

Clan Migrations

Before the government resettlement project of the late 1970s and early 1980s, the Kaure lived in a triangular area east of the Ihipo River, south of the Nawan River, and north of the Idenburg River.

Families were not originally organized in village units but were spread out along river and creek banks, near mountains or waterfalls, or near a sago plantation. Some clans used to live in more than one area, and some areas had more than one clan (see figure 2).

During the government resettlement project all the Kaure moved into the villages of Harna, Masta, and Wes (known together as the Lereh area), as well as Aurina about thirty miles distant from Lereh. Most clans that formerly lived south of the Yapola River and east of the Martaluk River moved to Wes and Aurina, while some moved to Masta but none to Harna. Clans that lived north of the Yapola River and west of the Martaluk River moved to Harna and Masta. The Yamle clan is the only clan with members who live in three villages.

Due to earlier migrations, at least eight Kaure clan names are found in surrounding language groups. All these names occur at locations near the former settlements of these clans (see far right column of figure 2). Most members of these migrated Kaure clans now have little knowledge of the Kaure language.

At Witi three languages are spoken by all inhabitants: Kaure, Sause, and Orya. Witi is not considered a Kaure village. Wes is a new village that was built by the government in the early 1980s to house some of the people who followed the government request to abandon their old areas of settlement.

Clan Name	Former Area	New Village	Non-Kaure Villages with these Clans
	At rivers and creeks:		
Bitaba	Pwara	Harna	Badrun, Ures
Pokoko	Pokoko	Harna	Badrun
Dalem	Ihipo	Harna, Masta	Pagai
Nakabi	Nakabi	Masta, Wes	
Hamun	Yakai	Masta, Wes	
Masita	Temiao	Harna, Masta	
Hirwa	Kwaisoa	Masta	
Lai	Takana	Wes, Aurina	
Kwarje	Takana	Wes, Aurina	
Kormasi	Pinabi, Plakija, Kope	Wes, Aurina	
Wati	Kope, Taku	Aurina	
Sita	Martaluk	Masta, Wes	
	At mountains:		
Auri	Pamohwi	Harna	Taja
	At waterfall:		
Koyao	Koyao	Harna	Badrun
	At mountain and river:		
Yamle	Kalelok (mt.) Sija (river)	Harna, Masta Wes	Witi
Kasu	Weikwaba (mt.) Pinabi (river)	Wes, Aurina	Pagai
	At sago plantation:		
Seh	Soar	Masta, Wes	Pagai
Yaplik	Soar	Wes, Aurina	

Fig. 2. Kaure migrations

Kinship Terminology

Kaure kinship terminology does not correspond to any of the standard types, but the cousin terminology follows the Iroquois pattern, that is, Kaure speakers differentiate cross-cousins from siblings but use sibling terms for parallel cousins. In the first ascending generation, ego's mother's younger sister is classified with ego's mother, but distinct descriptive terms denote each of ego's parents' other siblings (i.e., mother's older sister, mother's brother, father's older and younger brothers, and father's sister) as shown in figure 3.

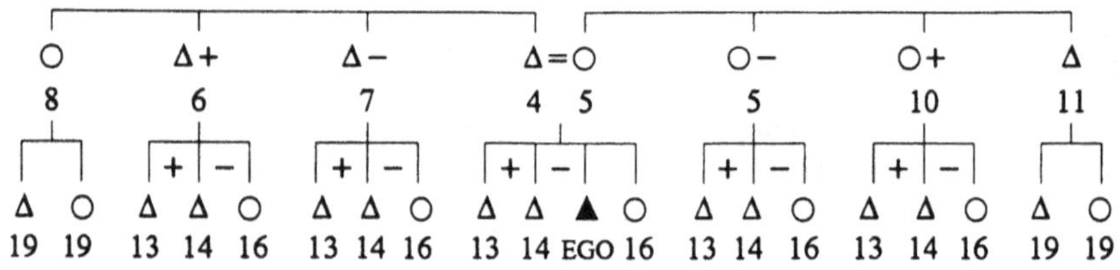

4.	*jik*	7.	*kadal*	11.	*baholai, kabwa*	16.	*neplai*
5.	*noa, ade*	8.	*neba*	13.	*dowi*	19.	*keli*
6.	*aseik*	10.	*ato*	14.	*semlik*		

Fig. 3. Kaure descriptive kinship system

The Kaure use basically a descriptive system for the first ascending generation while in ego's generation they tend to use classificatory terminology. There is a preferred tendency toward a more classificatory system (see figure 4) which may be derived using three rules of classification. While this paper primarily describes the broader descriptive system, the Kaure prefer to use the more simplified classificatory system unless the communication situation demands the use of the more detailed terminology.

Kaure classificatory terminology operates as follows. The terms used for siblings and parallel cousins can be extended to cross-cousins as in a Hawaiian system. The term for father can be used for father's brothers and may also be applied to other male members of the patrilineal kin group in the first ascending generation. The term for mother can also be used for her sisters and for other female members of her patrilineal clan in the first ascending generation. The following rules describe the relationship between the broader system and the preferred, more simplified usage.

1. Cross-cousins (in addition to parallel cousins) are classified with siblings.

2. All male members of father's clan who are in the first ascending generation are classified with father.

3. All female members of mother's clan who are in the first ascending generation are classified with mother.

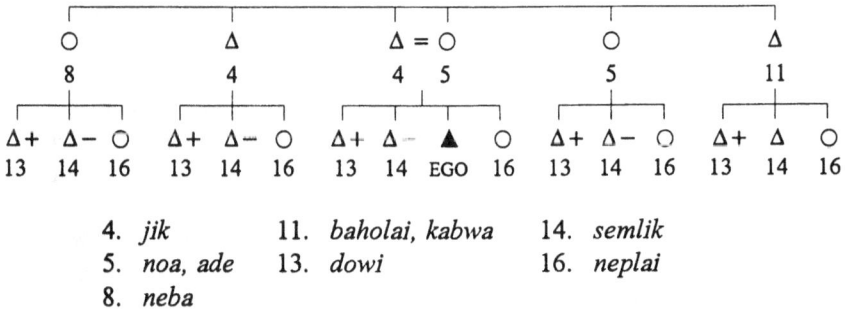

4. jik	11. baholai, kabwa	14. semlik
5. noa, ade	13. dowi	16. neplai
8. neba		

Fig. 4. Kaure classificatory kinship terminology

Consanguineal Kinship Terms

Kaure consanguineal kinship terms are, in principle, used for both address and reference, but only occasionally are these terms actually used in addressing people. They are all obligatorily possessed by either a preceding personal name or a prefixed pronoun, as in the following examples in which *na-*, *ha-*, *ne-*, or *nene-* are prefixed to *dok* 'child' or 'children'.[2]

na-dok	'my child(ren)', 'our (excl.) child(ren)'
ha-dok	'your child(ren)'
ne-dok	'his child(ren)', 'her child(ren)', 'their child(ren)'

---

[2] *dok* 'child' is the only kinship term that can be used without a preceding name and without a prefixed possessive pronoun, referring to any male. *na-noa* 'mother' and *da-jik* 'father' always have the prefixed pronoun, even when preceded by a personal name (e.g., *Piter nenoa* 'Piter's mother', *Piter dijik* 'Piter's father'). Notice that with the term *da-jik* 'father' the possessive pronouns usually change from *na-* to *da-* in the first person and from *ne-* to *di-* in the third person.

nene-dok	'our (incl.) child(ren)'
Piter dok	'Piter's child(ren)'

Forms throughout the remainder of the paper are cited without the possessive pronoun.

Kaure kinship terminology distinguishes seven generations of kinsmen. There are three ascending generations and three descending generations.

Grandkinsmen. The terms used for the second ascending generation are identical with those of the second descending generation (i.e., father's parents = son's children and mother's parents = daughter's children), except that the terms for the second descending generation can optionally be suffixed by *-nya* to indicate that it is a descending generation. In these generations sex is not differentiated, but matrilateral ascent and descent are differentiated from patrilateral ascent and descent. *asa* refers to paternal grandparents as well as son's children. *apeuk* refers to maternal grandparents and daughter's children. All collateral kinsmen and their spouses in these generations are also called by the same terms, *asa* and *apeuk*. Notice that in the second descending generation brother's daughter's children and sister's daughter's children are called *apeuk(nya)*, while *asa(nya)* refers to brother's son's children and sister's son's children as shown in figure 5.[3]

A single term is used to refer to kinsmen three or more generations above or below ego. The term, which is used reciprocally, is *kaeuk* 'ancestor' or 'descendant' (with the optional suffix *-nya* for the descending generations). Sex and matrilateral or patrilateral descent are not differentiated on these levels.

Parent and Child Generations. In the first ascending generation *jik* is the term used not only for ego's own father but also for the husbands of ego's

---

[3]Note that in ego's generation there are three rows, the first referring to the terminology used by a male ego, the second referring to terminology used by a female ego, and the third to that used by either male or female ego. Likewise, in the first descending generation there are two rows, the top one corresponding to a male ego and the other to a female ego. Also note that all referents (including marriage partners) in the second descending generation from ego are unspecified for sex. This does not imply that same-sex marriage is practiced among the Kaure.

In kinship charting, lines of descent are normally drawn from the marriage link symbol. However, in this figure they are sometimes drawn in between the symbols for two married couples, indicating that the offspring of either of these unions are classified in the same way with respect to ego.

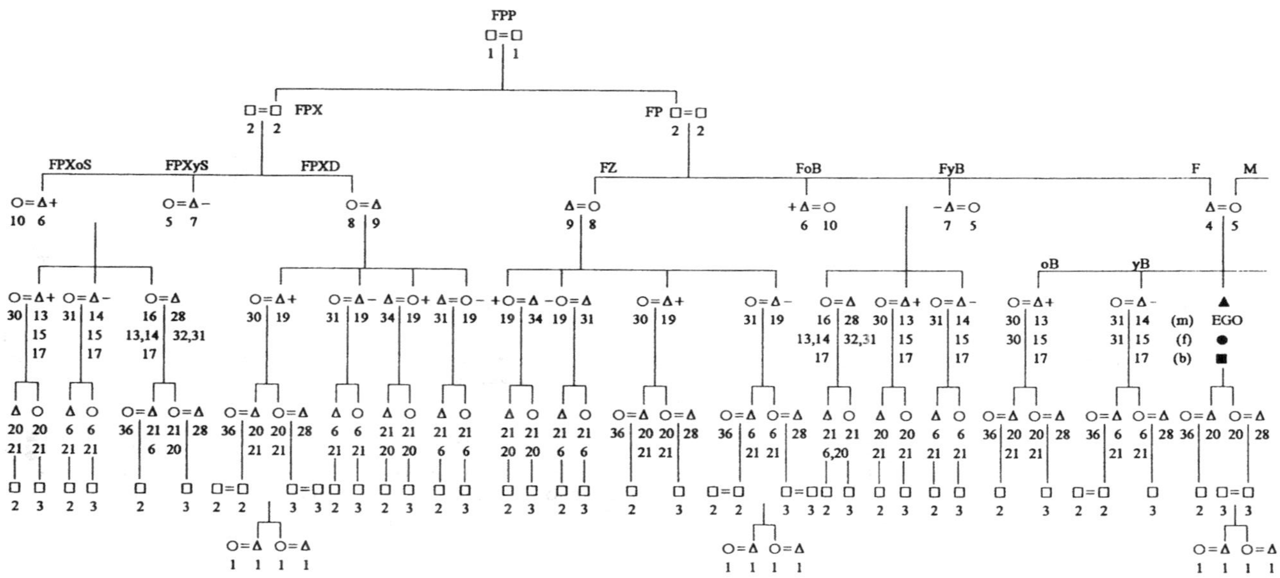

Fig. 5. Kaure consanguineal kinship chart (1 of 2)

1. kaeuk
2. asa
3. apeuk
4. jik
5. noa, ade

6. aseik
7. kadal
8. neba
9. nepan
10. ato

11. baholai
    kabwa
12. dole
13. dowi
14. semlik
15. nephu

16. neplai
17. pala
18. awiwen
19. keli
20. dok
21. kanon

28. asai
30. awai
31. niawa
32. sowai
34. siwai
36. nepli

Peter Barbarossa Dommel

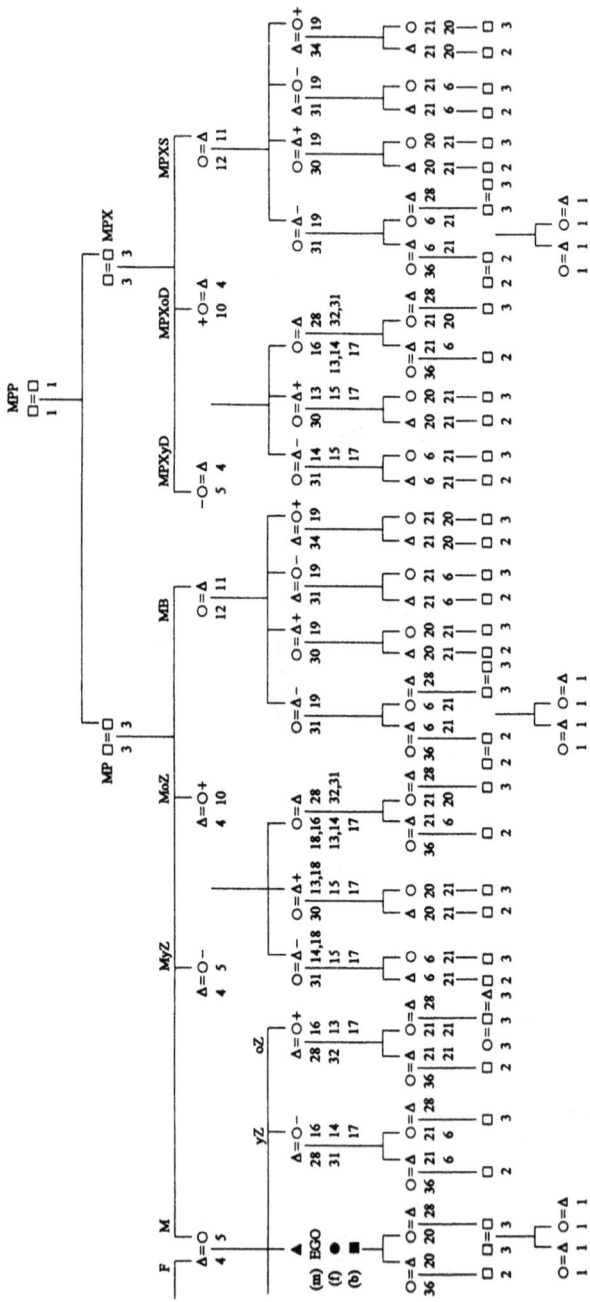

Fig. 5. Kaure consanguineal kinship chart (2 of 2)

B brother   D daughter   M mother   P parent   y younger

b both m/f   F father   m male only   S sister   Z sister

C child   f female only   o older   X sibling

mother's sisters. This term is also used in an extended sense for all men of any clan in the ascending generations as a term of respect. Father's brothers are usually differentiated according to relative age; *aseik* is father's older brother and *kadal* is his younger brother. Alternatively, the term for father, *jik,* may be used for either of them. Father's sisters are designated by one term only, *neba,* and their husbands are called *nepan.*

Ego's mother is usually *noa,* but an alternative term for mother is *ade.* These terms are also used for father's younger brother's wife and mother's younger sister. Furthermore, *noa* and *ade* can be extended to mother's older sister *(ato),* to father's older brother's wife *(ato),* and as terms of respect to any woman of any clan in any ascending generation. There are two terms for mother's brother, *baholai* and *kabwa.* Mother's brother's wife is called *dole.* All of these terms are used by a male and female alike (see figure 5).

Notice, however, that all these terms for parent's siblings can also be extended to one's parents' parallel and cross-cousins, that is, anyone for whom one's parents use the sibling and cross-cousin terms. Therefore, on the father's side *aseik* is not only father's older brother, but also father's parents' siblings' older son. *kadal* is father's younger brother and also father's parents' siblings' younger son. *neba* does not only denote father's sister but also father's parents' siblings' daughter. On the mother's side parallel rules apply. Besides mother's older sister, *ato* also refers to mother's parents' siblings' older daughter. *noa* is extended to mother's parents' siblings' younger daughter. *baholai* and *kabwa* refer to mother's brother and also to mother's parents' siblings' son.

In the first descending generation there is one term, *dok,*[4] for ego's own offspring. Sex and relative age can be expressed by additional modifiers, like *naplan* 'girl', *didok* 'boy' (lit. 'bow child', since only men have bows), *dipuk* 'boy' (lit. 'with bow'), *kolpi* or *subwa* 'big' (i.e., older), and *tainohlen* 'little' (i.e., younger). The term *dok* 'child' is also used to designate one's same sex older siblings' children, one's same sex older parallel cousins' children, and older same sex cross-cousins' children. A further extended usage of the term *dok* is to any member of any descending generation of any clan. Same sex younger siblings' children, therefore, may be called *dok,* but the term *aseik* is more precise. Since *aseik* is also the term used for father's older brother, it is reciprocal (i.e., ego calls father's older brother by this term and father's older brother calls ego, his younger brother's child, by the same term). Ego's opposite sex siblings' children are called *kanon.* The same terms apply to

---

[4]This term is apparently cognate with *Kemtuk do* (van der Wilden 1976:9).

ego's opposite sex parallel cousins' children.

Terms used for the children of ego's *keli* 'cross-cousin' are discussed under affinal terms in the following section since their designations are determined by the affinal terms.

Siblings and Cousins. In ego's generation parallel cousins are classed with siblings. Siblings of the same sex as ego are called *semlik* 'same sex younger sibling' or *dowi* 'same sex older sibling'. Parallel cousins of the same sex are called *dowi* if they are older than ego, and those who are younger than ego are called *semlik*. A male ego calls a female sibling or a female parallel cousin *neplai* 'sister' and a female ego calls a male sibling or a male parallel cousin *neplu* 'brother', not differentiating relative age. All siblings and parallel cousins of ego's lineage can also be called *pala* by speakers of either sex. Matrilateral parallel cousins (mother's sister's children) can alternatively all be called *awiwen* by a male ego. Spouses and offspring of parallel cousins are equated with spouses and offspring of siblings. All cross-cousins are *keli*. Their spouses are discussed under affinal terminology.

Kaure cousin terms are extended to cousins of the second degree of collaterality. Generally speaking, a second cousin is equated with a parallel cousin when the genealogical link between ego and alter is through ego's and alter's parents of the same sex. If the genealogical link is through their parents of different sexes, then alter is called *keli* 'cross-cousin'.

Affinal Kinship Terms

Kaure affinal terms of reference, like the consanguineal ones, may also be used as terms of address (although they are rarely used in this way). They are also obligatorily possessed as described above. In the paragraphs that follow, the affinal terms are presented without the obligatory possessive pronoun.

Affinal terms are used basically on two generation levels, the first ascending generation and ego's own generation. Spouses of parallel cousins are equated with spouses of siblings and the terms differ somewhat for male and female ego (see figure 6). For a male, the wife of his *dowi* 'older brother', 'father's brother's older son', or 'mother's sister's older son' is called *awai*. For a female, the husband of her *dowi* is called *sowai*. *nimwa* is the spouse of ego's *semlik* 'younger same sex sibling' or 'younger same sex parallel cousin' for both males and females. Male ego's sister's husband as well as the husbands of his parallel cousins are called *asai;* the same parallelism

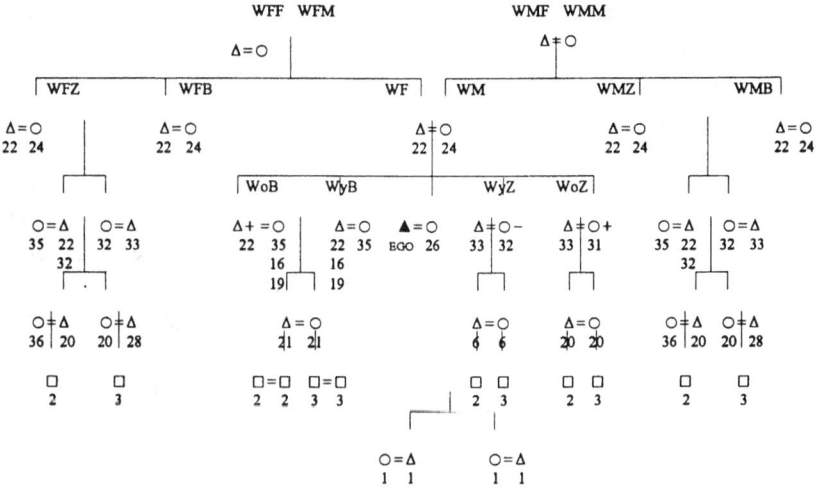

Kaure Male Ego

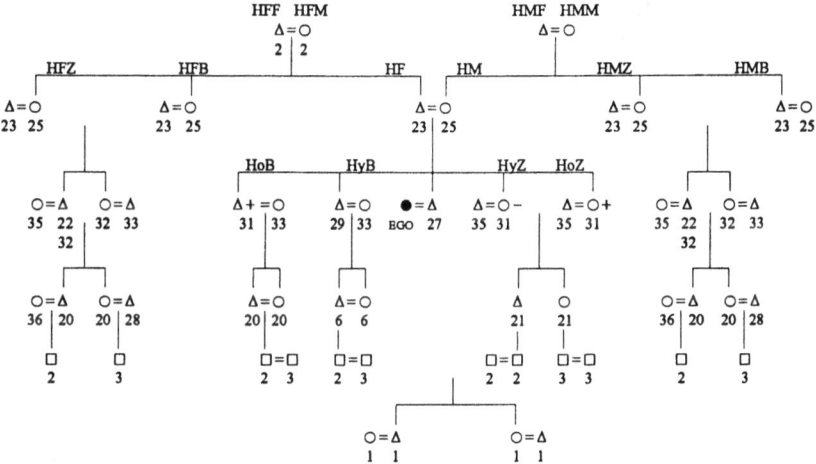

Kaure Female Ego

F	father	H	husband	B	brother	o	older
M	mother	W	wife	Z	sister	y	younger

1. *kaeuk*
2. *asa*
3. *apeuk*
6. *aseik*
16. *neplai*

19. *keli*
20. *dok*
21. *kanon*
22. *memai*
23. *kaeuktuk*

24. *neteik*
25. *deklik*
26. *dai*
27. *nokosai*

28. *asai*
29. *nalen*
31. *nimwa*
32. *sowai*

33. *syanwen*
35. *apwa, payan*
36. *nepli*

Fig. 6. Kaure affinal kinship chart

holds true for female egos. In a sister exchange marriage system a male ego's sister's husband could be the same person as ego's wife's brother *(memai)*. In such a case the consanguineal connection supersedes the affinal one, and ego refers to these people as the spouses of his siblings rather than as the siblings of his spouse.

The term *keli* is used for all cross-cousins, differentiating neither sex, relative age, nor descent. Sex and relative age of cross-cousins, however, are differentiated in the terms used for their spouses and children. An older female cross-cousin's husband is *siwai*. The offspring of *keli* and *siwai* are designated by the same terms as siblings' children according to sex and age relative to ego. A younger female cross-cousin's husband is sometimes called *siwai*, but more often *nimwa*. The wife of a male *keli* who is older than ego is called *awai*, which is the same term used for the wife of ego's older brother and for the wife of ego's older parallel cousin. The wife of a younger *keli* is called *nimwa*, the same term used for ego's younger brother's wife and for ego's younger parallel cousin's wife. These considerations relating to *keli* and their spouses hold true for male and female ego alike.

Ego's wife is called *nedai* 'his married woman' (or *nadai* 'my married woman'). When this term is extended to married women in general, it is not obligatorily possessed and is not used as a term of address. Instead, *noa* 'mother' is used.

There are three terms for the siblings of ego's wife. Ego's wife's younger sister is *sowai* and her older sister is *nimwa*. Ego's wife's brother is *memai*, the same term is used for ego's wife's father and all male affinal kinsmen of the first ascending generation. A male ego's mother-in-law is *neteik* as are also all the female affines of the first ascending generation. The wife of *memai* 'brother-in-law' of ego's generation, however, is called *neplai* 'sister' or 'female parallel cousin', or even *keli* 'female cross-cousin' because that is who she actually could be in a sister exchange marriage system. If there is no consanguineal connection between ego and his wife's brother's wife, she is called *payan*[5] (or its synonym *apwa*), the same terms used for ego's child's parents-in-law.

Ego's wife's siblings' offspring are classified with ego's own siblings' offspring. The children of ego's *nimwa* 'wife's older sister' are called *dok*, those of his *sowai* 'wife's younger sister' are called *aseik*, and those of his *memai* 'wife's brother' are called *kanon*. Correspondingly, the same holds true

---

[5]The Kaure term *payan* is apparently cognate with the term *bayan* used in the neighboring Sause and Orya language groups.

in reverse for a female ego's spouse's siblings' offspring, that is, her husband's older brother's children are called *dok,* his younger brother's children are called *aseik,* and his sister's children are called *kanon.*

There are two different terms for ego's children-in-law and two synony-mous reciprocal terms for ego's child's spouse's parents that are used by female and male ego alike. *nepli* refers to a daughter-in-law and *asai* to a son-in-law. These terms extend to the spouses of ego's sibling's children and to the spouses of ego's parallel and cross-cousin's children. The parents-in-law of the children of ego's siblings as well as those of the children of his parallel and cross-cousins are called either *apwa* or *payan,* not differentiating sex. These terms can be extended to all of spouse's collateral kinsmen in the first ascending generation.

For a female ego, the terms used for spouses of parallel cousins are identical to those used for sibling's spouses. Her older sister is her *dowi* who is married to her *sowai;* her younger sister is her *semlik* who is married to her *nimwa.* Though she uses only one term for brother, *neplu,* her older brother's wife is her *awai* while her younger brother's wife is her *nimwa.* Again, in sister exchange marriage, these terms supersede the connection a female ego has at the same time with her *nimwa* 'husband's sister'. Notice that *nimwa* is the term used for both husband's (younger) sister and for younger brother's wife, again reflecting the Kaure sister exchange system.

A female ego calls her husband *nokosai.* This term is unique and no other kinsman is so designated. Her husband's older brother is her *nimwa* and she calls his wife *syanwen,* while his younger brother is her *nalen* and she also calls his wife *syanwen.* Ego's husband's sisters are designated by the term *nimwa,* while she calls their husbands *payan* (or *apwa*). The spouses of ego's husband's female siblings could be ego's own male siblings in a sister exchange marriage, and in such cases the consanguineal terms supersede the affinal terms. Female ego's father-in-law is her *kaeuktuk;* her mother-in-law is her *deklik.* These terms are extended to all male and female affines in the first ascending generation.

There is no Kaure term for wife's grandparents as the Kaure do not consider ego to be part of that clan. Husband's paternal grandparents are called *asa* 'paternal grandparent' because the wife has married into their clan, but there is no kinship term for husband's maternal grandparents as ego did not marry into their clan.

For a summary of Kaure kinship terms see figure 7. This chart includes both consanguineal and affinal terms with their corresponding referents and an English gloss for the primary referent.

Consanguineal Terms

	Term	English Gloss	Generation	Consanguineal Referent	Affinal Referent
1.	*kaeuk*	great- grandkinsman	+3	PPP, PPPX,	PPPBW, PPPPZH, WPPP, HPPP, WPPPX, HPPPX, WPPPBW, WPPPZH, etc.
			−3	CCC	CCDH, CCSW, XCCDH, XCCSW, etc.
2.	*asa*	paternal grandkinsman	+2	FP, FPX,	HFP, FPZH, FPBW, SSW, SDH, XSSW, XSDH, FXCSW, FXCDH, etc.
			−2	SC, XSC	
3.	*apeuk*	maternal grandkinsman	+2	MP, MPX,	MPZH, MPBW, DSW, DDH, XDSW, XDDH MXCSW, MXCDH, etc.
			−2	DC, XDC	
4.	*jik*	father	+1	F	MZH, MPXDH
5.	*noa, ade*	mother	+1	M, MyZ, MPXyD	FyBW, FPXySW
6.	*aseik*	father's older brother, same sex younger sibling's child	+1	FoB, FPXoS,	
			−1	yBC, PXySC, PPXCySC, yZC, PXyDC, PPXCyDC	WyZC HyBC
7.	*kadal*	father's younger brother	+1	FyB, FPXyS	
8.	*neba*	father's sister	+1	FZ, FPXD	
9.	*nepan*	father's sister's husband	+1		FZH, FPXDH
10.	*ato*	mother's older sister	+1	MoZ, MPXoD	FoBW, FPXoSW
11.	*baholai, kabwa*	mother's brother	+1	MB, MPXS	
12.	*dole*	mother's brother's wife	+1		MBW, MPXSW
13.	*dowi*	same sex older sibling	0	oB, FBoS, MZoS, FPXSoS, MPXDoS, oZ, FBoD, MZoD, FPXSoD, MPXDoD	
14.	*semlik*	same sex younger sibling	0	yB, FByS, MZyS, FPXSyS, MPXDyS, yZ, FByD, MZyD, FPXSyD, MPXDyD	
15.	*neplu*	opposite sex sibling	0	B, FBS, MZS, FPXSS, MPXDS	
16.	*neplai*	opposite sex sibling	0	Z, FBD, MZD, FPXSD, MPXDD	
17.	*pala*	sibling	0	B, Z, FBC, MZC, FPXSC, MPXDC	
18.	*awiwen*	matrilateral parallel cousin (m)	0	MZC	

Fig. 7. Kaure kinship terms (1 of 3)

Consanguineal Terms

	Term	English Gloss	Generation	Consanguineal Referent	Affinal Referent
19.	*keli*	cross-cousin	0	FZC, MBC, FPXDC, MPXSC	
20.	*dok*	child (m)	−1	C, oBC, PXoSC, PPXCoSC,	WoZC, WPXCC
	(f)		−1	oZC, PXoDC, PPXCoDC	HoBC, HPXCC
21.	*kanon*	opposite sex sibling's child	−1	ZC, PXDC, PPXCDC, BC, PXSC, PPXCSC	WBC, HZC

Affinal Terms

	Term	English Gloss	Generation	Consanguineal Referent	Affinal Referent
22.	*memai*	father-in-law	+1		WF, WPB, WPZH,
		brother-in-law	0		WB, WPXS, HPXS
23.	*kaeuktuk*	father-in-law	+1		HF, HPB, HPZH
24.	*neteik*	mother-in-law	+1		WM, WPZ, WPBW
25.	*deklik*	mother-in-law	+1		HM, HPZ, HPBW
26.	*dai*	wife	0		W
27.	*nokosai*	husband	0		H
28.	*asai*	brother-in-law (m)	0		ZH, MZDH, FBDH, FPXSDH, MPXDDH,
		son-in-law	−1		DH, XDH, PXCDH, PPXCCDH, etc.
29.	*nalen*	brother-in-law	0		HyB
30.	*awai*	sister-in-law	0		oBW, PXoSW, PPXCoSW
31.	*nimwa*	sibling-in-law	0		yBW, PXySW, FZyDH, MByDH, FPXCySW, MPXCySW, FPXDyDH, MPXSyDH, WoZ, HoB, HZ,
	(f)				yZH, FByDH, MZyDH, FPXSyDH, MPXDyDH
32.	*sowai*	sibling-in-law	0		WyZ, WPXC, HPXC, FBoDH, MZoDH,
	(f)				FPXSoDH, MPXDoDH
33.	*syanwen*	sibling-in-law	0		HBW, WZH, HPXDH, WPXDH
34.	*siwai*	cross-cousin's husband	0		FZoDH, MBoDH, FPXDoDH, MPXSoDH
35.	*apwa,*	sibling-in-law	0		WBW, HZH, WPXSW, HPXSW,
	payan	child's parents-in-law			DHP, SWP

Fig. 7. Kaure kinship terms (2 of 3)

	Term	English Gloss	Affinal Terms Gener- ation	Consanguineal Referent	Affinal Referent
36.	*nepli*	daughter-in-law	−1		SW, XSW, PXCSW, PPXCCSW, etc.

Key to symbols:

B	brother	f	female only	o	older	X	sibling
C	child	H	husband	P	parent	y	younger
D	daughter	M	mother	S	son	Z	sister
F	father	m	male only	W	wife		

Fig. 7. Kaure kinship terms (3 of 3)

Terms Used in Address and Reference

Although Kaure kinship terms are extensive, they are hardly ever used as general terms of address and reference. Far more common is the use of the second-person personal pronoun in addressing another person, and Christian names are usually used in reference.

However, the following terms are frequently employed as general terms of address and reference alike:

nawen, nahan ke	friend, friends
naplan, napamelen	girl, girls
nanoa, nakamelen	woman, women
taman	boy, boys
kadela	namesake

As mentioned previously, *dai* is the term for ego's wife as well as for women in general. Correspondingly, *nemalon* means 'man', 'men', or 'people', and like *dai* cannot be employed as a term of address. Consequently, *nemalon* prefixed with the second-person possessive pronoun *ha-* 'your', means 'your clan (member)' or 'your group (member)', reflecting the patrilineal nature of Kaure social organization. *dai* prefixed with the same pronoun always means 'your wife'. If one wants to refer to a female member of the clan or the group, one employs *hanemalon* followed by the name of the person being referred to (e.g., *hanemalon Selpi* 'your fellow member Selpi').

Obligations and Restrictions

Kaure kinship terms reflect structurally defined patterns of social interaction between individuals. I now consider some of these social obligations and restrictions.

Dyads

The most important dyad in the Kaure culture appears to be that of father and son. The father is always the first to come to the aid of his son. It is he who instructs the boy in hunting, fishing, house building, garden work, and the like. The father, like all other male members of the clan, makes presents of betel nut, money, clothing, and pork to his son. The son in turn reciprocates, but never with pork or game that he has hunted himself (Rubel and Rosman 1978:5, 321). Such meat is taboo to his parents and to himself, and is given only to his siblings and parallel cousins. If the taboo is broken, the Kaure fear bad luck in future hunting endeavors.

The father-son dyad has reciprocal obligations, as the son is expected to obey his father and help him in his daily work. He is also expected to help his brothers, uncles, and cousins if they live nearby.

If a man dies, neither his son nor any member of his clan is permitted to help with the burial of the corpse. When a woman dies, neither her *natal* clan nor her husband's clan may help. (There are semiprofessionals among the Kaure who perform this service and receive food gifts for it.) Items like tools and weapons are usually inherited by the oldest son, but they can always be borrowed and used by his younger brothers. The father's house is given to the son who has the greatest need for it at the time of his father's death. Personal things, like pillows, sleeping mats, stringbags, are not passed on but placed on the grave of the deceased.

The mother is the one who instructs her daughter in skills such as sago processing, making stringbags (not done any more), garden work, and cooking. Daughters do not inherit, but share in the inheritances of their husbands.

A number of authors have pointed out that in many New Guinea cultures the dyad between ego and mother's brother is the predominant one (Sims 1986:25ff.; May 1981:10). This characteristic does not appear to be true for the Kaure, though there are social obligations between mother's brother and ego. Sometimes the *baholai* 'mother's brother' gives to ego his *ble na* 'traditional name' at birth. His Christian name is not given until much later by the pastor, who comes in from the city about once a year for the christening of all surviving infants. Mother's brother also teaches ego and may even negotiate for a wife for ego. However, he does not punish his nephew for unacceptable behavior; that is left to ego's father and older brothers.

At some point in his life *baholai* will give a shirt to ego with red betel nut saliva on it. This "gift" is accompanied by a verbal demand that ego must beat up his son, that is, ego's *keli* 'cross-cousin', shortly after the mother's brother's death. Before government contact, ego used to shoot an arrow into the thigh of his *keli*, but this practice has been replaced by a beating in recent times because of government intervention. On several occasions we have observed that these beatings inflicted more severe wounds than an arrow might have done. This beating is seen as a final punishment for any disobedience and grief the son may have caused his father during his lifetime. A good and obedient son may, however, be spared the beating. When *baholai* makes the arrangement with ego, he can point out which of his children shall receive the beating. This arrangement can be made with one or several of his sister's sons. The punishment can be meted out to one of mother's brother's children or to several, including daughters.

This type of arrangement is made not only with *baholai* but also between ego and his *neba* 'father's sister'. When she dies, ego may likewise be obligated to beat up her child, also his *keli* 'cross-cousin'.

Marriage

The rule of clan exogamy requires that a Kaure marry outside of his parental clans. Marriage partners may be taken from any other clan, with these further restrictions:[6] (a) ego may not marry his second cousins, i.e., any great grandchild (CCC) of any of his great grandparents (PPP), (b) ego may not marry the children of his parents' siblings' spouses' siblings, and (c) a member of the double clans Nakabi-Hirwa and Dalem-Wama may not take a wife from the other part of his double clan.

There is one case in which a man married the widow of his maternal uncle. This act caused great distress among the people and the couple was forced to live isolated in the forest for many years, their marriage considered illegitimate.

---

[6]Nimboran has one further marriage restriction—the partner may not be a member of the paternal grandmother's clan (May 1981:12). Kemtuk extends the restriction to one more clan, a so-called "friend clan" (van der Wilden 1976:11).

These extensive marriage restrictions account for the fact that an estimated fifty percent of the women now resident in the Kaure villages are from other ethnic groups in the area. However, if one wants to marry outside the language group, the ideal of sister exchange marriage still applies. If there is no sister available, any female parallel or cross-cousin qualifies, or if none is available the other party must wait until a younger sister or cousin matures. If a suitable exchange partner is available, the two weddings may be on the same day or in the same week. The sister exchange marriage system is gradually being abandoned because of the influences of church and government. The bride price payment alone, although traditionally used in addition to sister exchange, is slowly becoming the way of attaining a bride. The bride price is considerably higher if no sister or relative is given in exchange. In this case a transistor radio or tape recorder is often added to the bride price.

Out of sixty randomly chosen men, including one with multiple wives, twenty of the men gave "real" sisters (i.e., they had the same father), and four men gave parallel cousins. In the other cases, no sister or parallel cousin was available for exchange, so four men gave cross-cousins in exchange for a wife, one polygamous man gave the child of his first wife, one man gave his older brother's child, and two men gave more remote affinal kin (see, for example, figure 8). Four others did not exchange any relative at all and twenty-four took spouses from other language groups.

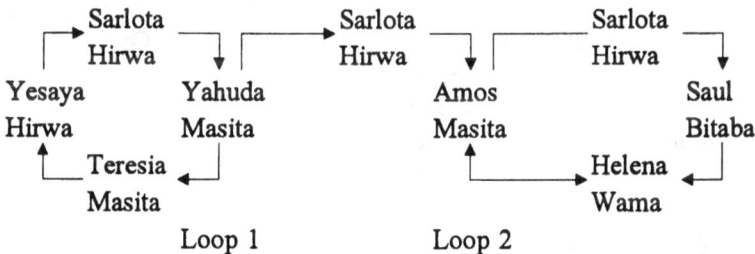

Fig. 8. Example of a sister exchange marriage

Thus, when Yesaya Hirwa received Teresia Masita as a wife from her brother Yahuda Masita, he gave his sister Sarlota Hirwa in exchange (figure 8, Loop 1). Since at that point Yahuda Masita was already married (to a woman to whose brother he had given his other sister Monika in exchange) and as he did not want a second wife, he passed Sarlota on to his younger brother, Amos Masita. Amos, however, declined to marry Sarlota and passed her on to Saul Bitaba, who in return gave his "sister" Helena Wama as a wife to Amos Masita (Loop 2). In other words, Amos was able to marry his wife because his sister was given in exchange by his brother to a third party. Saul Bitaba is the foster child of Helena Wama's parents; he retains his old name, but has the same rights in exchanging a sister as any blood brother of Helena would have had. However, other marriage restrictions and rights are different for him as a foster child, since he may not marry into either his foster clan or his birth clan. The bride price for Sarlota was paid by the Wama clan to the Hirwa clan.

A young man who wants to get married usually talks to his parents about his plans. As it is not appropriate for his own parents to engage in direct negotiations with the bride's parents, they send ego's *kadal* 'father's younger brother', *aseik* 'father's older brother', or *baholai* 'mother's brother' to open discussions with their prospective *payan* 'son's wife's parents'. If negotiations are successful, the wedding date will be set for the same week. The prospective bride can, however, refuse to accept a particular husband by weeping loudly in front of many witnesses before the marriage celebration.

For the actual marriage feast, food is provided by the groom's clan. The ceremony lasts one night and takes place either at the groom's parent's house or at the house of one of his father's brothers, where the bride is led by the groom's older brother's wife. The bride usually wears a special dress for the occasion, which is provided by the groom's parents or anyone else who has access to such a dress. The marriage is sealed when the bride and groom eat a sago meal together from one plate with one spoon. On the morning following the feast the newlywed couple moves to their own house, which is given to them by a relative of the groom. If no house is available, the couple will move in with the groom's parents until they have built their own house. In the afternoon of the day following the wedding, the bride's parents come to see their daughter. They remind her of her duties as a wife and that she must obey her husband.

The following morning is the time for paying the bride price. Formerly, various kinds of beads and shells for necklaces were given as well as stone axes imported from the highlands. Nowadays, beads and shells are still given, but not stone axes. They have been replaced by steel axes, knives, machetes, clothes, cooking utensils, plates and silverware, and most importantly by cash (formerly about 100,000 rupiah, but in 1991 it was as high as 1,000,000 rupiah or about 500 US dollars for outsiders to the area). These items are gathered together by all the groom's elder relatives, including older siblings and cousins. Bride price items are received by the bride's father who in turn will distribute them to all his relatives, regardless of age.

The bride price is not, however, always paid the day following the wedding. In fact, some men stay indebted to their wife's parents for a lifetime, never managing to pay the price fully. It is believed, however, that until the price is fully paid, the wife will remain barren. In cases of polygyny, another regular practice is to give to the second wife's clan as bride price payment, the newborn child of another wife (for whom the bride price has already been paid in full). These children are adopted and never returned to their biological parents. They have inheritance rights like any other child in their adoptive clan, but their marriage restrictions are the same as for any member in their biological father's clan except that they also cannot marry into their foster clan.

There are exceptions to the bride price payment. For example, a widower marrying a second time into his deceased wife's clan does not pay a second bride price to the same clan. Nor does a man marrying an old widow have to pay a bride price, though he does for a young widow. However, a young widow may be married without a bride price if it is to a man of her deceased husband's clan. A widow may not marry her dead husband's brother. Her children go to her deceased husband's clan if he has paid the bride price; they go to her own clan if the bride price was not fully paid at the time of her husband's death. If the wife dies, the children are fostered by a relative of her husband until he remarries and they are then returned to him.

Frequently, a widow is given to a man in another language group. The second husband pays the bride price for a young widow to her former husband's clan if the deceased man had paid the bride price in full to his wife's clan. If the deceased husband had not paid fully, the new husband pays the bride price to the woman's clan.

A second pattern for acquiring a wife is by elopement. Usually, however, the wife's father will go after the couple, bring them back home, and insist on payment of the bride price.

Divorce is infrequent because the bride price is relatively high and is not returned in case of a divorce, forcing the husband to collect and pay a second bride price for a new wife. A divorced wife returns to her parents, who will receive her back if no bride price payment has been made. If, on the other hand, the bride price was fully received, she can expect to be beaten by her parents, and taken back to her husband. Husbands take second wives if the first one is infertile but do not divorce the barren wife, though she may leave voluntarily. Relatively frequently, married women run away with men who are married to someone else. I have observed that these women usually return to their husbands after a few weeks or months, receiving only a possible beating or physical restraint for a time since the husband is usually desperate to get her back to avoid paying another bride price.

During childbirth the following people typically give help: husband's mother, husband's older brother's wife, husband's sister, and wife's younger sister. The husband, too, will be there mainly to give moral support to his wife. If the older sister and mother of the wife are present, payment for their help is expected; consequently, they are usually not asked to assist at the birth.

Taboos Reflecting Avoidance Behavior towards Affines

The taboos described here are distinct from the marriage restrictions enumerated above because of their mythological origin. Also, they are distinct from the many other Kaure taboos since they apply only to certain affinal kinsmen. All these taboos define various patterns of avoidance relationships. They fall into three categories: verbal taboos, food taboos, and taboos concerning other interpersonal behavior.

Our language associates indicate that these taboos began being abandoned in the late 1950s when government and church contact was made. Some Kaure stated that they do not submit to these taboos at all any more. In actual practice, however, we have observed that the taboos are still very much a part of their life. In our tape-recorded text materials, speakers time and again avoided certain words, substituting either Indonesian loan words or neologisms. The point is to avoid saying words that are homophonous with the traditional names of certain affines, even though they might have been long dead. There is some disagreement over the question of whether the name taboo only applies to the traditional *ble na* 'earth names' or whether it also applies to Christian names. Some feel that it applies in either case while others feel that the name taboo is restricted to traditional names only.

For example, Yordan Masita's traditional name is *Koseikpo*. Consequently, Yohanes Yamle and Simon Yamle do not pronounce the word *koseik* 'crocodile' since they are each married to Yordan's older brother's daughters. Neither may they pronounce the following: *kajel* 'deep' and *Soar,* the name of a vacated village, as the names of Yordan's two brothers, *Blejel* and *Soa-Soa,* sound similar to these words.

The Myths: "Nahai" and "Ahwansekeuk"

There are two myths which Kaure people always relate to kinship taboos, one about old Nahai, and the other about Ahwansekeuk. Both myths were told to us by several of the elderly or middle-aged men and it is believed that Nahai's visions still hold true today. An English summary follows:

> Old Nahai lived in the days when the earth had just been created, and there were no kinship related taboos. The people enjoyed great freedom. After the birth of his children old Nahai became paralyzed and his children had to carry him around in a basket. Whenever he wanted to go anywhere, he was carried by his children, even when he needed to urinate. One day old Nahai died. After two days, however, his children saw something moving under the sheet where the corpse had been put. When they lifted the sheet they found that their father had moved and had come back to life. So they sat him up. Old Nahai said, "Give me some water to drink." His children went to draw the water, and when they gave it to their father he rinsed his mouth and the bad mouth smell vanished. Then Nahai said, "Listen to what I have to say." Then Nahai proceeded to tell his children the visions he had had when he was dead. All these visions concerned future events in the Kaure area, especially regarding the arrival of outsiders, who should receive friendly treatment.

This myth is related to kinship taboos in that Nahai's era is viewed by the modern Kaure as a "golden age" since none of the kinship related taboos had been given yet and their lives were free of those irksome restrictions.

> A long time after Nahai had died for the second time, a man named Ahwansekeuk lived. Ahwansekeuk was a male cannibal who went down to the Idenburg river, then up the Naka river, and lived there in a cave that is called the Ahwansekeuk cave to the present day. He captured people who were lying in wait for birds and ate them. The people of the village became suspicious about their many fellow villagers vanishing when they saw their bones floating in the river. So two men decided to do something about it. They went together to the jungle, built a bird blind, and one of the men slept outside the bird blind, while the other kept watch inside. It was not long before they heard Ahwansekeuk approaching. He was disguised in leaves and weeds, and looked

like a devil. The two village men wrestled him down, beat him with a stick, stripped off his disguise, and were about to cut his throat, when Ahwansekeuk called out, "Don't cut my throat, but listen to what I have to say!" Then he proceeded to tell them all the taboos and consequences of transgressing them.

Taboos

All of the taboos handed down to the two village men by Ahwansekeuk are proscriptions against certain normal activities in the presence of specific affines. These proscriptions are delineated in figure 9 and the affines specified are listed in figure 10.

pronounce name of	eat food of
smoke cigarettes of	chew betelnut of
drink water of	drink water near
open and eat betelnut near	pass by near
step in footprints of	look into eyes of
share stringbag with	sit with
sit in place of	touch
speak in loud voice	break wind near

Fig. 9. Prohibited activities

Kaure avoidance relationships exist between affines of both the same and opposite sex. The avoidance taboos are in effect reciprocal between ego and anyone ego refers to by the affinal terms listed in figure 10.

The terms *nimwa* and *payan* designate more than one kinsman and are used reciprocally. For example, taboos that apply to ego's younger brother's wife also apply to ego's husband's older brother since both refer to each other by the term *nimwa*. The same reciprocity of taboos applies to parents-in-law and their children's spouses, though the kinship terms are not reciprocal. In other words, what a female ego cannot do in relation to her *keuktuk* 'father-in-law' and to her *deklik* 'mother-in-law', they cannot do in relation to her, their *nepli* 'daughter-in-law'. And likewise, what a male ego cannot do to his *memai* 'father-in-law' and to his *neteik* 'mother-in-law', they cannot do to him, their *asai* 'son-in-law'. The same reciprocity holds true for all other kinsmen who are addressed by the terms in figure 10. For instance, since *memai* is also the term for wife's brother, the same taboos apply to him, and reciprocally, to sister's husband, who is called *asai*.

Breaking these taboos is said to result in serious consequences for the health and well-being of the transgressor. As Ahwansekeuk pointed out, the breaking of any taboo will invariably lead to fatigue, loss of energy and motivation, a speeding up of the aging process, drop of body temperature, and sickness. Fear of these effects motivates the majority of the Kaure today to adhere to the kinship related taboos as passed down from Ahwansekeuk.

	Kin term	Reciprocal relationship		
Reciprocal Terms:	*nimwa*	yBW	↔	HoB
		HoZ	↔	yBW
		WoZ	↔	yZH
		FBySW	↔	HFBoS
		FZySW	↔	HMBoS
		MBySW	↔	HFZoS
		MoZySW	↔	HMZoS
	payan	SWF	↔	DHF
		SWM	↔	DHF
		SWF	↔	DHM
		SWM	↔	DHM
Non-reciprocal Terms:	*asai*	DH	↔	WF	*memai*
		ZH	↔	WB
		MZDH	↔	WMZS
		FBDH	↔	WFBS
	asai	DH	↔	WM	*neteik*
	nepli	SW	↔	HF	*kaeuktuk*
		SW	↔	HM	*deklik*

Fig. 10. Kaure affinal kinsmen affected by avoidance taboos

Summary

Kaure kinship relations and the terms that represent them are extensive. Ego differentiates many of his consanguineal and affinal kinsmen by age of alter relative to ego, sex of alter relative to ego, and sex of alter. Kaure speakers use these many descriptive terms only reluctantly, and prefer rather the extended classificatory usages of *dok* 'child', *noa* 'mother', *jik* 'father', *dowi* 'same sex older sibling', *semlik* 'same sex younger sibling', *neplai* 'sister', and *neplu* 'brother'. Many of the behavioral patterns described for the Kaure have also been found in other New Guinea societies (Shaw 1974:64, 198), but the beating of one's cross-cousin upon his father's and/or mother's death and the legendary origin of kinship related taboos appear to be unique to the Kaure.

References

Dommel, Peter R. and Gudrun E. Dommel. 1991. Kaure phonology. Workpapers in Indonesian Languages and Cultures 9:1–68.

May, Kevin R. 1981. Nimboran kinship and marriage. Irian: Bulletin of Irian Jaya 9(2):1–26.

Rubel, Paula G. and Abraham Rosman. 1978. Your own pigs you may not eat. A comparative study of New Guinea societies. Chicago: The University of Chicago Press.

Shaw, R. Daniel, ed. 1974. Kinship studies in Papua New Guinea. Ukarumpa, Papua New Guinea: Summer Institute of Linguistics.

Sims, Andrew. 1986. Ketengban kinship. Irian: Bulletin of Irian Jaya 14:15–44.

van der Wilden, Jelly. 1976. Kemtuk kinship. Irian: Bulletin of Irian Jaya 1:7–21.

Voorhoeve, C. L. 1975. Languages of Irian Jaya: Checklist. Preliminary classification, language maps, wordlists. Pacific Linguistics Series B 31.

The Social Functions of Polygyny in Relation to Sikaritai Kinship and Marriage

David L. Martin

Polygyny had long been a normal practice among Sikaritai people when indigenous missionaries from the highland Dani came to them in the early 1970s. Under the influence of these outsiders, polygyny was abandoned by large numbers of Sikaritai.

A revival of widespread polygyny began, however, in the mid 1980s, raising questions and sparking inquiry into just how polygyny was rooted in traditional Sikaritai social structure. The extent to which polygyny was directly related to kinship relations and marriage exchange patterns soon became clear. In taking another wife, a man was apparently not concerned about his own individual interests or merely endeavoring to gain prestige. Rather, after considering his kinsmen, both consanguineal and affinal, and being aware of the crucial role of exchanges in maintaining good clan relations, he was obliged to meet these diverse commitments according to Sikaritai values. In this context, the elimination of polygyny can be seen to produce certain negative impacts on Sikaritai society.

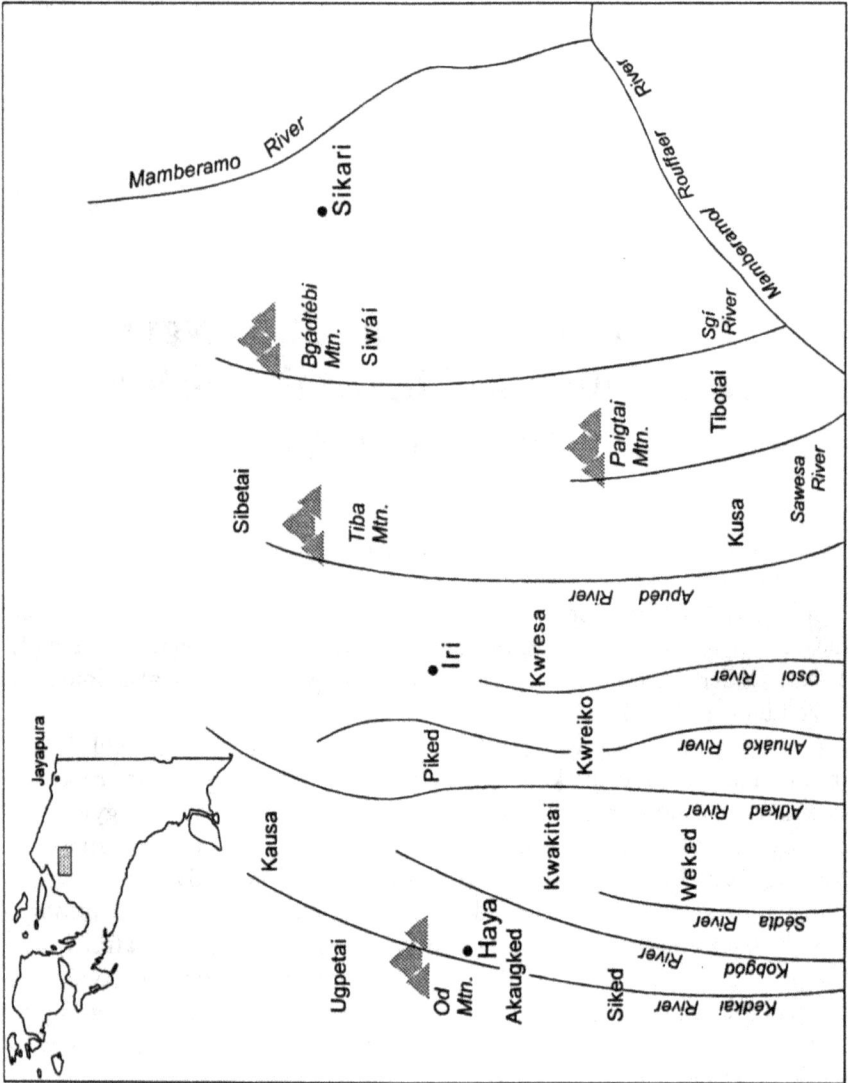

Fig. 1. Traditional Sikaritai settlement locations

In the pages that follow, I attempt to describe Sikaritai kinship and marriage, then look at the institution of polygyny as it is interwoven into Sikaritai society as a whole, and finally consider its function in the society.[1]

Before discussing Sikaritai social structure, however, I will describe briefly some of the other aspects of Sikaritai culture.

The Sikaritai

The Sikaritai people live in the Greater Lakes Plain region of Irian Jaya (see figure 1), through which the Mamberamo River flows. They number approximately 600 people and are settled in three main villages, located 150 miles southwest of Sentani, and west of the Mamberamo, in an area approximately 15 miles long and 10 miles wide. The area is lowland swamp, bordered by the Van Rees Mountains on the north. It is part of the District (Kabupaten) of Jayapura. The Sikaritai language has been identified in previous survey reports as Aikwakai or Ati, and has been classified by Voorhoeve (1975) as a member of the Trans-New Guinea Phylum, Tor-Lakes Plain Stock, Central Lakes Plain Family. Sikaritai people are traditionally animists, but since Christianity was introduced in the early 1970s, 20 percent have become baptized, approximately 60 percent are involved in Christian activities, and the majority consider themselves Christians.

---

[1]My family and I have been resident at the village of Sikari for extended periods since November 1979, studying the Sikaritai language and culture under the auspices of RBMU International. The data for this paper have been collected primarily during the past five years, with concentrated gathering during January–June 1989.

Special recognition is due to Batépid and Yan Siwáf/Maitemtai, a father-son pair, who contributed the most recent data resulting in the analysis presented in this paper. Most of the married men resident at Sikari helped by relating their genealogies as far back as they recalled.

Special thanks goes to Drs. Ken and Marilyn Gregerson, of the Summer Institute of Linguistics, who provided technical advice and expertise in analyzing and interpreting the data. This paper was written during an Anthropology Workshop, sponsored by the UNCEN-SIL Project, Indonesia Branch, Irian Jaya Program, of the Summer Institute of Linguistics, held at Danau Bira, during September–October 1989.

Social Groups

The Sikaritai are organized into two distinct groups of clans, which I shall call *phratries* (Schusky 1972:92).[2] Each phratry *(apuí)*[3] is identified with a specific geographical area and exhibits minimal dialectal variation with respect to the other phratry. These phratries also provide a framework for alliances in times of war. They might also be called "alliances" or "subtribes" to reflect their character as territorial units.

Each *atú* 'clan'[4] (Schusky 1972:90) traces its ancestry to one man, who lived on either a specific mountain or a specific river. The clan names are derived from these locations or from an animal involved in some incident between two clan founders.

According to Sikaritai legend (see appendix), the ancestors of all the clans originally lived together at Akuri, more or less central to the Central Lakes Plain region. The legends speak of a "golden age" in which the environment was still unblemished, food was plentiful and easily available, and problems were few, if any. Then one day a pair of brothers, who were the founders of two clans in the Siwai phratry, had a disagreement and went downriver by canoe, taking with them all the other ancestors and some earth from the original location. As they were floating down the Mamberamo river, they struck an ironwood tree in the middle of the River and their canoe was destroyed. They were, however, able to escape their predicament when a

---

[2]Since there are only two such groups of clans, I might also have called them "moieties," but I hesitate to do so since they function quite differently than the moieties of the Dani and Yali in the highlands. Also, there are extensions of the sister exchange system to Papasena and Eri, which are also, in fact, phratries. Therefore, I could refer to a system of four phratries, which would better fit the definition of phratry. These others, however, claim separate ancestry.

Peter Lawrence (1971:7) tabulates eleven general types of society. Of them, Sikaritai most closely aligns itself with the following two:

5. Tribal or district group societies: where a number of patriclans, without claiming a further common ancestor, form a named, war-making, political group and the whole society consists of a number of such groups.

6. Patriphratry societies: where a number of patriclans, claiming a further common patrilineal ancestor, form a named patriphratry, which may or may not be a war-making group, and the whole society consists of a number of such groups.

[3]The terms used in this paper are written in accordance with analysis of Sikaritai Phonology (Martin 1991).

[4]These groups could also be called "sibs" (Schusky 1972:92). I choose to call them "clans" to reflect the unilocal as well as the unilinear rule of descent.

strong wind swayed a branch of a palm tree, bringing it within their reach; they caught it and tied it to a branch of the ironwood tree in the river. Then all of them climbed onto the palm tree, cut the vine, and the palm tree bounced back into position, slightly inland from the river. From the palm tree, all the other ancestors descended from the various branches, and found their way to their traditional locations. The younger brother, however, climbed down to the base of the tree itself, and threw down the earth he had brought from Akuri, thus creating one of the three mountains at Sikari.

The legend then explains how the younger brother, after coming down the tree, stood with his sister on one mountain, while his older brother and another sister stood on an adjacent mountain. Having discovered that they were the only two pairs still in the immediate area, one pair came across and the men exchanged sisters. The implication is that other pairs of ancestors, having descended to adjacent locations, also exchanged sisters.

This legend details Sikaritai understanding of how the various clans came to live in their traditional locations and with whom (at least in part) they exchange sisters in the marriage exchange system. Understanding the interrelationships of clans together with the marriage exchange system gives the foundation for understanding the total social structure of the Sikaritai, which in turn would appear to be key to basic features of all the groups across the entire Central Lakes Plain Region. The belief that their ancestors originated from one location and that, even after separating, they still had close relations with each other gives the foundation for stability in all relationships.

Sikaritai express solidarity as a group by the use of two terms, taken from the legend referred to above. The base of the palm tree from which all the clan founders descended is known as *apuí*, expressing the idea of origin or beginning. The separate clans resulting from the ancestors climbing onto separate branches and going down to different locations are known as *tró atú* 'people branch'. Thus, the group now living as a unit at Sikari is known collectively as *tró apuí* Siwáí 'people originating from Siwáí', because each of the four clans originated from the same tree. Each of the individual clans is known as *tró atú*, e.g., *tró atú* Sibetai 'people of the branch Sibetai', and is associated with specific land. Similarly, people of the other "tree" (i.e., origin) are *tró apuí* Kausa, who in turn are also broken down into their own clans *(tró atú)*. The term *tró apuí* corresponds to phratry while *tró atú* corresponds to clan. The term subphratry refers to groups of clans which are within one phratry but are geographically distinct as a unit; there is no Sikaritai term corresponding to this unit. This system has the potential of relating any person from any group throughout the Central Lakes Plain to those at Sikari village/phratry. People of one phratry definitely consider themselves united, and there is a strong sense of "us" as opposed to "them" in another phratry. The two phratries, Siwáí and Kausa, form the backbone of Sikaritai society and particularly marriage exchange.

Residence is patrilocal, with a settlement consisting of the clan's adult men, their wives, and their children, extending at times over four generations. Upon marriage, women begin living in their husband's settlement, and unless widowed when elderly, they do not return to live in their natal settlement. Each clan has its own separate settlement close to the river and/or mountain where their original ancestor descended from the palm tree. A man's obligations to his father-in-law, however, lead him to spend extended periods with his wife (or wives) in the wife's settlement. This practice in turn encourages phratry endogamy so that traveling great distances is not necessary to fulfill these obligations. Marriage is clan exogamous but may be inside or outside of one's phratry.

Traditionally, Sikaritai settlements were distributed throughout the area as shown in figure 2.

Beginning in the early 1970s, airstrips were built in the Central Lakes Plain area and the people were encouraged by the government and Protestant missions to gather and form villages at the airstrip locations. It was at this time that all thirteen Sikaritai clans formed one large village at Sikari. This arrangement lasted only briefly, ending after a fight between the Siwáí and Kausa phratries. Two more villages were then formed, reflecting previous geographical divisions within the Kausa phratry and one more airstrip was built. In the early 1980s the Weked clan split off to form a small fourth village. Figure 3 details the clan and phratry composition of each of the Sikaritai villages. (Location of the villages is shown in figure 1.)

The Sikaritai were traditionally hunters and gatherers, but now they also grow small gardens. Sago and bananas are their staple foods, supplemented by fish (particularly at Sikari), wild pig, marsupials, rodents, turtles, birds, pandanus, breadfruit, papaya, coconut, pineapple, and occasionally crocodile. The raising of chickens, as well as gardening, has been introduced by the Dani missionaries and other outsiders, but the latter innovation is still rather foreign.

Traditional households are composed of a man and his wives, unmarried daughters, and uninitiated sons. The houses have three levels; the men stay on the top level, women in the middle, and cooking facilities are on the bottom. Each settlement has a separate men's house, which is off-limits to women, and a separate house for unmarried young men.

A newer type of residence houses the same nuclear family, but there is usually a separate cook-house. Most families also have a house close to their clan's traditional land, where they live for extended periods. Each clan has general rights to this land, and each family grows bananas and sago on it as well as hunts on it. Individual fruit trees are individual family property and are handed down patrilineally.

River/Location	Clan	Subphratry	Phratry
Sgí River upstream Bgádtébi Mountain	Siwáí/Maitemtai		
Apuéd River upstream Tiba Mountain	Sibetai		Siwáí
Apuéd River downstream Tiba Mountain	Kusa		
Sgí River downstream Paigtai Mountain	Tibotai		
Kédkei River	Kausa		
Od Mountain	Ugpetai Akaugked Siked	Kausa	Kausa
Kobgód River	Kwakitai		
Sédta River	Weked	Weked	
Osoi River	Kwresa		
Ahuákó River	Kwreiko	Idtai	
Adkad River (& lake)	Piked		

Fig. 2. Traditional Sikaritai settlements

Phratry/Dialect	Subphratry/Village	Clans
Siwáí	Sikari	Siwáí
		Kusa
		Sibetai
		Tibotai
Kausa	Haya	Kausa
		Kwakitai
		Ugpetai
		Akauked
		Siked
Kausa	Iri	Kwresa
		Kwreiko
		Piked
Kausa	Pui	Weked

Fig. 3. Present distribution of clans

Kinship Terms

Sikaritai kinship terminology reflects a modified Iroquois system. Cross- and parallel kinsmen are distinguished in the first and second ascending generations, ego's generation, and the first descending generation. Terms primarily extend bilaterally, not distinguishing lineal from collateral kin, except that kin traced solely through male links tend to be treated as siblings to a male ego.

Consanguineal Kinship Terms

Sikaritai consanguineal kinship terms are considered under the following four categories: grandkinsmen, distant grandkinsmen, familial terms, and sibling terms.

Grandkinsmen. For the second ascending generation, two terms are used: one primarily for male grandkinsmen, *kóg* 'grandfather', and one primarily for female grandkinsmen, *atá* 'grandmother'. These terms are used reciprocally with the second descending generation, that is, a child refers to his grandparent and is referred to by his grandparent using the same term. Thus, ego uses *kóg* for both of his grandfathers (i.e., FF and MF) and *atá* for both of his grandmothers (FM and MM). Ego's two grandfathers refer to their grandchildren of either sex as *kóg,* and his grandmothers refer to their grandchildren of either sex as *atá.*

kóg is further extended to refer to paternal grandfather's siblings (FFB and FFZ), as well as father's mother's sister's husband (FMZH), mother's mother's sister's husband (MMZH), father's father's sister's husband (FFZH), and mother's father's sister's husband (MFZH). Mother's father's brother (MFB) is also called *kóg,* but mother's father's sister (MFZ) is *atá.* *atá* is similarly extended to refer to grandmother's siblings, father's mother's brother and sister (FMB and FMZ) and mother's mother's brother and sister (MMB and MMZ), as well as father's father's brother's wife (FFBW), mother's father's brother's wife (MFBW), father's mother's brother's wife (FMBW), and mother's mother's brother's wife (MMBW). These extended applications are also used reciprocally by brother's child's child and sister's child's child (BCC and ZCC).

These two terms are also used between a son's wife (SW) and her husband's parents, and by extension with all their siblings and their spouses. They are thereby extended from second generation above and below ego to first generation above and below ego as well. Correlated with this usage is the fact that in most cases a son's wife is younger than he is, in fact closer to the age of his sister's children.

Distant Grandkinsmen. The two grandparent terms are further applied in the third ascending generation and above, with the addition of the adjectival suffix *kró* 'old'. This use only distinguishes sex, no bifurcation, probably because few if any Sikaritai have relatives of this generation living. Above the third ascending generation, the terms *kóg* and *atá* are combined with *kró* to create *atákogkró* 'ancestors'.

Familial Terms. The Sikaritai employ seven terms to designate kinsmen of the parent and child generations.

Four familial terms classify kinsmen of the first generation above ego. They are *awag* 'father', *aweg* 'mother', *ad* 'father's sister', and *abéid* 'mother's brother'. A fifth, *awag kwaré* 'father's brother' (*kwaré* 'not blood'), could be added, but since it is a compound involving *awag* 'father', it is considered simply as a compound, leaving a clearly bifurcate merging classificatory system.

These terms equate parallel kinsmen and distinguish cross-kinsmen. Thus, father's brother (FB) is referred to as 'father', and mother's sister (MZ) is referred to as 'mother'. In addition, there is a separate term for father's sister, and a distinct term for mother's brother, but father's sister can also simply be referred to as 'father'. In extending the terms to affines, FBW is 'mother' and MZH is 'father'. Then, reflecting the sister-exchange system, father's sister's husband is called 'father', and mother's brother's wife is called 'mother', just as they would be if father's sister married mother's brother. *awag* and *aweg* are both also referred to and addressed as *ai*.

For purposes of distinguishing between one's biological parents and their siblings or cousins, the suffix *-okwé* 'true' or 'real' can be added. It is also possible to single out father's brothers by the addition of *kwaré* 'not blood', but this form only distinguishes his consanguineal brothers from affinal brothers. The term *awag* 'father' optionally replaces *ad* in referring to father's sister, diminishing the distinctions slightly.

The term *túé* 'child' is the complement of *awag* 'father' and *aweg* 'mother'. It is used to refer to ego's offspring of either sex, with *húráre* 'male' or *húegso* 'female' added, if necessary, to differentiate sex. *túé* also refers to ego's male sibling's children (BC), children of his father's brother's son (FBSC), and children of his mother's sister's son (MZSC) and mother's brother's son (MBSC). Thus, ego uses *túé* to refer to first descending generation kinsmen of his own clan, of his mother's clan, and of his mother's sister's husband's clan, who have descended through male offspring of his generation. It is also used for males in the first descending generation of his father's sister's husband's clan (FZCS) and of his father's brother's daughter's husband's clan (FBDS).

The term *ariakó* 'nephew' or 'niece' is the complement of *abéid* and *ad*. It refers to ego's kinsmen of the first descending generation who are linked to ego with the first and final links being female. Thus, ego's sister's children of either sex are ego's *ariakó* and he is their *abéid*. Similarly, children of his mother's sister's daughter (MZDC) and his mother's brother's daughter (MBDC) are his *ariakó* as links are first through mother and finally through daughter. By extension, the children of any female *weyá* 'matrilateral parallel cousin' or female *abyá* 'cross-cousin' of the second or third degree are also *ariakó*, there being two female links. It is these *ariakó* who are considered first as prospective wives. Any *ariakó* is addressed as *duhuri*.

Finally, ego refers to father's sister's child's son (FZSS, FZDS) either by *túé* or by the term *túéta*, which is a combination of *túé* 'child' and the suffix *-ta* 'from' and may indicate that after two generations of female-related terms through connection with father's sister (FZ), now the relationship is returning to a male-centered link.

Sibling Terms. The greatest proliferation of Sikaritai kinship terms comes within ego's generation. These terms take into consideration sex of parent, relative age of alter to ego, relative age of parents, and sex of alter and ego. The terms can be arranged in levels, some having general range, others restricted range.

The most general terms relate to relative age: *aság* 'older sibling', *aprá* 'younger sibling', and *akadá* 'age-mate'. These terms are all used by those in ego's generation of both sexes to relate to siblings of both sexes in a general way. Ego also addresses and refers to father's brother's child (FBC) using these terms. *akadá* can also refer to twins.

The next term, *augtá*, distinguishes siblings on the basis of sex only. This term is used by a woman to refer to her brothers, and by a man to refer to his sisters. The use of this term may reflect the idea that women are only temporarily present in their parents' clan group and upon marriage will live with their husband's clan.

The next set of five terms further delineates the relative age distinction by differentiating a woman's sisters from a man's sisters (see figure 4). Thus, a female ego refers to her older sister as *áka*, while she refers to her younger sister as *awé*. Similarly, a male ego refers to his older sister as *arakúg* and to his younger sister as *orokgóg*. Female ego refers to her brothers using the general terms *aság* and *aprá*. Finally, male ego refers to his older brother as *débi*, while the general term *aprá* is used to refer to his younger brother. All these terms are alternate terms for *aság* or *aprá*, but are more descriptive in their denotation.

Sibling Relationship	Older	Younger
woman–woman	*áka*	*awé*
man–woman	*arakúg*	*orokgóg*
woman–man	*aság*	*aprá*
man–man	*débi*	*aprá*
sibling–sibling	*aság*	*aprá*

Fig. 4. Reciprocal sets of sibling terms

Finally, among ego's cousins a three-way distinction is made (see figure 5). Following the tendency to single out relationships following exclusively male links, patrilateral parallel cousins (FBC) are referred to directly with the terms *aság* 'older sibling' and *aprá* 'younger sibling'. The terms are applied based on the relative age of the linking parents, regardless of the cousins' actual ages. Thus, even if A is older than B but B's father was A's older brother, A is called B's younger brother. Matrilateral parallel cousins (MZC) are referred to as *weyá*. On the other hand, cross-cousins (both FZC and MBC) are *abyá*. Thus, FBC is classified as ego's sibling, MZC as ego's *weyá*, and both FZC and MBC as *abyá*. In terms of address, ego refers to all three of these relatives by the term *tejeró*, which is on a par with sibling.

Linking Parents	Older	Younger
father–father	*aság*	*aprá*
mother–mother	*weyá*	*weyá*
father–mother	*abyá*	*abyá*
mother–father	*abyá*	*abyá*

Fig. 5. Cousin terms

There is an interesting proliferation of terms distinguishing male and female kinsmen in ego's generation and the first descending generation. This profusion of terms may work together with the important role played by mother's clan and mother's mother's clan in sister exchange.

Figure 6 illustrates graphically the system of Sikaritai consanguineal relationships. The use of a " + " sign in the figure indicates that alter is older than ego and the use of " − " indicates that alter is younger.

Affinal Kinship Terms

Sikaritai affinal kinship terms distinguish the sex of ego and of alter. There are three groups of affinal terms: parent-in-law/child-in-law, sibling-in-law, and spouse terms.

Parent-in-law/Child-in-law. The two terms *akei* 'father-in-law' and *ahuri* 'mother-in-law', are used by a man to designate his wife's bilateral kinsmen of the parent generation. The two grandparent terms *kóg* and *atá* are used by a woman to designate her husband's bilateral kinsmen of the first ascending

Male Ego

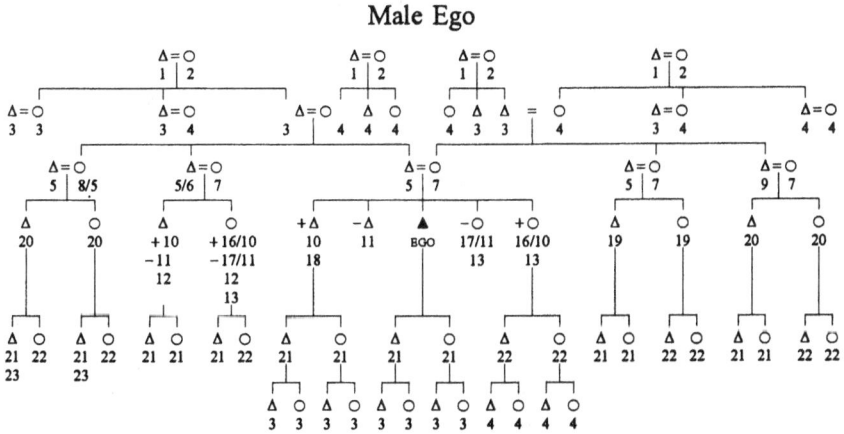

Female Ego (where different from male ego)

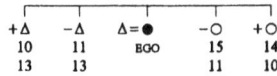

1. kógkróo		9. abéid		17. orokgóg
2. atákróo		10. aság		18. débi
3. kóg		11. aprá		19. weyá
4. atá		12. akadá		20. abyá
5. awag		13. augtá		21. túé
6. awag kwaré		14. áka		22. ariakó
7. aweg		15. awé		23. túéta
8. ad		16. arakúg		

Fig. 6. Consanguineal kinship chart

generation and are used reciprocally between her and her husband's parents. Thus, all siblings of ego's wife's father (WFB, WFZ) are ego's *akei* as well as his wife's parents' sister's husbands (WFZH, WMZH). Then, all siblings of ego's wife's mother (WMB, WMZ) are ego's *ahuri* along with his wife's parents' brother's wives (WMBW, WFBW). Further, all male ego's spouse's kinsmen in the second ascending generation and above are his *kóg* if male or *atá* if female.

The term *arod* 'son-in-law' is reserved by a woman's parents for her husband. This is its only use. It thus provides the counterpart for the grandparent/grandchild terms used by a man's parents for his wife.

Sibling-in-law Terms. There are nine terms used to denote affinal kinsmen of the same generation as ego and his spouse. The term *awá* 'sibling-in-law' is used to refer to all male ego's wife's consanguineal kinsmen of his generation. Thus, the children of all those to whom ego refers as *akei* and *ahuri* are his *awá*, and they are in fact referred to collectively as *bowákókéí* 'my siblings-in-law'. Thus, not only ego's wife's brother and sister but his wife's parent's siblings' children (WFBC, WFZC, WMBC, WMZC) are all *awá*.

Two additional terms, *díigká* and *húe*, both meaning 'wife's sister's husband', can be used in special situations to refer to WZH. They complete the group of terms for male ego to use in referring to his spouse's kinsmen.

On a more general level, the term *duká* 'brother-in-law' refers exclusively to male ego's sister's husband. The term for male ego's brother's wife is *atróka* 'sister-in-law', which is also used by a woman to mean 'husband's older brother'. The term *ará* is used by a man to refer to his sister's husband (ZH) or his wife's brother (WB), both classified as his sibling-in-law. Of the remaining two terms, *ahígja* 'brother-in-law' is reserved specifically for female ego's husband's younger brother, while *tráa* 'sister-in-law' corresponds by referring to male ego's older brother's wife or father's older brother's son's wife. Male ego's younger brother's wife as well as his sister's daughter's husband can be referred to by the term *borodá*, but it is not appropriate to address or to refer to either of these people by any term. The term *apgé* 'forbidden relationship' reflects that inappropriateness. *apgé* also includes the relationship between a woman and her husband's father's siblings' sons (HFBS, HFZS). The term *petakurí* 'give-take' (exchange-mate) refers to any of a woman's husband's sisters. It reflects the ideal in the exchange system—men exchange their sisters for wives.

Spouse Terms. A man normally uses the term *túg* 'wife' when referring to his wife. If he has more than one, he designates them in the order in which he took them. Thus, the first is *túg sígkad* 'preceding wife', the last *túg kódko* 'later wife', and if there is another, she is *túg éregtó* 'middle wife'. A woman refers to her husband as *té* 'husband'.

The term *túg* is frequently used by an older brother for his younger brother's wife, as in *beprá túg* 'my younger brother's wife'. Similarly, he refers to his sister's child's husband as *bariakó té* 'my sister's child's husband'. This usage bypasses prohibitions to referring to these people.

Figure 7 illustrates the affinal relationships among the Sikaritai, while figure 8 summarizes the full set of kinship terms with their consanguineal and/or affinal referents. The numbers in the first column of figure 8 that have a prefix of "C" refer to the consanguineal chart (figure 6) and those with a prefix of "A" refer to the affinal chart (figure 7).

Kinship Behavior

Sikaritai behavior between kinsmen as well as between kin groups can be summarized by the statement, "We help each other." Mutual help is accomplished for each dyad through teaching, giving food, giving physical labor, or simply being available to help when needed (e.g., to hunt for food or to build a house or a boat). This could mean being physically present or "on call" at any time. Such working together forms the backbone of the Sikaritai social system as a whole, and is directly related to the success of marriages, war alliances, and the survival of society.

Grandkinsmen

Grandparents give advice to their grandchildren who in turn are kind to their grandparents by giving them food when they see they are in need. Grandparents often help to care for their grandchildren when their son is gone hunting or their daughter-in-law is out getting sago, other food, or just firewood. If a daughter lives in a nearby settlement, grandparents may care for her children as well. In the past this relationship often was terminated by war, and now it may be by natural or accidental death of either grandparent or grandchild. There are currently many more grandmothers than grandfathers, and their primary role is that of helper to their children and grandchildren.

Male Ego

Female Ego

Siblings' Spouses, Children's Spouses

1. *akei*	7. *arod*	13. *borodá*
2. *ahuri*	8. *duká*	14. *apgé*
3. *kóg*	9. *ará*	15. *túg*
4. *atá*	10. *atróka*	16. *té*
5. *awá*	11. *ahígja*	17. *petakurí*
6. *díigká, húe*	12. *tráa*	

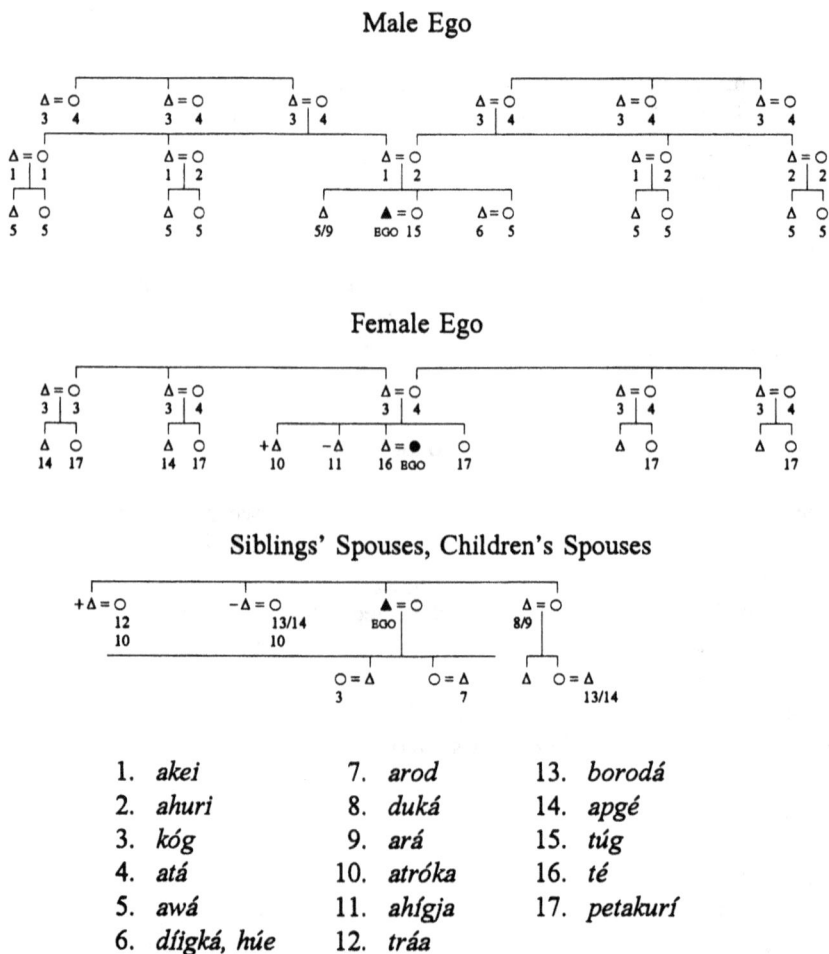

Fig. 7. Affinal kinship chart

Ref	Term	Generation	Closest Kin Designation	Consanguineal Referent	Affinal Referent
C1	kógkróo	+3	great-grandfather	FFF, FMF, MFF, MMF	
C2	atákróo	+3	great-grandmother	FFM, FMM, MFM, MMM	
C3	kóg	+2	grandfather	FF, MF, FFB, FFZ, MFB man's CC, man's BCC	FMZH, MMZH, FFZH, MFZH
		−2	grandchild	woman's BSC	
A3		−1	daughter-in-law		SW,
		+1	father-in-law		HF, HFB, HFZ, HFZH, HMZH, WFF, WMF, WFFB, WMFB, WFMB, WMMB, WFFZH, WMMZH
C4	atá	+2	grandmother	FM, MM, FMB, FMZ, MMB, MMZ, MFZ, FFZ woman's CC, ZCC, woman's BDC	FFBW, MFBW, FMBW, MMBW
		−2	grandchild		
A4		−1	daughter-in-law		SW
		+1	mother-in-law		HM, HMZ, HMB, HMBW, HFBW, WFM, WMM, WFFZ, WMFZ, WFMZ, WMMZ, WFFBW, WMMBW
C5	awag	+1	father	F, FB, FZ	FZH, MZH
C6	awag kwaré	+1	father's brother	FB	
C7	aweg	+1	mother	M, MZ	MBW, FBW
C8	ad	+1	father's sister	FZ	
C9	abeíd	+1	mother's brother	MB	
C10	aság	0	older sibling, patrilateral parallel cousin	oB, oZ, FoBC	
C11	aprá	0	younger sibling, patrilateral parallel cousin	yB, yZ, FyBC	
C12	akadá	0	age-mate, peer, patrilateral parallel cousin	twin, B, Z, FBC	
C13	augtá	0	opposite sex sibling	man's Z, FBD woman's B, FBS	
C14	áka	0	older sister	woman's oZ	
C15	awe	0	younger sister	woman's yZ	
C16	arakúg	0	older sister	man's oZ, man's FoBD	

Fig. 8. Kinship terms (1 of 2)

Ref	Term	Gener- ation	Closest Kin Designation	Consanguineal Referent	Affinal Referent
C17	*orokgóg*	0	younger sister	man's yZ, man's FyBD	
C18	*débi*	0	older brother	man's oB, man's FoBS	
C19	*weyá*	0	matrilateral parallel cousin	MZC	
C20	*abyá*	0	cross-cousin	FZC, MBC	
C21	*túé*	−1	child	C, BC, FBSC, MZSC, MBSC, FZCS, FBDS	
C22	*ariakó*	−1	nephew/niece	ZC, MBDC, MZDC, FZCD, FBDD	
C23	*túéta*	−1	nephew	FZCS	
A1	*akei*	+1	father-in-law		WF, WFB, WFZ WFZH, WMZH
A2	*ahuri*	+1	mother-in-law		WM, WMB, WMZ WMBW, WFBW
A5	*awá*	0	wife's sibling		WB, WZ, WFBC WFZC, WMBC, WMZC
A6	*dlígká, húe*	0	wife's sister's husband		WZH
A7	*arod*	−1	son-in-law		DH
A8	*duká*	0	sister's husband		man's ZH
A9	*ará*	0	sister's husband, wife's brother		man's ZH, WB
A10	*atróka*	0	brother's wife, husband's older brother		man's BW, HoB
A11	*ahígja*	0	husband's younger brother		HyB
A12	*tráá*	0	older brother's wife		man's oBW, man's FoBSW
A13	*borodá*	−1	sister's child's husband		man's ZCH
A14	*apgé*	0	younger brother's wife		man's yBW
A15	*túg*	0	wife		W
A16	*té*	0	husband		H
A17	*petakurí*	0	exchange-mate		HZ

Key to symbols:

F	=	father	S	=	son	C	=	child
M	=	mother	D	=	daughter	o	=	older
B	=	brother	H	=	husband	y	=	younger
Z	=	sister	W	=	wife			

Fig. 8. Kinship terms (2 of 2)

Parent-Child

A parent's relationship with his or her child is one of warmth and concern for the child's well-being. A child's mother gives him food and love and cares for him in such a way as to ensure he reaches adulthood. A father's role is primarily one of discipline and making sure the child follows in the paths of character set by the ancestors. In the past a high infant mortality rate discouraged parents from becoming too emotionally attached to a child until he was old enough to be responsible for his own well-being. A father rarely beats a child; discipline is more verbal, with emphasis on correcting bad habits.

Fathers are responsible to take over "raising" their sons when they reach preadolescence, weaning them of dependence on women, guiding them to physical maturity, and introducing them to the adult man's world of ritual, magic, and war. Mothers are available to their daughters as they reach puberty and approach marriage. Their role is more that of advisor, being there to answer questions rather than actually teaching them how to carry out a woman's role.

Thus, the parent-child relationship changes as the child enters adolescence, with fathers concentrating on sons while mothers devote themselves more to daughters. This scheme remains in effect throughout the children's adult lives, with fathers helping sons and mothers helping daughters; it later reverses itself to sons helping fathers and daughters helping mothers. Sons, particularly, are obligated to care for their parents in old age, assisted by their wife or wives. Sons of the same father but different mothers cooperate in caring for these mothers. Daughters, in turn, help their husbands care for his parents. Sons-in-law complete the circle of care by caring for their parents-in-law. This pattern goes along with the ideal marriage, where a woman marries outside her father's clan but within his phratry. Though residence is patrilocal, she is close to her mother's settlement and therefore able to help her. At the same time, her husband is close to his parents-in-law and can fulfill his obligations to them.

Same Sex Siblings

An elder brother acts in many ways as a substitute father to his younger brother(s). What a father is to his oldest son, that older son is to his younger brothers.

Thus, whereas an oldest son's marriage is arranged by his father, that older son helps to arrange his younger brothers' marriages. A father teaches his first-born about women, while the first-born helps to teach his younger brothers. It is normal for an older brother to teach his brothers the finer points of hunting, fishing, planting bananas and sago, and making bows and arrows. An older brother also is involved in his brothers' initiation. A pair of sisters acts toward each other on the same basis, with older teaching younger.

Upon a man's death, his younger brother takes responsibility for caring for his children. If this brother is not living, the next younger brother will assume this task. In the event that there are no brothers living, his oldest son, provided he is socially an adult, will assume the duties.

Opposite Sex Siblings

Behavioral expectations between a man and his sisters and between a woman and her brothers are those of mutual benefit for each other. However, opposite sex siblings are forbidden to work together (*togtákó kobadwa tébíyáa* 'opposite sex sibling work together forbidden'). On the other hand, regardless of whom a brother or sister marry it is the duty of siblings to take care of each other throughout life. Thus a brother is expected to go fishing for and share food out of his garden with his sister. A sister, in turn, who discovers her brother is hungry will cook food for him to satisfy his hunger. If she knows her brother is in need of sago, she will go and pound sago to make sago pudding for him and thus help him out. Obligations are more easily carried out if siblings live in the same or nearby villages, but they still apply even when villages are distant.

Upon marriage, spouses are aware of the close relationship between cross-siblings. Thus, if for some reason a wife is unable to provide food for her husband, his sister will go pound sago and make sago pudding for him with no protest from his wife. The brother-sister relationship remains intact regardless; nothing can interfere with it. It is abnormal for a man to favor his wife over his sister.

Similarly, a man works together with his wife's brother(s) *(duká)* on house-building, boat-building, and planting bananas and sago in the same way that the man and his own brothers work together. This reciprocity again reflects the underlying concept that through marriage and exchange the clans are united.

Cousins

Both cross- and parallel cousins normally treat each other as brothers and sisters. Father's brother's children are in fact called by the sibling terms *(aság, aprá, akadá,* and *augtá),* but the other cousins also relate in much the same way.

They give food to each other, such as pig from a hunt, fish, sago, and bananas. Female cousins may go to pound sago together, while male cousins may go.hunting or fishing together. They assist each other in house-building, canoe-building, planting bananas and sago, and in general in the tasks that men work on together with their brothers and women work on together with their sisters. Opposite sex cousins are forbidden from working together in the same way that opposite sex siblings are. Cousin relations are merely extensions of brother-sister relations, with slightly lowered expectations and emotional bonds.

In the first descending generation, children of cousins relate to one another in much the same ways as their parents do. The distinction is widened slightly, however, as children of male cousins relate more closely than do those of female cousins.

Mother's Brother-Sister's Son

Unlike many patrilineal societies in Melanesia, the Sikaritai place very little emphasis on the mother's brother-sister's son relationship. It could be summarized by saying that the general mutual helping rule is in effect in this relationship. A nephew will go hunting together with his maternal uncle, help him build a house, plant fruit trees, and all the things he would do with his own father. If they meet on the trail somewhere, the nephew normally gives his uncle some food. Otherwise, there is nothing unique about the behavior between the two men.

Father's Brother—Brother's Child

On the other hand, a child's father's brother *(awag kwaré)* has a special relationship with his brother's son or daughter *(túéta* or simply *túé* 'child'). The child is obligated to do whatever the uncle says without questioning. A man must help his *awag kwaré,* in priority over other relatives. A girl sees him as equivalent to her father. He is involved in arranging her marriage, and if he picks out a husband for her or agrees with someone else's choice, she must go along with that decision.

Adoption

In the past, when war was a way of life and women died more frequently in childbirth, it was not uncommon for numerous children to be orphaned. Even now there are several children at Sikari whose biological parents are dead.

In accordance with the Sikaritai priority of levirate marriage, whereby an older brother's widow is preferably taken by his younger brother, a child should ideally remain in his father's clan. Thus, his adoptive father is his father's brother, and family relationships and connections are virtually the same.

If, however, a widow's dead husband has no younger brother or any extended brothers (FBS) to marry her, she may be taken by someone from a clan other than her dead husband's clan. In such a case, the child will assume the clan name of his adoptive father and technically be absorbed into that clan. His adoptive father has the social option of choosing which clan the child will belong to as an adult. If, however, the dead father's clan thinks that the adoptive father is not caring for the child's mother adequately, they may demand that the child be returned to his father's clan to fit into their exchange scheme when he reaches marriageable age.

A second situation in which a child could be adopted would be that of a childless couple. A husband and wife who have not yet been able to have a child may ask the husband's brothers and sisters who have children to give them a child. If there is a shortage of children in the clan, none will be given, but in most cases they are expected to help. A child adopted in this way is not considered the child of the adoptive parents. Rather, they only raise him, and when he reaches adulthood, he is considered the child of his biological parents. Rarely will an unrelated family give a child to a couple, but in such a case the child would be known as their *túé kidá* 'following child' as opposed to *túé*.

Marriage

The rules of Sikaritai marriage are inseparably linked to kin relationships and behavior toward one's kin, both consanguineal and affinal.

The Sikaritai marriage system is built on sister exchange (*húegso kurípetawa* 'take-give girls'), a sister being defined as any female in male ego's clan or his mother's clan. As such, any female in those two clans is not a potential marriage partner. Rather, a man looks for a girl outside his clan and his mother's clan who has a relative who according to the same definition would be her brother. If her agnatic kin are agreeable, he then exchanges his "sister" with that man. Marriage is viewed primarily as a contract between two clans rather than between two individuals. It is essential to maintain a balance between the clans by exchanging some women in every generation. Furthermore, according to the rules of exchange, a man may have more than one prospective spouse, and he is expected to marry any prospective spouse of marriageable age when there are no bachelors available. With that broad definition, let us look at the details.

Physical Preparation and Qualifications

A girl is considered ready for marriage if she has had her first menstrual period and has proved herself to be a good cook, food and firewood gatherer, and sago pounder. When she begins her first menses, she tells her mother and is sent off to the forest to build her own menstruation house, where she will go every month thereafter. She stays there until her menstrual period is finished, then bathes, puts on a new loincloth, throws away the bark with blood on it, and returns to her parents' house. After her first menses and when her breasts are developed, she is considered ready to be taken in marriage.

A man is ready for marriage when he is able to grow a beard, has proved himself a good hunter, housebuilder, fisherman, boatbuilder, and, most importantly, knows how to work together with his father and brothers. First, however, he must become an adult and be purified from contact with women, particularly his mother. This ritual takes place outside the settlement in the *kwá tébí* 'forbidden house'. The man moves out of his parents' house and into the *kwá tébí*, usually with a small group of age-mates, and begins bathing several times a day to purify his body from contact with women. Later, several men from his clan and other related clans begin blowing the sacred flutes to invite the spirits to come and teach the young men in the house. In this way, over an extended time (and involving greater complexity than I am able to treat here), the young man is initiated into the secrets of Sikaritai ritual and magic. When he comes out of the house, having learned the body of knowledge known only to adult men, he is considered to be an adult. Most men assume a new name at this time and regardless of relative age call each other *bgadé* 'my age-mate'. After this initiation a man waits until his beard is fully developed, and then he is qualified to take a wife.

Candidates for Marriage

In deciding whom he will marry, a man considers two different groups of candidates. First, his mother's relatives (from her natal clan) and his extended relatives who fit in the category of grandkinsmen *(atákokéí)* are his *aráketawa* 'hand-holders'. It is absolutely forbidden to take a wife from this group. Secondly, those from the clan which owes his clan wives are his *tória,* i.e., the group including his ideal marriage partner. This woman is ideally a girl from one's mother's mother's clan who is neither in the group descended from her father's father *(kógkokei)* nor in the group descended from her mother's father *(atákokéí)*. The system is thus "characterized by 'positive' marriage rules. They not only say whom one may NOT marry, they specify also whom one SHOULD marry." (Fox 1967:199)

The closest kin a man may marry is his mother's mother's *ariakó* (this is at the bottom of the list of preferred potential spouses). These possibilities are illustrated in figure 9 and include: mother's mother's sister's daughter's daughter (MMZDD), mother's mother's sister's son's daughter (MMZSD), mother's mother's brother's daughter's daughter (MMBDD), mother's mother's brother's son's daughter (MMBSD), mother's mother's brother's son's daughter's daughter (MMBSDD), mother's mother's brother's son's son's daughter (MMBSSD).

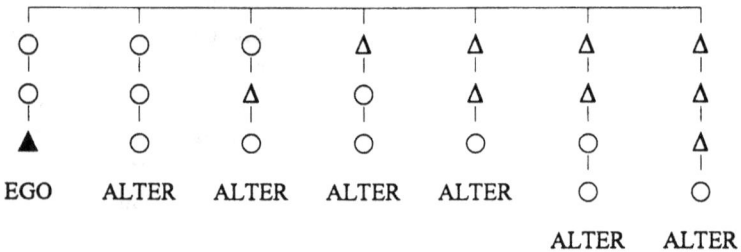

Fig. 9. Closest kin marriage partners

It is common, however, for a man to be considerably older than his bride at the time of his marriage. The population figures for the current and previous generations at Sikari (see tables 1 and 2) show a relative balance of males to females. The discrepancy in age at marriage, however, offsets this balance. A man's wife may be, in theory if not in fact, in the first descending generation from him. This girl is classified as her husband's *ariakó* 'sister's child' and thus is a generation below him—his *ariakó* from his mother's mother's clan. If her descent is through his mother's mother's brother's daughter (MMBDD), she would be in a different clan from mother's mother. What is important, then, is her descent from mother's mother's clan. Father's sister's daughter's daughter (FZDD) and father's father's brother's daughter's daughter's daughter (FFBDDD) are also classified as *ariakó;* so if such an *ariakó* also has connections with mother's mother's clan, she would be an acceptable marriage partner. There are cases of a man taking his father's mother's father's brother's son's son's daughter (FMFBSSD), i.e., his father's second cross-cousin's daughter. Thus, although there is only one female link, the common ancestor is in the third ascending generation. In essence, then, the ideal in choosing a wife is to take an extended cross-cousin from mother's mother's clan in order to maintain balance together with her exchange in marriage to mother's father. Figure 10 portrays some of the relationships for potential spouses.

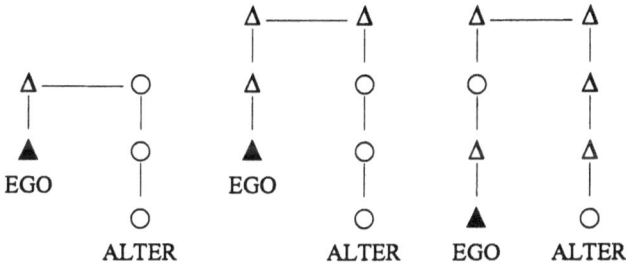

Fig. 10. Acceptable marriage partner

Thus, neither a man's mother's clan nor his own patrilineal clan are acceptable places to look for a wife. But in looking for a "sister" to exchange, both of these groups may have possible candidates. For the men in any of the four clans at Sikari, (Siwáí, Kusa, Tibotai, Sibetai, i.e., Siwáí phratry), it is preferable to take a wife from one of the other three clans within Siwáí phratry. This practice is in keeping with the logistics of keeping

contact with in-laws and also with the original sister exchange system established by the clan founders. If this option is not possible, the next choice
would be one of the clans of Kausa phratry, who speak the same language.
If none of these clans have a girl whose marriage into the clan would keep
the exchange system in balance, one may go outside the language group, first
to Eri, a village speaking a related language, and then to Papasena, a
different language group. If there are absolutely no candidates for exchange
and a man is anxious to take a wife, he may take one and promise his first
daughter in exchange to her clan. Legitimate exchanges outside these four
groups are rare. Tables 1 and 2 portray the variation in male-female child
balance between the clans of Siwáí phratry at Sikari. Such variation keeps
exchange patterns complex and may, together with generational skewing and
exchange ideals, contribute to the frequency of polygyny (see section below).

Clan	Married Men	Bachelors	Married Women	Male Children	Female Children	Total
Siwáí	15	1	20	24	34	94
Kusa	5	3	9	13	3	33
Sibetai	10	2	14	26	19	71
Tibotai	7	5	11	15	14	52
Kausa	2	5	2	0	0	9
Papasena	2	0	3	0	0	52
Total	41	16	59	78	70	264

Table 1. Population balance in current generation at Sikari

Clan	Married Men	Married Women	Male Children	Female Children	Total
Siwáí	10	14	18	14	56
Kusa	4	5	10	10	29
Sibetai	5	8	14	11	38
Tibotai	11	12	11	11	45
Kausa	3	4	7	3	17
Total	33	43	60	49	185

Table 2. Population balance in previous generation at Sikari

A Sikaritai man considers the following questions when choosing a wife:

1. Is there an *ariakó* in his mother's mother's clan who is ready for marriage?

2. Are the original exchange pairs established by the clan founders (i.e., Siwáí-Tibotai, Kusa-Sibetai) out of balance?

3. Does he have a sister *(augtá)* who needs a husband?

4. Does he have a brother *(aság/aprá)* who needs a wife?

5. Is there a prospective wife in the Siwáí phratry whose exchange would balance out that part of the system?

6. Is there a prospective wife in the Kausa phratry whose exchange would balance out that part of the system?

7. Does the Eri or the Papasena phratry owe his clan any women (i.e., have they taken women without completing an exchange)?

A given man looking for a wife may consider any one, some, or all of the above questions. In some cases, one factor may outweigh the others; in other cases, they may all interact to choose that particular man's prospective spouse. There is potential overlap in the categories, complicating the data considerably. If there is any doubt as to whether or not the man and woman are too closely related, their families gather and try to determine a common ancestor. If they cannot recall one, the marriage goes forward.

Table 3 summarizes the source of wives for the current generation of men at Sikari.

Mother's mother's clan	8
Mother's mother's phratry	6
Own clan (incest)	1
Original exchange pairs	13
Siwáí phratry	14
Kausa phratry	14
Papasena	16
Eri	4
Outside	5

Table 3. Sources of wives at Sikari

The system that thus becomes evident is a combination of extended cross-cousin marriage and dual organization marriage, concerning which Levi-Strauss (1969:102) states:

> Dual organization, therefore, defines a very general class within which it is permissible to choose a spouse, while the system of cross-cousin marriage determines very precisely the individual whom one is obliged to marry. Dual organization is a global system, binding the group in its totality. Marriage between cross-cousins seems a very much more special process; it is a tendency rather than a system. It is the highly specialized formula for a system which has its beginnings, still poorly differentiated, in cross-cousin marriage. The two institutions are in contrast, one being crystallized, the other flexible.

Thus, the ideal of extended cross-cousin marriage is just that, an ideal. If not realizable, a man has recourse to marriage within the overall system of the Sikaritai social structure, i.e., via the two phratries. Going outside these two phratries is apparently a recent innovation, but even that follows the dual system of geographical proximity (i.e., very rarely does a man from the Kausa phratry take a wife from Papasena, or a man from the Siwáí phratry take a wife from Eri; see figure 11). The system thus seems to be in a state of expansion while holding to duality.

In looking for a "sister" to exchange, a full sister is the ideal. This notion is reflective of the legend referred to earlier, in which the two brothers exchanged sisters to start two of the clans. If none are available, however, a man may go to his father's brother's children, i.e., his *aság/arakúg* or *aprá/orokgóg* who are not his siblings. If this group has no girls of marriageable age, he goes to the clan at large. Failing that, he approaches his *aráketawá* (i.e., his mother's relatives) and asks their help in providing a girl for him to exchange for a wife.

This system is in keeping with the two types of direct exchange (Fox 1967:200–204). Systematic direct exchange is characterized by "overall exchange between such large groups as clans, lineages, and moieties" (Fox 1967:200). Statistical direct exchange involves "true" relatives. Delayed exchange, on the other hand, involves one clan giving a woman to the other, but the exchange is not carried out until the next generation or possibly two generations later. What is important is that it is eventually completed.

In this regard, a study of 118 men who took wives at Sikari reveals the statistics that follow. Forty marriages (34 percent) involved direct exchanges (i.e., a man from one clan gave a woman from his own clan to a man from another clan, who returned a woman from his own clan). Thus only two clans were involved. Thirty-six marriages (30 percent) involved indirect exchanges, involving a third or possibly even a fourth clan. Thus, a man gave a woman from his own or his mother's clan to a man who returned a woman from his own or his mother's clan. Two of the men (2 percent) have agreed to give offspring in the next generation, or the following generation (i.e., delayed direct exchange). Seventeen marriages (14 percent) involved marrying a widow who had already been part of an earlier exchange, so no further exchange was necessary. Fifteen men (13 percent) have not yet carried through an exchange; they are either waiting for a suitable candidate or hoping the wife's clan will not insist on their rights. Four marriages (3 percent) involved either capturing the woman in a raid or marrying one who had been captured when young, and thus no exchange was necessary. Two cases (2 percent) were where a man secretly took a wife from his own clan (both cases are labeled incest, *betúéd kobadpeí*). Two men (2 percent) have taken wives from outside the area totally.

Any of the above methods (except for the penultimate one) of obtaining a wife are acceptable, and the man and woman are considered legally married. However, those involving the exchange of two women are the norm at present. Women who have been exchanged by any of the above principles refer to each other as *petakurí* 'give-take' (exchange-mates). *petakurí* can also refer to any of a woman's husband's sisters. Table 4 summarizes these varieties of exchange.

Form of Exchange	Siwáí Phratry	Kausa Phratry	Papasena/Eri Phratry
Direct (2 clans)	18	6	16
Indirect (3–4 clans)	11	15	10
Delayed direct	0	0	2
Not yet exchanged	4	6	2
Widows	8	4	5
Captured	0	1	3
Own clan	2	0	0
Outside area	2	0	0

Table 4. Types of sister exchange at Sikari

The above statistics show that it is important to complete a marriage exchange. In fact, 80 percent of exchanges were completed or arrangements have been made to complete immediately, or as soon as possible. The 15 percent who have not carried through can expect friction between the two clans involved. The rule that wife-givers are usually superior to wife-takers (Fox 1967:202) is clearly in effect among the Sikaritai. In the past, when raids were allowed, it was one method of collecting on an I.O.U. At present it is still acceptable for one clan to "kidnap" a girl from a clan which owes it a woman to complete an exchange on that basis. The system on the surface is simple, but details and interaction of the seven factors listed previously can lead to many and varied problems. Figure 11 shows the geographical relationships of the two Sikaritai phratries to other groups. These distinctions were crucial not only for marriage exchanges but also for alliances in time of war.

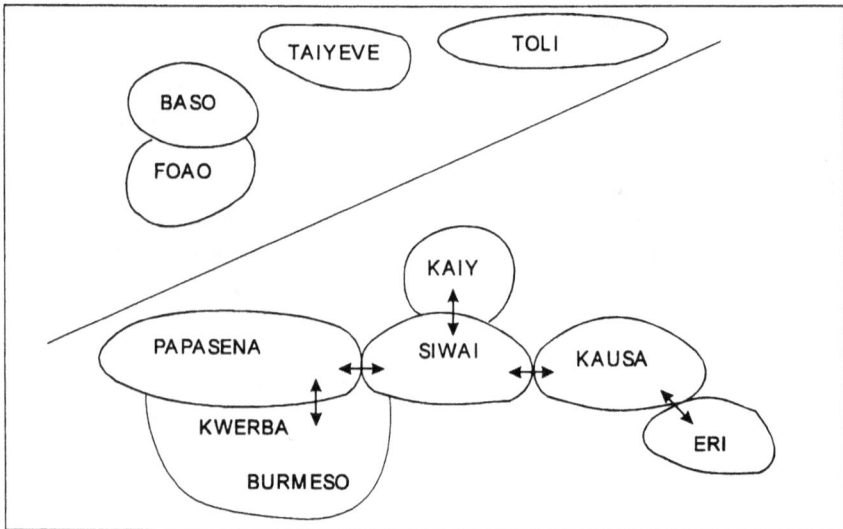

Fig. 11. Marriage exchange and war alliances

Marriage Arrangements

Sikaritai parents are continually aware of imbalances in the exchange system and may consider possible spouses for their children when they are still young. In the process of arranging an older child's marriage they may consider an exchange involving a younger sibling who is not yet ready for marriage. However, they rarely arrange marriages before their children are physically ready to marry. Until that time they concentrate on teaching their son or daughter what he or she needs to know to be a good husband or wife when the time comes. A son, then, learns how to hunt, fish, build a house and canoe, and plant bananas and sago by doing these things with his father, his father's brother, and his own brothers. A daughter learns how to pound and process sago, make sago pudding, gather food and firewood, carry water, and cook by helping her mother and sisters. When the son has a fully developed beard, he chooses a girl who is in his *tória,* has breasts, and has begun menstruating. It is considered important that a girl be taken as soon as possible after her first menses. In some cases a man may choose a girl who has no breasts yet, in which case he must wait until she matures before taking her as wife.

If the man's father thinks he is waiting too long, he might suggest a girl, but most young men are allowed to choose for themselves. The candidates are quite restricted in number and he is well aware of who they are, so he is qualified to make his own decision. He must, however, consider the priorities listed above. In that sense, then, his choice becomes a group decision.

A man may not directly ask his prospective wife's parents if he may marry their daughter. He first tells his older brother (or his father if he is the oldest son), who then approaches her parents with the proposal. If her parents refuse to give her, he must accept their decision. If they agree, he prepares to take her as his wife. In rare cases a man may ask a woman first, before their parents discuss the situation.

A father is normally responsible only for arranging his oldest son's marriage. The oldest son is then responsible for arranging his younger brother's marriages. A mother decides when her daughter is ready for marriage. Then, both the girl's father and mother, together with her oldest brothers, are involved in arranging her marriage.

The order of marriage for both sons and daughters follows their birth order. That is, older brothers marry before their younger brothers and older sisters before their younger sisters. When an arrangement has been made for an older sister to marry a particular man, even if he has not yet actually taken her as his wife, her younger sister is then free to be taken.

When a young man is considering marriage, his father will counsel him to observe how his prospective bride helps her mother with pounding sago, gathering food and firewood, and cooking. This behavior is an indication of how she will perform after her marriage. Similarly, a girl's parents will advise her to watch closely how her prospective husband helps his father and brothers hunt, fish, and build houses and canoes. If he is not a good helper he should not be considered, since one of the roles of a good husband is to help his in-laws. A father will also encourage his son to work hard so that girls will consider him an eligible husband. If he is lazy, they will not be interested in him.

Engagement Period

  After an agreement is reached, it is traditional for the prospective bride and groom to exchange gifts of clothing and tools and to eat together while avoiding sexual relations. It is understood that once an agreement with the parents is reached, physical involvement, although not considered ideal, is allowable. It is not considered in the same way as adultery *(ahuéd peyáwa)* would be which is a punishable offense, but it would not be in line with tradition and the ancestors. If a girl and boy have intercourse before an agreement for marriage has been settled by the parents, their parents express surprise, but will likely decide they should marry. The exchange system usually has the upper hand, i.e., if there is a suitable exchange couple available, they will be married. The marriage may also be arranged with a potential exchange at a later date, as explained above.

  Prior to marriage a young man becomes aware, of course, that his father and his older brothers are having sexual relations with their wives. If he has no "true" (same mother and father) brothers, he learns about matters of sex from his father's brother's *(awag kwáré)* sons as well as from his father. Here again, an older brother is responsible to teach his younger brother how to handle his wife physically. There is no actual instruction about intercourse, but insights into its negative results are typically given, e.g., intercourse makes a man skinny, his skin bad, and takes away his blood, making him weak. So if a man wants to be strong, he should not have intercourse with his wife too often. Particularly, if he needs to work hard (e.g., build a canoe), he should abstain from sexual intercourse or risk becoming too weak to work as he should. This instruction is an extension of what is learned at the ceremonial men's house *(kwá tébí)* during initiation. When the man is on the verge of taking a wife, he is ready for more detailed instruction.

The Marriage Ceremony

The marriage ceremony is as rooted in the Sikaritai origin legends as the concept of sister exchange itself. The final event in the legend of the two brothers going downriver from Akuri to Bgádtebi is the exchange of their two sisters. This exchange was ritually sealed by the sisters making cigarettes (*sawé ígjuwa* 'tying tobacco') and giving them to their new husbands.

This ceremony then becomes the visible sign that a young man is taking a girl as his wife. The bride must first consider all the brothers (older, younger, age-mate siblings) of her husband-to-be and make enough cigarettes for his father and each of these brothers. She then gives the appropriate number to her husband, and he in turn passes them out to all those he calls brother (*aság, aprá, akadá*). This gift satisfies her duty to her male in-laws. Next, she makes sago pudding (*bói suwa*), sufficient to feed all her husband's female relatives (his *augtá* 'sisters'). Ideally, she makes enough so her relatives as well as his can eat together and be satisfied, but if sago is scarce she prepares less. Once she has delivered the cigarettes and the sago pudding has been eaten, the couple are considered married. It is at this time that the woman ceases to be a *húégso* 'unmarried girl' and becomes a *túg* 'woman, wife'. The couple takes up residence in their own house in the husband's settlement. In the rare cases when a man takes a wife before a completed exchange (*wésó kwríwa* 'free take'), they may take up residence in the wife's settlement. This, however, is a temporary arrangement until a suitable exchange is completed. The length of time they stay in the wife's settlement depends on exchange arrangements.

Husband-Wife Behavior and Responsibilities

The husband-wife relationship is one of mutual caring and helping. A husband's role is to hunt, fish, plant bananas and sago, and in general make certain his wife has enough food and a house in which to live. His wife is responsible to pound and process sago, draw water, gather food and firewood, and cook good food, with special attention to making sure there is sago pudding available frequently. If they carry out their individual duties properly, they will be able to enjoy each other physically. *igjékobad hosukewá* 'work-helping together' is the key to the relationship. A husband expects his wife to work hard, and then he will be motivated to "play" (i.e., have sexual relations) with her. A wife connects working hard with pleasing her husband so that he will desire her sexually. However, he must restrict his sexual involvement with her in order to have the strength to fulfill his other responsibilities to her.

One of the wife's most important duties is to bear children for her husband's clan. If unable to do so, she may be returned to her natal clan if an exchange has not been completed. This practice is rare, however. A more common solution is to adopt a child or take a second wife. A wife is not punished for inability to bear children, but her husband feels short-changed.

If a wife does not cook enough food or if she cooks food which is not to her husband's liking, he may beat her with a vine. If she refuses to submit to him sexually, he may become angry and beat her or rub a certain rough tree leaf *(iyei)* on her skin as punishment. He is clearly in control of their physical relationship, and if she resists he may punish her or force her to have sex. In such cases he may respond to her lack of submission by taking a second wife.

A woman's parents and siblings keep close watch on her husband to make certain he is treating her properly. If they observe him treating her harshly and there has not yet been an exchange made for her, they may demand that he return her to them. A completed exchange, however, renders this impossible.

Affinal Behavior

Husband with Wife's Relatives. A man's relationship to his wife's relatives seems to be even more important than that with his consanguineal relatives, with the exception of the brother-sister dyad discussed earlier. This relationship is again based on mutual helping and giving, but the balance is in favor of the wife's family. Since there is no brideprice paid at the time of marriage, these obligations function as a virtual replacement of such (i.e., compensation for the wife's services and for her progeny).

A man is obligated, first of all, to provide a girl to his wife's clan in exchange for her. Following that, he must help his father-in-law *(akei)* any time he can. If he knows his *akei* is building a house, he will volunteer to help. If his *akei* is building a canoe, planting bananas, sago, or taro, he will make himself available to help. If he shoots a pig, he must give the largest portions to his father-in-law and brothers-in-law *(awá)*, even before considering his immediate family. He may give his *akei* an axe or a bush knife without any request, just to make a good impression. It is this voluntary help which demonstrates to his father-in-law that he is a good son-in-law *(arod)* and thus a good husband for his daughter.

A man has a very constrained relationship with his wife's mother *(ahuri).* They must use only kin terms *(ahuri* 'mother-in-law' and *arod* 'son-in-law') in referring to and addressing each other. However, their relationship is not one of avoidance. They are free to converse with each other and, in fact, if there is a hint of avoidance in their contact, the man's *ahuri* will think he is having problems with his wife.

A man is expected, along with helping his father-in-law, to be available to help his wife's brothers in the same way. Thus, he must work together with the males in his wife's family as much if not more than with those in his own family. This responsibility carries through the oneness of the clans initiated at the marriage ceremony.

If a man's wife dies, he normally goes and stays temporarily with her parents and siblings. They go hunting together, plant food together, eat together, and share their grief with one another. This activity completes the husband's obligations to his wife's family, and if they release him to go back to his clan after this period, he is free of further obligations. In many cases, however, after this period, his *akei* and *ahuri* will decide to give freely *(wésó begwa,* i.e., without requesting an exchange) another of their daughters to him. This act is at the same time a seal of approval of his relationship with his first wife and with them and also a pledge of continued support between the two clans. (There are no such cases presently among the Sikaritai.)

Wife with Husband's Relatives. A woman has an open relationship with her husband's parents, perhaps symbolized by their referring to and addressing each other by the reciprocal grandkinsmen terms. A son's wife pounds sago with her mother-in-law; however, if the mother-in-law is old, her daughter-in-law may get sago without her but will make sure they work together on making sago pudding once she returns home. The important thing is that they work together.

She has a similar role with her husband's sisters (his *augtá*), i.e., working together with them in gathering food, cooking, and gathering firewood. She has become an integral part of her husband's clan through marrying him and so must do her share of the work. She refers to anyone in this group as *petakurí* 'exchange-mate', and they may in fact have been exchanged with her natal clan. Unless the two clans are in the Siwáí phratry, however, and thus live in close proximity, a woman has little contact with her husband's *augtá.*

A wife's relationship with her husband's brothers is one of distance. She is forbidden to refer to or address his younger brother *(ahígje).* She may give him food, but he may not have anything to do with her. A wife's older brother-in-law is also in the category of forbidden relations *(apgé)*, but she may also give him food if that is all they have to do with each other.

Marriage of Widows and Widowers

Sikaritai past practice of war, together with illness and disease, led to a large number of men and women losing their spouses. The consequence to the exchange system and marriage as a whole is great.

As mentioned before, practice of the levirate, whereby a man marries his older brother's widow, is common among the Sikaritai. This practice has the effect of keeping the woman, who was obtained in an exchange, in the clan. In addition, for men who have no sisters *(augtá)* by any definition and thus have no possibilities for an exchange, taking a widow is an easy solution for marriage. Furthermore, when an older man's wife dies and he needs a wife to finish raising his children who are not yet adults, taking a widow is a natural answer.

Sikaritai girls are only exchanged in marriage once. Therefore, if they are widowed and taken by a second husband, there is no further exchange necessary. It is considered a necessity for a young widow, with or without young children, to marry again in order to protect her from the sexual advances of young unmarried men. Older widows whose children are young may or may not marry again. If they do not, they may live separately in their own house or with one of their grown children.

Most widowers feel they need to take another wife in order to have someone to carry out the household duties that are a woman's responsibility. They may either marry a widow or complete a sister exchange for an unmarried girl, depending on their age (i.e., most parents are reluctant to give their daughter to an old man whose blood is old *(sag kró)* and is unlikely to father more children).

Adultery

Sikaritai define adultery *(ahuéd peyáwa)* as sexual relations between a married woman and a man who is not her husband. Intercourse between unmarried young people is not considered *ahuéd peyáwa*, but neither is it considered normal or ideal.

Intercourse between father and daughter, mother and son, a man and his brother's wife, or a woman and her husband's brother are all considered *ahuéd peyáwa* and the normal punishment is death for both parties. This penalty underscores the seriousness of the institution of marriage among the Sikaritai.

If a man and woman commit adultery, the woman's angry brothers ask her if her husband, whom they arranged for her to marry, is not satisfactory, causing her to look for another man. The man's brothers normally are not angry with him but usually suggest that he take the woman as his wife. The woman's husband, if he discovers the adultery immediately, may simply discipline her with words (*túgkó pgidówa* 'fight with (his) wife'), beat her, stab her with an arrow, or slash her with a bush knife. However, if she persists in adultery, her husband will take his bow and arrow and shoot her himself. Or he may kill her in a less obvious manner through sorcery. If he can find the guilty man, he will also shoot him. Sometimes no opportunity is given to remedy the situation and the two people are killed immediately.[5]

Some of the relatives of the man may decide that it is better for him to take the woman as his wife—then they can have intercourse legitimately rather than secretly, and death will not be necessary. This action would necessitate a divorce, which is seen as socially undesirable. This solution may also lead to further trouble and possible fighting between the woman's first husband and her new husband. There are no cases of this practice among living Sikaritai. The most common solution, therefore, seems to be death for both the woman and the interloper.

War, Allies, Wives, and Marriage

In the past, when war and raiding were a way of life in the Greater Lakes Plain Region, they served to maintain the balance of men to women. The main purpose of raiding, however, was not to capture wives or children, but rather to avenge a death which was suspected to be a result of sorcery by men in the village raided.

As is still the case, Sikaritai men (and women) get angry very quickly and often pick up bush knives or bows and arrows to attack someone. Until recent years, the method of attack was to gather together related men from several clans in the Siwáí phratry with possible reinforcements from the

---

[5]Another Sikaritai legend relates an incident of adultery between an unmarried man from Burmeso and a married woman from the Siwáí clan. The legend ends when the woman's relatives split her in half, beginning with her vagina. It graphically portrays the consequences of adultery.

Kausa phratry and raid the offending clan settlement (Papasena, Taiyeve, Toli, etc.). After killing several men in retaliation for some previous grievance or a recent attack, they consider any need they may have for future marriages. If they do have need, they carry off as many women as they need and return to their settlement. If they decide they have enough women at present, they kill the women and children belonging to the men whom they killed in the raid and return home.

A clan's allies in war were for the most part those clans with whom they exchanged wives. However, if a clan was raided by one of the clans with whom they exchanged women and from which there were wives in the settlement, the husbands of these women, since they had stock in both warring clans, would stand in the middle attempting to make peace. Thus, the wives who had married in from the attacking clan played an important role in preventing war.

The Social Functions of Polygyny

What role does polygyny play in Sikaritai kinship relations and marriage as these systems have been described? It is an integral part of both systems. It provides a means for preserving the stability of sister exchange as the foundation of marriage. It protects widows, who otherwise might be without support in the society. It also provides a means of producing offspring when a man and his wife are incapable. It prevents unmarried young men and women from being involved in premarital sexual activity by providing for the girls to be married as soon as they come of age. In contrast, abolishing polygyny could lead to the disintegration of the entire social fabric. Let us consider, then, the roles polygyny plays among the Sikaritai people.

The Role of Marriage in the Sikaritai Social System

Marriage, in addition to legitimizing normal sexual activity, involves the physical care and protection of women—a crucial responsibility of Sikaritai husbands. Furthermore, both husband and wife have separate and distinct duties within marriage. Husbands do the hunting, building, and planting, while wives cook, pound sago, gather food and firewood, and bear children.

But perhaps equally as important as these factors, marriage exists to unify the clans specifically through sister exchange. Thus, each clan, as established in the origin legends, exchanges wives with certain other clans, thereby ensuring good relations between them. This relationship is especially evident in a husband's obligations to his wife's entire family and by extension to her entire clan. As these two clans unite around two people, their longevity is ensured in turn by children born of the union.

Marriage, therefore, functions on the individual level between a husband and his wife. It functions on the family level between a couple and their children. It also functions on the clan level between a couple and their separate clans. Finally, it functions to unite clans into larger groups.

Frequency of Polygyny

Of the current generation of forty-three married men resident at Sikari, fifteen (35 percent) have more than one wife. Of these, three men have three wives. One man had two wives at one time, but the first wife died, leaving him monogamous. Two of the fifteen took widows of their older brothers. One of the fifteen took another man's bride in revenge for continued adultery between his wife and the prospective groom. Another took a second wife to offset his guilt in having taken a "sister" *(augtá)* from his own clan as his first wife. Of the twenty-eight monogamous men, seven are married to a second or third spouse, following the death of the first and, in some cases, the second spouse. Two men, one young and one old, are widowers looking for another wife but so far unsuccessfully. There are at least ten young men whom the society considers of marriageable age who are still bachelors. One young man has been asked to take a wife, but refuses. One physically handicapped man has no wife.

In the previous generation, that is the fathers of the forty-three (married) men currently living at Sikari, eleven of thirty-three men had more than one wife (33 percent). In addition, three of the thirty-three had more than one wife, but the first wife died before taking the second. Another man had had two simultaneously but divorced the second. These data are summarized in table 5. The category of polygamous men includes any man who has ever had at least two wives simultaneously and the monogamous category includes any man who has ever been married, even if he may not be at the present time.

These statistics conform to Hillman's prediction (1975:88) regarding societies which practice simultaneous polygyny, that "it will always be found that at any one time monogamous unions actually outnumber polygamous ones, although, at the same time, monogamous unions will usually tend to be potentially polygamous." As we see below, societal reasons for taking another wife dictate that every Sikaritai man be open to the option of doing so. Thus, although 65 percent of current households are monogamous, all of them have the potential of becoming polygamous. It is interesting to note that only one of thirty men (3.5 percent) at Haya and three of fifteen (20 percent) at Iri, the other two Sikaritai villages, are polygamous.

	Current Generation	Previous Generation
Total polygamous men:	16	12
Two wives	12	11
Three wives	3	0
Formerly two wives	1	1
Total monogamous men:	27	21
Second/Third wife	7	3
Widowers	2	
Total unmarried men:	10	
Physically handicapped	1	

Table 5. Polygyny at Sikari

Reasons for Polygyny

Historical/Mythical Context. We have seen that both sister exchange and elements of the marriage ceremony are an important part of the Sikaritai origin legends. The same is true of polygyny. *Húkig/Hútebi,* an important Sikaritai ancestor, had two wives. *Húkig* is also the spiritual advisor to men on how to handle their wives. Thus, if a man's wife commits adultery, he consults *Húkig* first and should follow his advice. In case of war, *Húkig* also advises men whether or not to return an attack. *Húkig* thus constitutes a pervasive presence and role model for Sikaritai men, including expectations about the ideal in marriage.

Quite apart from mythic norms of marriage, there are also social forces at work among the Sikaritai culture that make polygyny a viable option. The Sikaritai say, "If a girl is available in my *tória* (the clan which exchanges women with my father's clan) and there are no bachelor candidates in my clan, a married man takes her." The basic underlying factor in such availability is not an imbalance of birth rate for male and female children (tables 1 and 2). Rather, it lies in the fact that the society requires that girls marry immediately after their first menses while men are up to ten years older than women when they marry, thus skewing the generations in regard to husband's and wife's ages. With this basis, some further reasons why a Sikaritai man takes a second wife follow.

1. The first wife is barren. As in any society, there are childless couples at Sikari. It is assumed if a monogamous pair have no children that the woman is infertile. If a sister exchange has not yet been carried through, it is permissible for the husband to return the woman to her parents and take another wife. However, if the exchange is complete, his common response is to take a second wife when a suitable candidate becomes available. This second wife may or may not be from the same clan as the first wife. If, however, the second wife also has no children, the process stops, the assumption being it is the man who is infertile.

2. A brother dies, leaving a widow. The levirate system is very evident among the Sikaritai. It is not demanded that a man whom the deceased referred to as *aprá* 'younger sibling' take his widow, but it is normally expected. Of course, since the terms *aság* 'older sibling' and *aprá* 'younger sibling' are extended to patrilateral parallel cousins, there may be a number of men who are eligible to take the widow. This eligible list, however, is prioritized to give first option to the "true" younger brothers of the deceased, beginning with the oldest of them. Since, of course, there is no guarantee that the younger brother who takes the widow is not already married when his older brother dies, polygyny is a natural result of this practice.

By contrast, however, it is not acceptable, because of restrictions on a man's relationship with his younger brother's wife, for an older brother to marry his younger brother's widow. A younger brother, either biological or extended, would have first option.

3. The first wife's inability to carry out her other roles when menstruating, pregnant, and during the postpartum period. A further reason for polygyny arises because a husband must not eat food prepared by his wife during the final stages of pregnancy. Even after giving birth, she must remain in a separate place until the fluids of the birthing process stop flowing. A monogamous husband is, under these conditions, deprived of his wife's help, companionship, and sexual favors for rather long stretches of time. Furthermore, after she has several children, the care of these children while she is in birth confinement brings added pressure on the family.

4. The first wife's inability to carry out her other roles while caring for many children. A similar situation occurs when a man's wife must choose between getting sago or taking care of the children. The acceptable Sikaritai solution is to take another wife. The first wife, in fact, often suggests this solution to her husband. However, if she is not in agreement, she is apt to be jealous of her husband's attention to the second wife and conclude that he no longer cares for her.

5. The lack of unmarried men. As previously mentioned, there are times when a man is asked to take a second or third wife. For example, if a man's brother is in need of a wife and he has a daughter of marriageable age, he will ask someone from his *tória* (the clan which exchanges women with his clan) to provide an exchange. If there are, however, no unmarried men in his *tória,* an already married man may acceptably take the man's daughter as a second or third wife. It is important that a woman be married almost immediately after her first menses; otherwise, it is assumed she will not be a virgin at marriage, which bears social stigma. Unmarried girls past their menses are considered "fair game" by men if they are not married and it is considered better socially to become a second (or third) wife than to remain unmarried and be viewed as promiscuous.

A similar case would be one in which a man's *tória* took a wife freely *(wésó kwrípi),* i.e., without providing a woman in exchange. It is expected that they will complete an exchange at a later time. Therefore, when this clan has a suitable girl available, a man may take her as his second wife, if all the men in his clan are already married.

6. The first wife is lazy or overworked. A possibly selfish but acceptable reason for adding a wife is found in a case where the first wife does not pound enough sago, or in general does not work hard enough to please her husband. This problem is compounded if she has several small children and is preoccupied with caring for them. Here again, a husband is unwise to take another wife against his first wife's wishes. However, the logistics of feeding and caring for his family may override her objections.

7. The desire for more children. A further reason for taking more than one wife is the desire of the husband to have many children in order to insure continuation of the clan and to cement relations with other clans through exchange.

8. As a reward for good relations with one's in-laws. In keeping with the obligations of a man to his wife's family, it is normal practice for a father-in-law to observe his son-in-law's behavior toward him. If he approves of the way he assists with projects and in general is a contributor to the family welfare, the father-in-law may offer him a younger daughter as an additional wife. This proposal, of course, also cements relations between the two clans and ensures continued favorable contact.

Of the above reasons, only point 6 could be considered somewhat personally motivated. In keeping with the usual Sikaritai emphasis on the group as opposed to the individual, the needs of the clan as a whole and its relations with other whole clans take first priority in marriage as in everything else. The ideals to be reached are: (1) assuring that girls are married immediately following puberty and (2) completing sister exchange cycles. Sikaritai society clearly "represents the genius of many generations who discovered, invented, borrowed, and integrated the elements available and useful to them for existence in their bioclimate" (Hillman 1975:58).

To Be or Not To Be Polygamous

Approximately fifteen years ago, the Sikaritai were told that polygyny was not good and must be abandoned. The majority complied but were uncertain about the reason for this new view of marriage. Then, two or three years ago they began questioning their earlier decision and many have revived the practice.

The dilemma of the Sikaritai, as they face competing norms of marriage, dramatizes the observation that "newly accepted elements, not harmoniously integrated into the whole culture, can even initiate a process of disintegration and dehumanization" (Hillman 1975:66). This view is currently reflected in the breakdown of traditional morality in the face of outside demands for monogamy. Whereas traditionally a man with a pregnant wife or newly delivered or nursing child may have had a second wife to satisfy his sexual needs, he now tends to look elsewhere.

It is not the purpose of the present paper to moralize or propose social engineering solutions. The Sikaritai themselves will make these decisions. It does, however, seem rather clear that there is not yet a suitable substitute to replace the function of polygyny in the overall Sikaritai system.

Summary

The Sikaritai social structure, kinship system, and system of sister exchange marriage all combine to produce a complex system of interaction.
The two phratries at the foundation of the system give stability to all these
interactions. Sister exchange, both within and outside one's phratry, is rooted
in the kinship system, having its ideal realization in extended cross-cousin
marriage.

Although strongly patrilineal in descent, Sikaritai men must, in the context
of sister exchange, also consider their matrilateral relationships in choosing
a wife. This fact, in combination with the balance of males to females and a
potential ten-year age gap between a husband and his wife, leads naturally
in many cases to social pressure on a man to take a second wife.

Sikaritai society is in a state of change, influenced by contact with Indonesian culture and society and increased contact with other similar cultural
groups in the Greater Lakes Plain. Time will reveal what changes this
contact will bring on their kinship relationships, marriage system, and the
practice of polygyny.

Appendix

The Legend of Sikaritai Clan Origin

Went down. Our ancestors went down.
The ones who came from the snake went down from there.
Some went from Kaisra, and others went from Og Junction.
There, they lived at Akuri.

Then the older brother opened a white ant nest and put it out.
Then the older brother having gone, watched far away.
Didn't come. The mouse didn't come.
Then the older brother went back to sleep.

Then the younger brother took his bow and went.
He saw a mouse eating the ants. Then he shot it.
Having killed it, he removed its insides with his knife, butchered, baked, ate
it, and went home to sleep.

After he went, the older brother jumped down to see the nest.
Blood was all that was left.
He went up and saw the mouse's jaw hanging in the doorway.

Then the older brother put the younger brother, who had eaten the mouse
and had put a knife in his armband, in a canoe.
They both crossed over, untied the canoe, and pushed off from the land.
They went down the Mamberamo.

Now the ironwood tree where we tie our canoes now, it then stood in the
middle of the river. They collided with it, and they could hear the water
rushing by.

They woke up and saw, "We're in the middle of the Mamberamo. How will
we get out?" Then climbed up and lived in the ironwood tree, and ate
nothing but ironwood leaves and became very thin. There was a palm tree
at Bgadtebi. The wind blew it upstream so it was placed neatly down on the
ironwood tree.

Then the younger brother, who ate the mouse, stood and held a palm tree branch, opened his armband, and with the vine tied it to the ironwood branch. Then he, the older brother, and all the other brothers jumped onto the palm tree. Then he cut the vine and the tree bounced back into place. It swung back and forth and finally stood straight again.

Then all the brothers went down the separate branches to the land below. Some went to Bgadtebi, some to Sawesa, others to Bgida, others to Tiba.

There were two brothers and two sisters. One set left on Bgadtebi, the other left on Tiba. The two mountains were opposite facing each other.

Then the brothers went hunting, and the sisters went to get sago. They saw there were no other people. The sisters went up and cried.

Then the brothers came up, and shouted, "Are there other people over there?" They answered, "No, no people." The one on Bgadtebi called, "Come over here." So the brother and sister came across, carrying food (cassowary).

Then the sisters rolled cigarettes. Then one gave hers to the Bgadtebi brother, the other gave hers to the Tiba brother. Then they started living together here.

References

Fox, Robin, 1967. Kinship and marriage: An anthropological perspective. Harmondsworth, England: Penguin Books.

Hillman, Eugene. 1975. Polygamy reconsidered: African plural marriage and the Christian churches. Maryknoll, NY: Orbis Books.

Lawrence, Peter. 1971. Introduction. In Ronald M. Berndt and Peter Lawrence, (eds.), Politics in New Guinea, 1–34. Nedlands, Western Australia: University of Western Australia Press.

Levi-Strauss, Claude. 1969. The elementary structures of kinship. James Harle Bell, trans. Boston: Beacon Press.

Martin, David L. 1991. Sikaritai phonology. Workpapers in Indonesian Languages and Linguistics 9:91–120.

Schusky, Ernest L. 1972. Manual for kinship analysis. 2nd ed. New York: Holt, Rinehart and Winston.

Voorhoeve, C. L. 1975. Languages of Irian Jaya: Checklist. Preliminary classification, language maps, wordlists. Pacific Linguistics Series B 31.

A Look at Cohesion, Mutual Obligation, Reciprocity, and Social Interaction among the Meyah

Gilles Gravelle

Kinship among the Meyah determines who may marry whom, whom one may depend upon for help in the collection of bride wealth, and where one stands in the authority structure. It establishes new marriage lines, and generally provides balance and security in society through the reciprocal relations of each kinsman.[1]

[1]Information for this paper was gathered over a period of three years during intermittent stays in the northern coastal Meyah village of Nuni. More intensive research was done during the months of July and August 1989 with Meyah language associates in Manokwari. I wish to thank our Meyah friends who have invited us to live in their village and observe their way of life. I am especially grateful to Mesakh Tibyai, Bastian Salabay, and Yosef Dowansiba for their help in the research for this paper. Research was conducted using the Meyah language as the principle medium of communication.

A special thanks to Marilyn Gregerson and Joyce Sterner whose suggestions and editing remarks were of invaluable assistance in writing this paper. Sims (1986) provided a helpful model in formatting this paper.

Background

The Meyah people live in the eastern part of the Bird's Head, in the Manokwari district of Irian Jaya. Numerous villages may be found deep in the highlands and valleys of the Arfak mountains (see figure 1). There are also many villages along the northern coast of the Bird's Head bordering the Amberbaken language area to the west, and extending east as far as the regional center of Manokwari. Due to the government's translocation program, higher population density may be found in the northern coastal lowlands as well the coastal zones. There are an estimated ten to twelve thousand Meyah people, with 35–40 percent living within the urban areas.

Outside contact with the Meyah dates from the time the first ships came into Manokwari (Dorey) Bay in 1705 as well as in 1793 (Kamma 1981:85). The Meyah, from early history until now, have been looked upon as an aggressive and warlike people. They formed alliances with the Hattam and warred against the Biak/Numfor people which resulted in their takeover of the Manokwari peninsula and surrounding coastal lands, where they still live today. Wallis (1869:504) makes reference to the Meyah in his classic book *The Malay Archipelago*.

Today the Meyah still live a seminomadic existence. The poor soils of the Arfak mountains have forced them into low intensity agriculture in addition to some hunting and gathering. Their main staple is the cassava root, supplemented by plantains and leafy vegetables. They usually plant one garden a year, and if that garden does not yield enough food, they will travel to different areas seeking relatives who may have a greater food supply. They also hunt birds, wild pigs, and tree marsupials, all of which are still abundant in the coastal areas.

The traditional Meyah village consists of one Meyah patriarch and his extended family. There are four to seven houses that make up such a village. Due to the translocation programs much larger population units (*desa* in Indonesian) have resulted in several extended families or lineages living together in one village. These newer *desa* may number up to 300 people.

Meyah is classified as a Papuan language and part of the East Bird's Head phylum level stock. They form their own Meyah family level isolate (Voorhoeve 1975:49). The closest related language to Meyah is Moskona at 68 percent lexical similarity (Gravelle 1985).

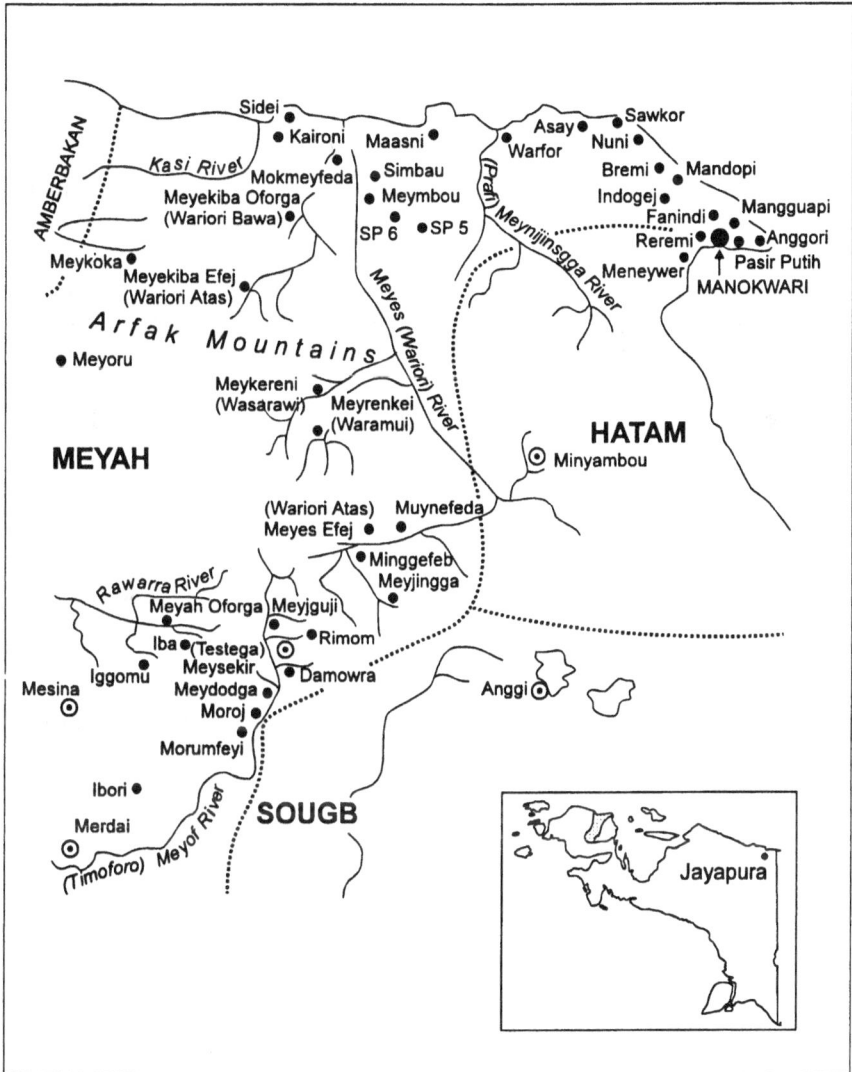

Fig. 1. Meyah village locations

Other spellings[2] and names for Meyah are: Meax, Meah, Meyaj, Mejach, Arfak, and Mansibaber, the latter being the Biak/Numfor name for the Meyah (Grimes 1988:496).

Meyah Social Structure

The Meyah trace their origin to a common ancestor. However, that ancestor is too far removed to be traced within their genealogy. The common ancestor of all Meyah people is widely believed to be a woman call Ejemes. She is the offspring of a dog named Tibyai. She married a man from what is now known as Iggomu, a Moskona area. It is popularly believed by the Meyah that her offspring were the first Meyah; thus they refer to her as their grandmother.

There are three levels that form the Meyah social hierarchy, as shown in figure 2.

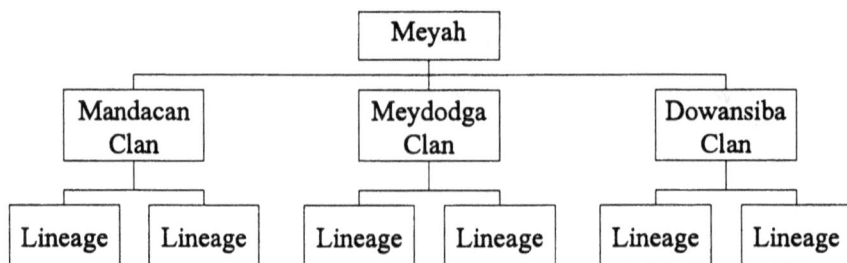

Fig. 2. Meyah social hierarchy

The first level is the whole Meyah group, which is segmented into three patrilineal descent groups called CLANS. The three clans, Mandacan, Meydodga, and Dowansiba,[3] all have separate founders and originate from a particular territory within the Arfak mountains. Each clan is comprised of

---

[2]The spelling of the Meyah words in this paper reflects the Meirenkei and Meyes area dialects. Some words may have variation in spelling within other dialect areas. The spelling also reflects the phonological analysis done by Gravelle and Gravelle (1988) and orthography testing by Gravelle (1990).

[3]The Dowansiba clan was originally called Ejameren. After forming an alliance with the Dowansiba clan of the Manikion people, they intermarried and the Ejameren name was no longer used. The alliance has long since ended, but the Dowansiba name is still used by the Meyah clan.

several LINEAGES, which are based on traceable ancestry that may go back four or five generations. The original ancestors of lineages are frequently male siblings.

The Meyah may marry within the clan but must marry outside of their own lineage, that is, their local blood line. Historically the lineages went by one of the three clan names but were further distinguished by the name of their territory. This distinction helped them to know which blood line a person belonged to. However, within the last eighteen years many of the lineages under the Mandacan clan have changed their lineage name. This change of nomenclature may be due to the modern geographical diversity of the Meyah clans and lineages (see figure 3). Some also say that the Mandacan name carries a bad reputation because of the uprising of 1965–1971, in which the Mandacan clan were heavily involved.

As mentioned above, members of a lineage do not necessarily all reside in one village or local geographical location. Due to various reasons several members may be living in the area of a different lineage. In the village of Nuni, of the sixty-two households, thirteen belong to the one local lineage of the Mandacan clan, six are from the Bomoi lineage of the Dowansiba clan, and forty-three from the Yoom lineage of the Dowansiba clan.

The lineages that have taken on new names, such as Isba or Salabai, are easier to identify. An Isba cannot marry a Salabai, and vice versa. However, for those lineages that still use their original clan names, the lineage and territory must be first examined to see if they are of a single descent group or not.

Meyah Kinship Terms

The Meyah kinship system is basically a Hawaiian system on all generation levels for consanguineal kinsmen but deviates only in the first ascending generation with a descriptive term for mother's brother. Terms for the spouses of parents' siblings are distinct from consanguineal terms. In ego's

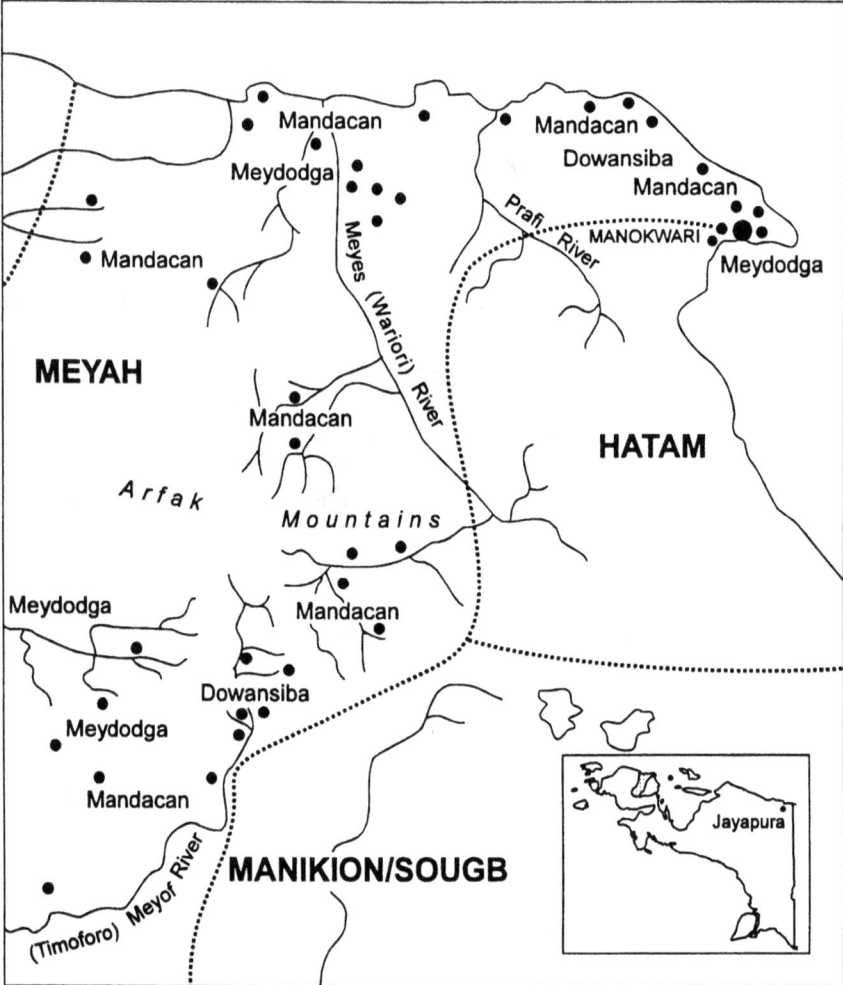

Fig. 3. Meyah clan locations

generation, relative age and sex are marked for both consanguineal and affinal kinsmen.[4]

Consanguineal Kinship Terms

Meyah consanguineal kinship terms are found in figures 4 and 5. They cover four generations of kinsmen. Relative age and sex is marked in ego's generation for both parallel and cross-kinsmen.

Grandkinsman Generation. Explicit lineal relations extend only through the second ascending generation. The term used for grandparents is also used for ancestors beyond the grandparents' generation. An alternate term used for ancestors too distant to recall is *runa ensis* 'the people of old'.

There are two terms denoting ascending grandkinsmen by sex. The terms extend bilaterally to all collateral relatives and their spouses of the grandkinsmen generation. The first term is *indimowa* which refers to ego's male bilateral kinsmen of the second ascending generation. The second term is *indawa* which refers to ego's female bilateral kinsmen of the second ascending generation. The reciprocal term for *indimowa* and *indawa* is *edebesa* 'grandchild'. It extends to collateral kinsmen of either sex in the second descending generation.

Parent-Child Generation. There are five terms that classify the kinsmen of the first ascending generation. These terms extend bilaterally to all collateral kinsmen of the parent generation, and denote sex. They are: *akeina* 'father', *ameina* 'mother', *edeina* 'mother's brother', *edkeina* 'mother's sister's husband', and *edmeina* 'father's brother's wife'.

The term *akeina* applies to ego's biological father as well as to all his father's brothers. The term *ameina*, applies to ego's biological mother as well as bilaterally to all ego's parents' sisters. The term *edeina* refers to mother's brother and extends to all males of ego's mother's lineage of the parent generation. Any one that ego's mother refers to as brother is referred to as *edeina* by ego.

---

[4]Kinship terms in this paper are written in first-person-singular possessive form. All kinship terms in Meyah are inalienably possessed. The word is formed by the combination of a stem plus a prefix for person. There are eleven pronouns that form nine different ways to inflect a kinship word stem. The stem for child is *esa.* Inflected for first-person-singular the prefix *ed-* is added thus deriving the root *edesa* 'my child'. See the appendix for a complete list of inflected kinship terms.

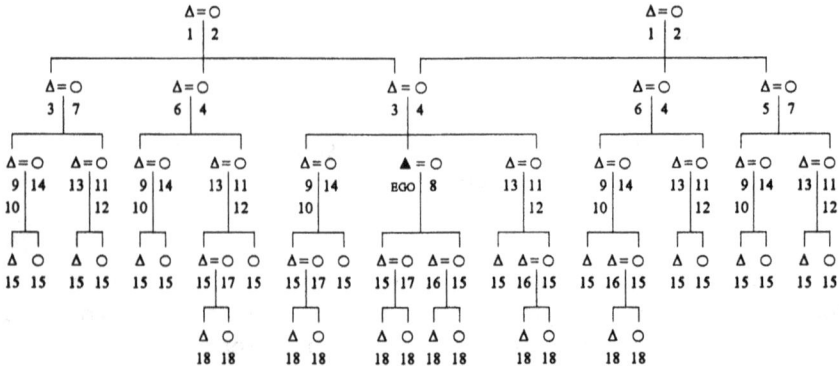

1. *indimowa*   grandfather
2. *indawa*   grandmother
3. *akeina*   father
4. *ameina*   mother
5. *edeina*   mother's brother
6. *edkeina*   parent's sister's husband
7. *edmeina*   parent's brother's wife
8. *edohona*   wife
9. *edkosa*   same sex younger sibling
10. *edkora*   same sex older sibling
11. *ediesa*   opposite sex younger sibling
12. *ediera*   opposite sex older sibling
13. *edcosa*   same sex sibling-in-law (ms)
14. *eduisa*   opposite sex sibling-in-law
15. *edesa*   child
16. *edfina*   son-in-law
17. *edgona*   daughter-in-law
18. *edebesa*   grandchild

Fig. 4. Consanguineal kinship chart (male ego)

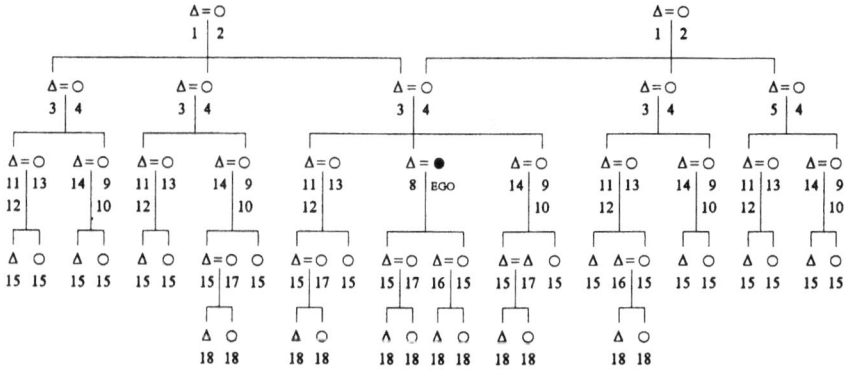

1. *indimowa* — grandfather
2. *indawa* — grandmother
3. *akeina* — father
4. *ameina* — mother
5. *edeina* — mother's brother
8. *edohina* — husband
9. *edkosa* — same sex younger sibling
10. *edkora* — same sex older sibling
11. *ediesa* — opposite sex younger sibling
12. *ediera* — opposite sex older sibling
13. *edfebesa* — same sex sibling-in-law (fs)
14. *edulsa* — opposite sex sibling-in-law
15. *edesa* — child
16. *edfina* — son-in-law
17. *edgona* — daughter-in-law
18. *edebesa* — grandchild

Fig. 5. Consanguineal kinship chart (female ego)

The Meyah use separate terms to distinguish their male and female collateral relatives of the parent generation from their spouses. As already stated, ego's father's brothers are referred to as *akeina* 'father', but the spouses of ego's father's sisters are *edkeina* 'father's sister's husband'. The term *ameina* extends collaterally to all of ego's female relatives of the parent generation. However, the spouses of ego's mother's brothers are referred to as *edmeina* 'mother's brother's wife'.

The term *edesa* is the reciprocal of *akeina, ameina, edeina, edkeina,* and *edmeina.* The term extends bilaterally to all males and females of the child generation. It also extends affinally to all offspring of ego's spouse's siblings. The term does not designate relative age or sex. Normally in discussing children the Meyah just use the general term for child. But if the relative age must be distinguished, then the Meyah use the term *osumbohka* 'first born'; other terms delineate second born and third born. The rest of the children then are called by the corresponding number, e.g., four, etc. To distinguish sex of alter the term *orna* 'male' or *ojaga* 'female' is placed after the word child. Meyah also has a plural marker *-ir*. When suffixed to *edesa* it becomes *edeser* 'children'.

Sibling Terms. The Meyah use two sets of sibling terms that extend bilaterally to all collateral kinsmen of ego's generation. The terms form a reciprocal set and delineate sex and age of alter relative to ego. The first set of terms is *edkora* 'same sex older sibling' and *edkosa* 'same sex younger sibling', while the second set is *ediera* 'opposite sex older sibling' and *ediesa* 'opposite sex younger sibling'. These terms are used precisely, in that the sibling in question must actually be older or younger than ego. For collateral kinsmen there is no seniority granted relative to the age of parents' siblings.

Affinal Kinship Terms

Meyah affinal kinship terms are presented in figures 6 and 7 while figure 8 summarizes both consanguineal and affinal terms with their referential scope and nearest English equivalents. Affinal terms of ego's generation denote the sex of ego and of alter. For male ego, affinal terms are used for ego's generation as well as for the first ascending and descending generations. The first ascending generation uses one reciprocal term and ego's generation uses a set of two reciprocal terms. For female ego, there is one reciprocal term for the first ascending generation and two reciprocal terms for ego's generation.

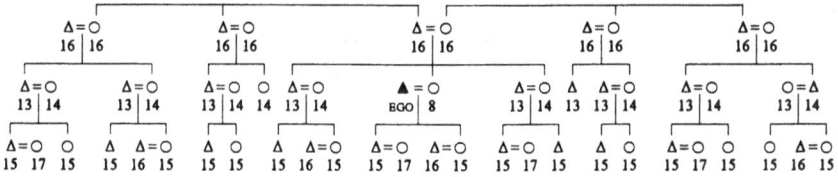

8.	*edohona*	wife
13.	*edcosa*	same sex sibling-in-law (ms)
14.	*eduisa*	opposite sex sibling-in-law
15.	*edesa*	child
16.	*edfina*	son-in-law; parent-in-law (ms)
17.	*edgona*	daughter-in-law

Fig. 6. Meyah affinal kinship (male ego)

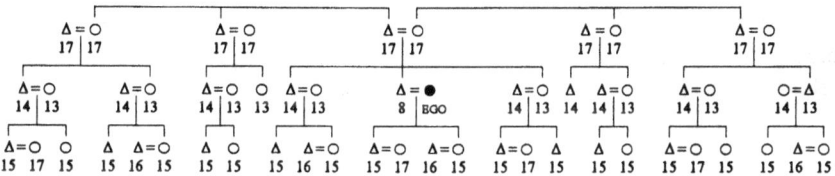

8.	*edohina*	husband
13.	*edfebesa*	same sex sibling-in-law (fs)
14.	*eduisa*	opposite sex sibling-in-law
15.	*edesa*	child
16.	*edfina*	son-in-law
17.	*edgona*	daughter in law; parent in law (fs)

Fig. 7. Meyah affinal kinship (female ego)

Parent-in-law/Child-in-law Terms. The term *edfina* 'parent-in-law', extends to all of ego's spouse's bilateral kinsmen of the parent generation. The term identifies ego's sex as male. *edfina* is used reciprocally between a man and his spouse's parents and their siblings and their spouses regardless of sex. The term *edgona* 'parent-in-law' extends to all of female ego's spouse's bilateral kinsmen of the parent generation. *edgona* is used reciprocally between a female and her spouse's parents and their siblings and their spouses regardless of sex.

Sibling-in-law Terms. For male ego, the term *edcosa* 'brother-in-law' is used reciprocally between ego and his wife's male relatives of her generation. The term is used irrespective of relative age and extends to his wife's sisters' husbands.

For female ego, the term *edfebesa* 'sister-in-law' is used reciprocally between ego and her husband's female relatives of her generation. The term also extends to her husband's brothers' wives.

Ego uses the term *eduisa* 'sibling-in-law' in addressing his or her spouse's siblings of the opposite sex. It is used irrespective of relative age.

There is one term used by both male and female ego in referring to the offspring of his or her collateral affinal relatives of the child generation. The term is *edesa* 'child'. It is the same term that ego would use for his own biological offspring. It extends collaterally to all of ego's spouse's bilateral relative's offspring of the first descending generation.

Spouse Terms. In Meyah there are two terms of reference for spouse. The first one is *edohona* 'wife'. It is the term used by a male ego in referring to his spouse. If he has more than one wife, he refers to each one using the Meyah count nouns for human beings according to whom he married first, second, and so on. The terms are *edohona osumbohka* 'first wife', *edohona endeis* 'second wife', and *edohona osuira* 'third wife'.

Other terms ego may use to address his wives are *edohona ojona* 'mature wife' for his first wife, and *edohona oforoka* 'immature wife' or 'young wife' for his other wives. These terms are used irrespective of age. The second wife may be older than the first, but she is still referred to as the immature wife. This signifies a more subservient position to the first wife.

The term *edohina* 'husband' is used by female ego in referring to her spouse. All wives address their husband as *edohina*. The first wife refers to her cowives as *mohona edkosa* 'younger sister wife'. This term applies even if the second and third wives are older than the first. Likewise the second and third wives refer to the first wife as *mohona edkora* 'older sister wife'. This again demonstrates the seniority the first wife has over her cowives.

Term	Gener-ation	Nearest English Translation	Scope Consanguineal	Affinal
indimowa	+2	grandfather	FF, MF	
indawa	+2	grandmother	FM, MM	
akeina	+1	father	F, FB	
ameina	+1	mother	M, MZ, FZ	
edeina	+1	mother's brother	MB	
edkeina	+1	aunt's husband	MZH, FZH	
edmeina	+1	uncle's wife	MBW, FBW	
edfina	+1	parent-in-law (ms)		WF, WM, WFB, WFZ, WMB, WMZ, WFBW, WFZH, WMBW, WMZH, DH, BDH, ZDH
	−1	son-in-law		
edgona	+1	parent-in-law (fs)		HF, HM, HFB, HFZ, HMB, HMZ, HFBW, HFZH, HMBW, HMZH
	−1	daughter-in-law		SW, BSW, ZSW
edohona	0	wife		W
edohina	0	husband		H
edkosa	0	same sex younger sibling	B, FBS, FZS, MBS, MZS, Z, FBD, FZD, MBD, MZD	
edkora	0	same sex older sibling	B, FBS, FZS, MBS, MZS, Z, FBD, FZD, MBD, MZD	
ediesa	0	opposite sex younger sibling	Z, FBD, FZD, MBD, MZD, B, FBS, FZS, MBS, MZS	
ediera	0	opposite sex older sibling	Z, FBD, FZD, MBD, MZD, B, FBS, FZS, MBS, MZS	
edcosa	0	same sex sibling-in-law (ms)	ZH, MZDH, MBDH, FZDH, FBDH	WB, WZH, WFBS, WMBS, WFZS, WMZS, WFBDH, WMBDH, WFZDH, WMZDH

Fig. 8. Kinship terms (1 of 2)

Term	Generation	Nearest English Translation	Scope Consanguineal	Affinal
edfebesa	0	same sex sibling-in-law (fs)	BW, MZSW, MBSW, FZSW, FBSW	HZ, HBW, HFBD, HMBD, HFZS, HMZD, HFBSW, HMBSW, HFZSW, HMZSW
eduisa	0	opposite sex sibling-in-law	BW, MZSW, MBSW, FZSW, FBSW, ZH, MZDH, MBDH, FZDH, FBDH	WZ, WBW, WFBD, WMBD, WFZD, WMZD, WFBSW, WMBSW, WFZSW, WMZSW, HB, HZH, HFBS, HMBS, HFZS, HMZS, HFBDH, HMBDH, HFZDH, HMZDH
edesa	−1	child	S, D, BS, BD, ZS, ZD, FBSS, FBSD, FZSS, FZSD, FBDS, FBDD, FZDS, FZDD, MBSS, MBSD, MZSS, MZSD, MBDS, MBDD, MZDS, MZDD	WBS, WBD, WZS, WZD, WFBSS, WFBSD, WFZSS, WFZSD, WFBDS, WFBDD, WFZDS, WFZDD, WMBSS, WMBSD, WMZSS, WMZSD, WMBDS, WMBDD, WMZDS, WMZDD
edebesa	−2	grandchild	SS, SD, DS, DD, BSS, BSD, BDS, BDD, ZSS, ZSD, ZDS, ZDD, FBSSS, FBSSD, FBDSS, FBDSD, FBSDS, FBSDD, FBDDS, FBDDD, FZSSS, FZSSD, FZDSS, FZDSD, FZSDS, FZSDD, FZDDS, FZDDD, MBSSS, MBSSD, MBDSS, MBDSD, MBSDS, MBSDD, MBDDS, MBDDD, MZSSS, MZSSD, MZDSS, MZDSD, MZSDS, MZSDD, MZDDS, MZDDD	WBSS, WBSD, WBDS, WBDD, WZSS, WZSD, WZDS, WZDD, WFBSSS, WFBSSD, WFBDSS, WFBDSD, WFBSDS, WFBSDD, WFBDDS, WFBDDD, WFZSSS, WFZDSS, WFZDSD, WFZSDS, WFZSDD, WFZDDS, WFZDDD, WMBSSS, WMBSSD, WMBDSS, WMBDSD, WMBSDS, WMBSDD, WMBDDS, WMBDDD, WMZSSS, WMZSSD, WMZDSS, WMZDSD, WMZSDS, WMZSDD, WMZDDS, WMZDDD

Key to symbols:

F = father	M = mother	B = brother	Z = sister
S = son	D = daughter	H = husband	W = wife

Fig. 8. Kinship terms (2 of 2)

Reciprocal Behavior and Expectations of Key Relationships

In studying Meyah kinship from an outsider's point of view one may choose only to elicit the basic terminology employed by the Meyah in distinguishing kinship relations. Of critical importance, however, is how individuals interact with one another in the key relationships discussed below. As is the norm with most kinship oriented societies, the kinship terms are more than just a label to distinguish one individual from another. They are a type of flag that signals how one person is expected to relate to another. As mentioned in the introduction, it is the kinship bonds that decide who an individual may depend on and who he may be obligated to. These bonds are very strong among the Meyah. They supersede any outside relationship with a nonclan member, even if they share a common language.

For the Meyah, every action, every request, and every form of assistance that is given is strictly governed by the reciprocal relationship involved. From the time a child begins to know who his key relatives are, he is instructed to develop those relationships by assisting these key relatives in any way he can. Thus he is already starting to build liability in others that he will be able to reclaim later on in life.

edeina *'maternal uncle'* and edesa *'sister's son'*

It is common in most Papuan societies that the relationship between mother's brother and sister's son is a highly important one. For the Meyah as well, it is a crucial relationship.

Because the Meyah are a patrilineal society, all nurturing, material wealth, and assistance is provided to ego by his father and his other agnatic relatives. Ego's mother is technically an outsider who does not help to provide for her own offspring through her consanguineal relatives. Ego's link to his mother's familial wealth and assistance is technically not through her but through her brothers. She has become the human property of another clan. And because of the great amount of wealth paid to her extended family for her, she must serve wholly her new affinal relatives.

But through the mother's brother-sister's son relationship, her familial relatives are still meeting her needs, although indirectly. The things that she cannot provide for her male offspring are provided by her brothers. Thus the material and emotional link is maintained.

Around the time ego is five years old and knows who his maternal uncle is, he begins to develop his relationship with him. He goes and lives in the same house as his mother's brother for one to two months at a time. He is still quite small, so the relationship is one-sided. His uncle will provide food for him, take him along to the gardens and generally treat him as his own biological son. He gives him affection, and makes small bows and arrows for him.

When ego is more mature he will seek out advice and assistance in important matters from his mother's brother. His maternal uncle will teach him about the spirit world, and about who their common enemies are. He will also teach him the traditional songs and how to avoid improper contact with women. When ego is ready to marry he will approach both his father and his maternal uncle for help in the collection of bride wealth. In this way the material wealth is reciprocated back to ego's father's relatives from the time that ego's mother's relatives received the bride price paid for her.

Once ego has fully matured (about 18–20 years old) he is expected to reciprocate for all the help and nurturing his uncle gave him while he was growing. He now must aid his mother's brother by working in the garden, assisting in house building, and helping to provide occasional wild meat. It is not uncommon for the mother's brother to request his sister's son's help in the collection of bride wealth for himself, another of his kinsmen, or perhaps his own son. Even though ego is not obligated to any of his mother's other collateral relatives, he is obligated to his mother's brother. Thus through his maternal uncle's request he is still meeting the needs of other members of his mother's lineage.

akeina *'father' and* edesa *'son'*

Because Meyah is a patrilineal society, the most crucial relationship is ego's relationship with his father. Although ego's relationship to his mother's brother is very close, his relationship to his father is of greater importance.

The father holds the key to knowledge and experience that he will pass on to his son in order to help insure his survival in a complicated and sometimes hostile world. He teaches him the importance of being honest with others and assisting them in any way he can. It is of utmost importance that he develop a close relationship with as many of his father's relatives as possible.

The father begins to teach his son early on about how he should act around others in order to avoid offending someone in a serious way. The father and his brothers have the primary responsibility in disciplining ego. It is ego's father and his kinsmen that would suffer the wrath or anger of another offended clan. His mistakes could cost his father a large amount of wealth paid to compensate for the offense. If the offended party does not demand compensation, he will resort to sorcery or poison and the offense may result in sickness or death.

He teaches him the history of their lineage and clan, where they came from, the important locations of their ancestral villages, and the myths relating to those ancestors. He will be careful to instruct him concerning special food taboos as well as how to avoid offending certain spirits by his actions. He will tell him about their common enemies and the history of ongoing vendettas in order to avoid further antagonism with those groups.

He will take him to the gardens and show him how to clear land and build pig fences around the new garden. He will demonstrate how and when to plant food. He will take him on hunting trips into the forest and teach him the technique of hunting birds and wild pigs. Because inheritance is handed down through the father, ego's father will be careful to point out what land belongs to him, and what parts will be parceled out to the son when he marries. The son will also inherit debts that are owed to his father. So the father will tell him to whom he may go to collect material wealth in times of need.

edkora *and* edkosa *'same sex siblings'*

Because the Meyah do not distinguish between siblings and their parallel and cross-cousins, the relationships between ego, his siblings, and his cousins are on much the same level. Siblings and cousins are treated alike.

There is a fairly close bond between male siblings and cousins. They will frequently spend time together playing or making bows and arrows to take hunting. When one has a task to carry out, he will depend on his brothers to help him in it. They will accompany each other when taking short or long trips to town or to the interior or coastal areas.

If ego has done something wrong or is angry with somebody, he will usually confide in his same sex siblings. They may together plan to carry out revenge against an offender. There are cases in which a Meyah, wanting to murder another person, requested his own brother's help in carrying out the task. (Such a case may or may not involve retaliation for the killing of a relative by another party.)

If ego is in need of an item of clothing, he may ask his siblings to help provide it for him. They will usually share most of their common household items.

Generally, an older sibling is given responsibility for his younger siblings. He must watch over them, and assist them in making toys or small play tools. He must also help provide for their food if the parents are not around.

ediera *and* ediesa *'opposite sex siblings'*

The sister and brother relationship represents a special one for the Meyah. Because the Meyah have no distinction for cousin, ego's sisters and his female cousins are treated alike. Before a sister is married, she spends a great deal of her time assisting her brothers. If her brothers are younger, she is responsible for carrying them around, cooking for them, and helping to guard over their general welfare. Frequently this provision of care is looked upon as a burden by the older sister who would just as soon leave her siblings behind during her outings.

If the brother is older but not married, she must assist him in his garden, repair his clothes, and make string bags for him. She makes his rain capes, tends his pigs, and generally provides many of the kinds of services that a wife would provide. Once her brother is married, she may help care for his children in addition to other duties. However, once she is married, she is no longer obligated to help her brother.

Her older brother, in turn, is her protector. He watches over her physical welfare and assists her in carrying out the more laborious tasks. She will eventually play an important role in enabling him to marry. Once she is married the bride wealth transferred to her kin group will later be used to provide a bride price for her brother's marriage. Thus her physical welfare is important to her brother.

van Baal (1975:76) suggests that the sister has claims concerning her brother's protection for her and eventually for her sons as well. This obligation, he says, is due to the exchange of bride wealth between groups[5] and provides a possible explanation for why the sister serves her brother so much before marriage and why he becomes obligated to her and her children later on. He is her only link to her familial kinsmen that she may depend on for assistance.

---

[5]In van Baal's book *Reciprocity and the Position of Women* he presents an interesting viewpoint. He suggests that through a woman's marriage she places her brother in a debt position. Also through marriage she establishes a reciprocal debt relationship between her husband and her brother. Both of them benefit by her willingness to marry.

Other Relationships

indimowa *and* indawa *(grandkinsmen).* The relationship between ego and his grandkinsmen is a close one. However, it is not really one of reciprocity. Ego's grandfather will help in his nurturing and provide a relationship of affection and joking. He will advise ego in the areas of the spirit world and recount historical events as well as popular myths. He will teach him the qualities of a good wife and how to go about choosing one. He may occasionally help in the collection of bride price for his grandson.

Ego will help his grandparents by bringing them food and firewood, and by providing folk medicines for them. He will occasionally live with them for several weeks at a time in order to enjoy their affection.

mendes *'purchased child'.* It is common for the Meyah as well as other groups of the eastern Bird's Head to purchase children. The child is called *mendes* 'purchased child'. The Meyah mostly purchase children from the Moskona people located to the south of the Meyah area. The Moskona are considered poor, and they must occasionally sell children in order to attain the crucial eastern cloth *(kain timor)* that is an essential part of bride wealth. The Meyah are considered rich in eastern cloth, as well as other forms of bride wealth. Therefore, they do not sell their children to other groups or even to kinsmen.

Both male and female children are purchased. The female is the more valuable because of her service and the eventual bride wealth that her parents receive when she marries. It is for this reason that wealthy Meyah will purchase a female *mendes;* when she is married they will receive more material returns on their investment than they originally paid for her. The Meyah use the phrase *mendes meka* 'father of purchased children' to refer to men who own many *mendes.* The term also applies to other types of wealth such as pigs or eastern cloth.

mendes are usually purchased at the age of four or five years. An older child may rebel and seek to return to his original kinsmen. Once the *mendes* is purchased, all ties to his or her kinsmen are severed. He or she has become the sole property of the purchaser and no longer has any claims to his or her blood relatives' wealth or inheritance.

How the *mendes* fits into her new kinship relationship is strictly up to those who purchased her. One family may treat her as a slave, using her to perform tasks without receiving the affection or compensation that a biological daughter may receive. Others will treat her as a part of the family, giving her the same affection and benefits that the other children receive. If a child is diligent and works hard, she may become well accepted by members of the family. If she is lazy or troublesome, she may be sold to another person.

Ego relates to his sibling *mendes* as he would his own biological sibling. They both use the terms of sibling for each other. The main difference between the two is that a *mendes* does not have the customary reciprocal relationships with his adopted collateral relatives. Neither mother's brother nor any other consanguineal kinsmen have any obligations towards the *mendes*. His benefits, if any, come strictly from his adopted nuclear family.

In turn, when the female *mendes* marries, all the bride wealth received for her does not have to be distributed among the father's extended family. If a male *mendes* wants to marry, the adoptive father may not approach his key relatives for assistance in the collection of bride wealth. The burden is his alone.

ereiriri *'stepchild'*. If a widow with children remarries, her children, though they are called *ereiriri* 'stepchild', still belong to their father's lineage and clan. If the child is female and is living with her mother's new affinal kinsmen when she marries, the bride price paid for her will go to her father's relatives and not her stepfather and his relatives.

If the child is male, he still remains part of his father's lineage. The lineage members will assist him in collecting his bride price. His stepfather may also provide assistance, but he is under no obligation to do so. Once the child is older he will begin to develop closer relationships with his deceased father's collateral relatives.

Within the stepfamily setting, the child will still be treated as a normal part of the family by his stepsiblings. They may develop a reciprocal relationship that falls more under cooperation than mutual obligation. They may eventually help each other in the collection or payment of bride price. The term *ereiriri* seems to signify to his mother's affinal relatives that they do not have a reciprocal relationship and all that it entails even though he is living in their local kin group.

edfina *'parent-in-law'*. Upon marriage male ego establishes what seems like a one-sided relationship with his *edfina* 'parents-in-law' and his other affinal kinsmen. Ego's affinal kinsmen do not have any kind of reciprocal relationship with ego's collateral kinsmen.

Even though the main bride price has been paid, ego will remain in debt to his *edfina* as long as his wife is alive. Ego's *edfina* may make many requests of his son-in-law whenever he wishes. Ego will frequently be called upon to help clear a garden or build a house. His *edfina* may discover that ego has come into some material wealth and he will request part of that for himself.

The rationale behind *edfina*'s behavior is that he has lost a valuable helper as well as her progeny when his daughter marries. He now expects continual compensation for that loss. Ego cannot look to him to help him meet his own material needs. He may only look towards his own relatives for assistance.

In the early days of his marriage ego must be careful to show good will and generosity to his *edfina*. If he does not live up to his *edfina*'s expectations, then his *edfina* may decide to annul the marriage and give back the bride price. However, once offspring are born, ego's *edfina* may no longer annul the marriage. On the other hand, he can still make life difficult for ego.

If ego mistreats his wife with severe physical abuse, his affines, particularly his father-in-law and brothers-in-law, will be very angry and seek immediate retribution. This type of offense is compensated by the payment of goods by the husband and his family to his wife's affines. If the marriage is of several years standing, the offender or one of his close relatives may be killed in retribution.

If ego's wife dies, he is no longer obligated to his *edfina* as long as he remains single. If he decides to marry once again, he must first make a final payment of bride price items to his *edfina*. After making this payment, he is released from his obligations to his *edfina* and is free to marry. Then he must collect the bride wealth items for his new wife. Because this situation causes a material burden for the male, it often takes years before he can remarry.

Meyah Marriage

Marriage is one of the most important events in a Meyah person's life. For a woman, it is a time when she breaks with her familial kinsmen and goes to live with a group of strangers that will always consider her an outsider. It is a time when a young man may begin to reclaim the many favors he has given to his key relatives for so many years. It is a time that he, with the help of his father and his mother's brother as well as other collateral kinsmen, work together to collect the large amount of bride wealth that will be paid.

During the collection of the bride wealth some people will have to pay off long-standing debts. The groom and his close kinsmen will become indebted.

It represents the formation of new kinship lines along with a new set of reciprocal relationships. Months of discussion among the consanguineal relatives of both parties will take place until a bride price can be agreed upon. It is a time of tension for both parties. If the two parties cannot come to an agreement over the amount of bride price, then the marriage never takes place, leaving either disappointment or relief for the bride and groom as the case may be.

Choosing a Wife

There may be a number of reasons for arranging a particular marriage. Sometimes the kinsmen of two lineages may want to form an alliance, so they will arrange a marriage between a male and female member of the lineages involved. Sometimes two different families may want to match their children in marriage for economic reasons. Or as in most cases, the man has seen a woman that he is attracted to.

He will first approach his father and his mother's brother and inform them of his desire to marry a particular woman. If the father is agreeable, he will approach the family of the woman his son desires in order to discuss the matter. After a time of deliberation they will inform the man's father of the amount of bride wealth they desire in exchange for the woman. The groom's father will bargain with the woman's family. If they can not come to an agreement, the marriage may not take place. Or the prospective groom may convince his father that the woman is worth the price.

The Collection of Bride Price

The prospective groom's collateral relatives are obligated to help him collect the bride wealth. He will approach his parallel and cross-cousins, his father's siblings, and importantly, his mother's brother. If the prospective groom has led the exemplary life style that he was taught by his father and his grandfather, he has built up a large amount of credit with respect to his relatives and may now count on them to supply his needs.

His relatives will travel great distances to contact other kinsmen in order to collect the eastern cloth and pigs that make up the bulk of the bride payment. One man's extended family helped him collect the following items for his bride price: six large pieces of eastern cloth *(kain timor)* of three different types, 13 large pigs, 50 bolts of store-bought cloth, 15 arm bands, 13 antique necklaces, two watches, two large radio/cassette players, plus 200,000 rupiah (about $115 U.S.). Of all the types of bride price collected, the eastern cloth is the most crucial. Without it a man may not marry. The collection of all of the items of bride wealth could span several years once the initial payment of the *kain timor* is made.[6]

Once all the items are collected in one place, the father of the groom informs the bride's father that everything is ready. The father of the bride and many of his key relatives come to the groom's village with the bride-to-be. After they arrive, they begin to examine all the items. If they are satisfied, they hand over the bride and collect their bride wealth.

Following the exchange a feast is given by the groom and his extended family. Large amounts of food are provided to insure that nobody from the bride's party goes back to their village hungry. Such an event would result in a serious loss of face for the groom's family.

Once the bride's family has collected their wealth and left, the groom takes his bride into his house, or his father's house if he has not built one yet. Soon after the marriage is consummated. The bride assumes the name of her husband's clan or lineage if the name differs from hers.

In line with the patrilineal nature of their society, residence after marriage tends to be patrilocal. In some cases when a couple is first married, the groom will go and live with his father-in-law's family. This practice is occasionally done so that the groom can start out his marriage relationship with his affinal relatives on a good footing. He may spend two to three months with them, assisting his father-in-law in the gardens or doing other labor intensive tasks. After a time the groom will return to his own village with his wife and begin house building.

The wife's relationship with her *edgona* 'parents-in-law' is a close one. Since they are the ones who helped the groom collect his bride wealth, they also have claims to his wife's services. The relationship with the mother-in-law is especially close. The mother-in-law will treat her daughter-in-law as a daughter. She values the daughter-in-law's help around the house and in the gardens. The bond can become so close that tensions may develop if the husband wants to leave the area with his wife for an extended period of time. In one case a man got a job in the interior, but his mother would not allow

---

[6]According to Meidema (1988) this is the reason the Kebar people, who border the Meyah to the west, marry more women into the Meyah than the Meyah marry into the Kebar. Because the Kebar, like the Moskona, lack enough eastern cloth to meet the marital needs of their young men, they exchange their women for the crucial eastern cloth.

him to take his wife because she depended on her help and companionship so much.

Exchange Marriage

Exchange marriage among the Meyah does not occur frequently. However, at times a lineage from the mountain area will approach a lineage from the coastal areas and propose a marriage exchange in order to establish a trade relationship. The lineage from the mountains will purchase the wife from the lineage from the coast. However, the family supplying the bride will not directly purchase back a bride. That will be left to another family within the lineage. If no bride is bought, the wealth exchange would be kept within the same two families. There would be no new items of wealth to distribute to other relatives.

The Meyah have exogamous patrilineages and they are expected to marry into other clans or language groups. In the village of Nuni, out of sixty-seven heads of households, only six have married into another language group. Most of the mixed marriages occur along the language group borders with the Manikion, Hattam, Mai Brat, and Kebar peoples. The Meyah do not marry the Moskona.[7]

Sister exchange, that is, a brother and a sister of one patrilineage marrying a sister and brother of another patrilineage is reported to be rare.

Marriage Constraints

The Meyah may not marry anyone in their own patrilineage. Also, they may not marry anyone with whom they share a common ancestor in the +2 generation, including anyone of their own generation or anyone of the first descending generation or of the first ascending generation.

A man may marry the offspring of his wife's kinsmen of the parent generation or of his own generation. He may also marry his wife's sister, or his brother's wife or her sister. He may marry his cousin of at least the second degree of collaterality, i.e., one who shares a common ancestor in the +3 generation.

In accordance with levirate marriage, if a male ego's brother dies, he must marry his brother's (or cousin's) wife. The widow may not marry anybody

---

[7]The Moskona are the closest related language to Meyah (68 percent). But the Moskona are considered poor and not a profitable group to marry into.

except one of her husband's kinsmen. This limitation is primarily due to the bride price that was paid for her. To marry into another lineage would upset the bride price balance that exists. If there are no male affinal relatives to marry, she is then free to marry into another lineage. However, that lineage will have to pay the bride price to her affines. This practice causes some complications with her consanguineal relatives as well. They will also seek payment to establish a new reciprocal relationship with their new son-in-law. If the levirate marriage is made, all these complications can be avoided.

In some cases a person is forbidden to marry someone from a certain clan or lineage. It is not due to blood ties but to certain myths or hostilities that exist between those groups. Traditionally, if a woman married into a clan or lineage from another village and died within a short time, her lineage would avoid marrying into that clan or lineage again because of the bad omen.

Divorce and Other Complications

The Meyah use the term *oroun sons* 'bring back' or the euphemism *odou sons* 'my liver returns to me' for divorce. During the early months of marriage, if the groom's affinal relatives are making too many demands on him, he may decide his new wife is not worth the trouble. He will take her back to them and demand the bride wealth back. Conversely, if a man is not meeting the ongoing material and physical expectations of his affines, they will bring the bride wealth back and demand the woman be returned.

If a wife commits adultery, the husband will take her back to her family and demand that the bride price be returned and the marriage terminated. Her consanguineal relatives must return the bride price. They will then go to relatives of the man involved in the adultery and demand payment of the same type of wealth for the offense. If the offender does not pay, it may result in bloodshed.

If a husband discovers that his wife is not a virgin, her value has decreased in his eyes. He will go back to her relatives and demand that some of the bride price items be paid back. Again her relatives will seek out the offending person and demand payment to balance out what they have lost.

A Meyah man will not divorce his wife if he discovers that she is infertile. Also, it is not considered grounds for asking some part of the bride price back from her consanguineal kinsmen. The childless couple may seek out a relative who has several children and ask to be given one to raise up as their own. The husband may marry a second wife for procreation, or accept the situation and go on living without children.

Inheritance

Since the Meyah are a patrilineal society, most of ego's inheritance is handed down from his father. However, some land is also handed down to ego from his maternal uncle. His contribution is less significant than ego's father's. Perhaps this gift represents mother's brother's last form of assistance to his sister's son.

When ego is ready to start his own garden, his father and his maternal uncle will each give him a parcel of their own lands. When his father or his maternal uncle dies, the remainder of that person's lands will be divided among his male siblings and his other sons. It is a way of ensuring that every one gets some land for gardens. Other physical assets such as houses, animals, debts owed, or bride wealth will also be distributed among the deceased man's brothers and his sons.

Summary

The Meyah kinship system is basically a Hawaiian system on all generation levels for consanguineal kinsmen, but deviates only in the first ascending generation with a descriptive term for mother's brother. Terms for the spouses of parents' siblings are distinct from consanguineal terms. In ego's generation relative age and sex are marked for both consanguineal and affinal kinsmen.

It is clear that the interaction and reciprocal relationships between ego and his key relatives are crucial. They provide a sense of balance and security, and they help to insure his survival as well as to provide him with the basic material needs to marry and continue his own lineage.

Material wealth plays a very important role in this general balance in society. It is what maintains solidarity within consanguineal and affinal relationships. Without the payment of wealth for marriage and other social functions, many of the relationships would quickly dissolve. The wealth is what constrains individuals to cooperate with one another.

Appendix
Kinship Terms Marked for Person

1ps	2ps	1plex 3ps	1plinc	1dualinc	1dualex	2dualex 3dual	2pl	3pl
Grandfather (Male Ancestor)								
indimowa	ebimowa	meimowa	emimowa	naimowa	maimowa	geimowa	imowa	rimowa
Grandmother (Female Ancestor)								
indawa	abowa	mawa	emwa	nawa	mawa	egawa	eiwa	eraw
Father								
akeina	mekeb	meka	emka	naka	maka	geka	ika	rika
Mother								
ameina	mosib	mosu	emsu	nasu	masu	gasu	isu	risu
Mother's Brother								
edeina	ebdeina	medeina	emdeina	nadeina	madeina	eigedeina	ideina	rideina
Father's Sister's Husband; Mother's Sister's Husband								
edkeina (first person only differs)								
Father's Brother's Wife; Mother's Brother's Wife								
edmeina (first person only differs)								

(continued)

	1ps	2ps	1plex 3ps	1plinc	1dualinc	1dualex	2dualex 3dual	2pl	3pl
Parent-in-law (ms); Son-in-law	edfina	ebfina	meifina	emfina	nafina	mafina	eigefina	ifina	rifina
Parent-in-law (fs); Daughter-in-law	edgona	obgona	mogona	emgona	nagona	magona	gogona	igona	rigona
Wife	edohona	abhona	mohona	emhona	nahona	mahona	eigehona	ihona	rihona
Husband	edohina	ahwina	mahona	emhina	nahina	mahina	eigehina	ihina	rihina
Same Sex Younger Sibling	edkosa	obkosa	mokosa	emkosa	nakosa	makosa	gokosa	ikosa	rikosa
Same Sex Older Sibling	edkora	obkora	mokora	emkora	nakora	makora	gokora	ikora	rikora
Opposite Sex Younger Sibling	ediesa	ebiesa	meyesa	emiesa	nayesa	mayesa	eigeyesa	eyesa	eriyesa
Opposite Sex Older Sibling	ediera	ebiera	meyera	emiera	nayera	mayera	eigeyera	eyera	eriyera

(continued)

	1ps	2ps	1plex 3ps	1plinc	1dualinc	1dualex	2dualex 3dual	2pl	3pl
Same Sex Sibling-in-law (ms)	edcosa	obcosa	mocosa	emcosa	nacosa	macosa	eigecosa	eicosa	ercosa
Same Sex Sibling-in-law (fs)	edfebesa	ebfebesa	mefebeda	emfebesa	nafebesa	mafebesa	eigefebesa	eifebesa	erfebesa
Opposite Sex Sibling-in-law	eduisa	obuisa	moisa	emuisa	nasa	masa	eguisa	eioysa	yuisa
Child	edesa	ebesa	efesa	emsa	nasa	masa	gesa	isa	risa
Daughter-in-law	ediyba	ebdiyba	mediyba	emdiyba	nadiyba	madiyba	eygediyab	eyadeiba	riyba
Son-in-law	edgona	ebgona	megona	emgona	nagona	magona	eigegona	eigona	ergona
Grandchild	edebesa	ebdebesa	medebesa	emdebesa	nadebesa	madebesa	eigedebesa	eidebesa	erdebesa

References

Gravelle, Gilles. 1985. Meah lexical statistic survey. Universitas Cenderawasih and the Summer Institute of Linguistics. ms.

————. 1990. Orthography testing in Meah. Irian: Bulletin of Irian Jaya 18:125–42.

———— and Gloria Gravelle. 1991. Meah phonology. Workpapers in Indonesian Languages 10. Cenderawasih University and Summer Institute of Linguistics.

Grimes, Barbara F. 1988. Ethnologue. 11th ed. Dallas: Summer Institute of Linguistics.

Kamma, F. C. 1981. Ajaib di Mata Kita. Seri Gereja, Agama dan Kebudayaan Indonesia. Nomor 7. BPK Gunung Mulia.

Miedema, Yelle. 1988. Anthropology, demography and history. A shortage of women, inter-tribal marriage relations and slave trading in the Bird's Head of New Guinea. BIJDRAGEN. pp. 495–509.

Sims, Andrew. 1986. Ketengban kinship. Irian: Bulletin of Irian Jaya 14:15–45.

van Baal, Jan. 1975. Reciprocity and the position of women. Anthropological Papers. Amsterdam: Van Gorum.

Voorhoeve, C. L. 1975. Languages of Irian Jaya: Checklist. Preliminary classification, language maps, wordlists. Pacific Linguistics Series B 31.

Wallis, Alfred Russel. 1869. The Malay Archipelago. London: MacMillan and Company.

Edopi Kinship, Marriage, and Social Structure

Yun Hwa Kim

In 1975 when Voorhoeve published *Languages of Irian Jaya*, the Edopi language[1] (also now known as Dou or Elopi) was not included. It is only within the past decade that the Edopi people, who are traditional hunters and gatherers, have had some contact with outsiders, and the vast majority of Edopi are still monolingual.

The Edopi people, numbering about 750, live in the Western Lakes Plain in Kecamatan (subdistrict) Mulia, Kabupaten (district) Paniai in Irian Jaya, Indonesia.

The word *edopi* is made up of two morphemes *e-* 'we' and *dopi,* the vernacular name for the Tariku river, and means, literally, 'we of the Dopi river'. Until recently they lived along that river, which was formerly known as the Rouffaer river. From the mid-1970s the Edopi have been encouraged by several mission groups to form villages, which was also in line with standard government policy. There are four main villages: Kordesi, Dohu, Iratoi, and Dueita (see figure 1).

---

[1]According to the *Index of Irian Jaya Languages* (Silzer and Heikkinen 1984), Edopi is classified as a Papuan language, Trans-New Guinea Phylum, Northern (Border-Tor-Lake Plain) Subphylum-Level Superstock. Neighboring languages are Tause, Kiri-kiri, and Turu 1. The Iau dialect of Turu is the most closely related language. For a discussion of Edopi phonology see Kim and Kim (1989).

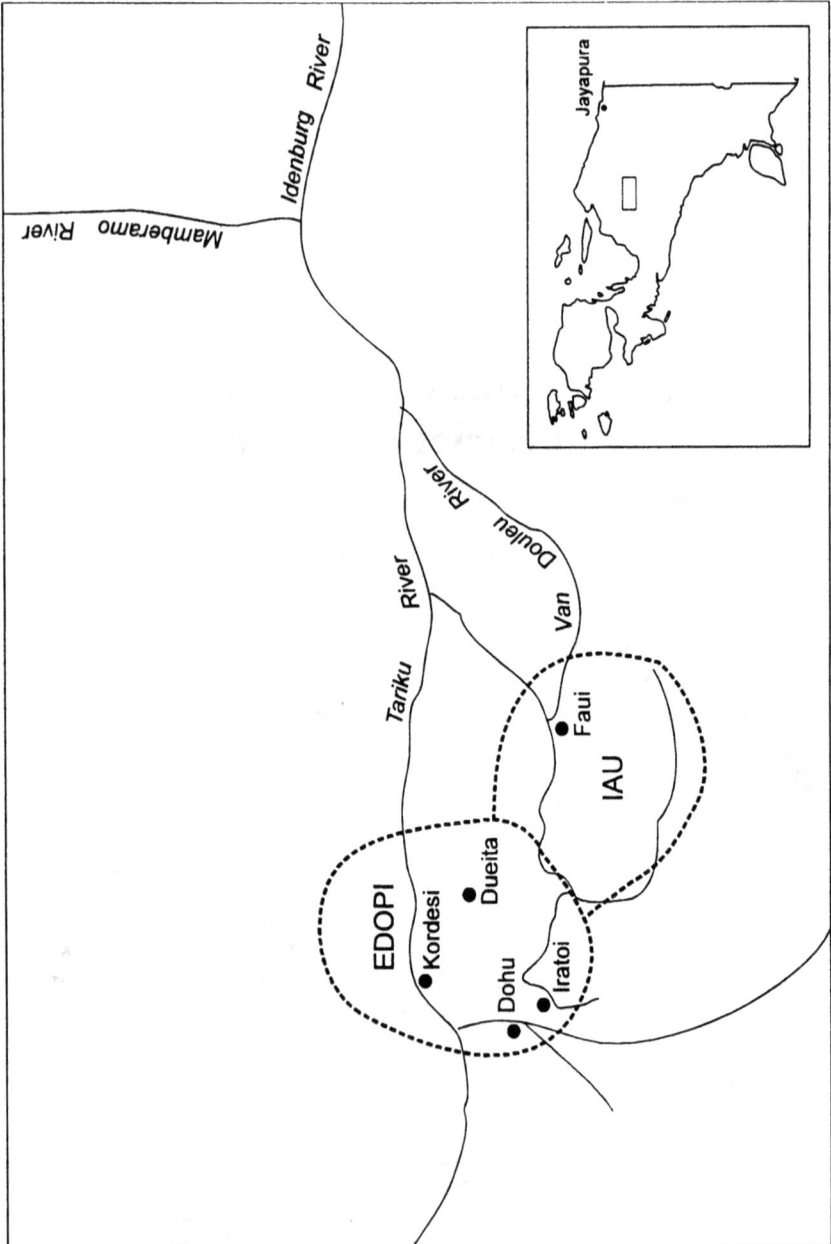

Fig. 1. Villages of the Edopi language group

As mentioned above, the Edopi are hunters and gatherers. Their staples are sago, bananas, and breadfruit. River fish, wild pig, and sago grubs supplement their diet from time to time. Recently the gardening of peanuts, maize, and sweet potatoes was introduced from the outside and, though Edopi in some areas are planting these crops, the terrain near Kordesi is swampy and not very suitable for gardening, so only a few Edopi attempt to do so there.

The paragraphs which follow describe some aspects of Edopi social structure, kinship, and marriage. The data were gathered at the village of Kordesi.[2]

Social Structure

The concept of forming villages is new to the Edopi. Just a little more than a decade ago there were no villages; the Edopi lived in isolated hamlets on the land belonging to their clans. Even now the village is a secondary residence as they shift back and forth between the village and their traditional hamlets. The village of Kordesi, for example, was formed in 1977 when an airstrip was built and Dani evangelists arrived from the highlands to live and work in the area.

The Edopi are divided into two territorial divisions. Within each division, certain clans are closely aligned with certain other clans with whom they unite for common defense and the exchange of women. I call these groups of allied clans *phratries*.

[2]My husband, Eui Jung Kim, and I began our study of the Edopi language in October 1987 under the auspices of the cooperative program of Cenderawasih University and the Summer Institute of Linguistics. Data for this paper included a comprehensive analysis of all kin relationships of people now located in the village of Kordesi. It was written during a six-week workshop held in September and October 1989 led by Drs. Ken and Marilyn Gregerson.

I wish to thank our good friends Hokuahea and his wife Kore, Tobias and his wife Toroku, Taitera, and other Edopi speakers from the village of Kordesi for their willing help. Also I wish to acknowledge the helpful comments by Ken and Marilyn Gregerson and David Brooks as well as the valuable suggestions and encouragement from Janet Bateman and my husband while drafting this paper. Ivor Green (1986) presents a list of Edopi (Dou) kinship terms. Edopi patterns of kin behavior share much in common with the neighboring Iau (Bateman 1983).

Divisions

The whole group in Kordesi is divided into two territorial units: *tee buri* 'upstream people', and *tee be* 'downstream people' (see figure 2). The Usa, the Uri, the Hoiti, the Touda, the Doho, and the Siri comprise the "upstream" group, while the Korobai, the Hoisa, the Tou, the Kariota, the Baisi, the Touborosi, the Sita, and the Toru make up the "downstream" group.

There is no history of war between these two groups; rather, they sometimes united for war against outsiders. However, there has been fighting between some of the smaller groups within each division. There are no cultural or dialectal differences between the two divisions.

The village of Kordesi was formed on land near the border of the two divisions. It is basically organized according to this binary division, that is, the downstream people live on the downstream side of the village and the upstream people live on the upstream side (see figure 3). Actually this idea was suggested by a Dani evangelist who was involved in the founding of Kordesi village, but I believe that the Edopi accepted his suggestion because it fell in line with their own way of thinking. Although five men from the upstream group built their houses in the area occupied by the downstream people, in every case it was because they had married women from the downstream group and had promised to build their houses in the half of the village where their parents-in-law lived. Additional evidence for these divisions is found in their marriage patterns. Also, each of the two groups has their own separate bachelors' house, one upstream and two downstream, as sleeping quarters for boys from the age of about eight until they marry.

Traditionally, there was no concept of a headman among the Edopi, all the adult male members of a clan having equal status. Recently, however, village representatives *(koranu)* have been appointed by the Indonesian government. In Kordesi, four representatives were appointed. However, the *koranu* do not have much real authority in regard to village affairs.

Phratry

An Edopi phratry[3] is an unnamed cluster of clans, consisting of two or three different clans (see figure 4). In the past, when one clan had a problem with another clan from a different phratry, the other clans within its phratry

---

[3]Since both clans and phratries are really also territorial units, I might have used the term "hamlet" for "clan" and "allied hamlets" for "phratry" (Shaw 1974).

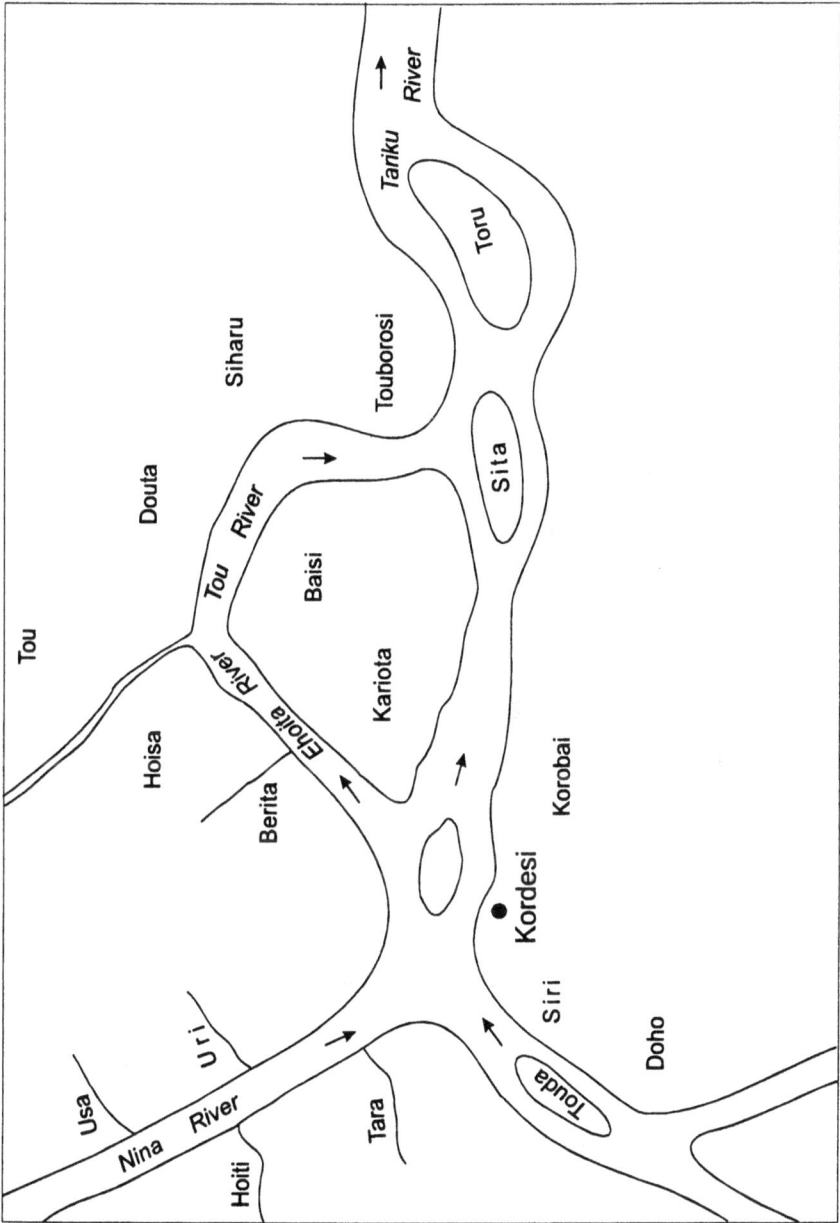

Fig. 2. Kordesi clans

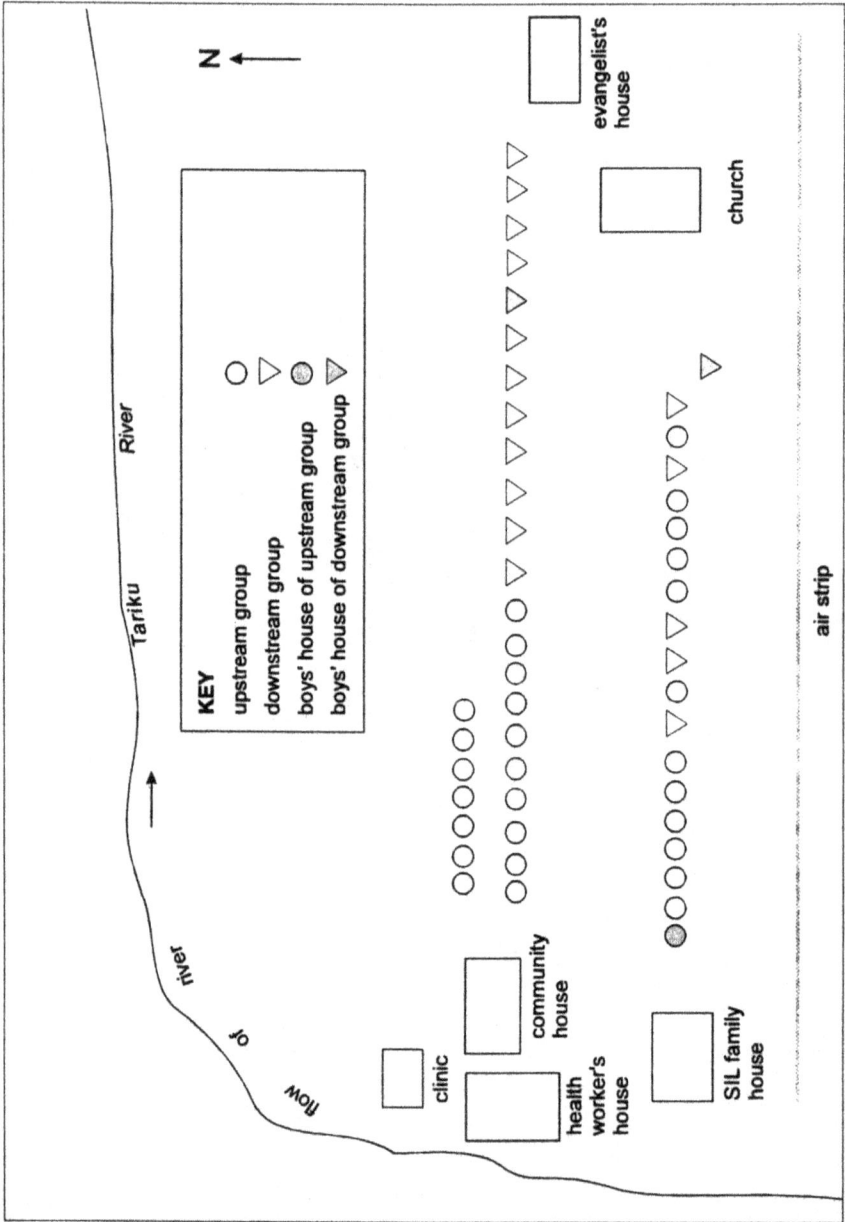

Fig. 3. Residence pattern in Kordesi

would immediately band together against the other phratry. At times, two or more phratries banded together to protect their common interests against any outside group. Most problems arose from disagreements over the marriage of widows (see the section on marriage which follows) and stealing food from other clans' land. For example, when hostilities broke out between the Touda clan and the village of Dohu, the Doho and the Siri banded with the Touda against Dohu. But when an attack came from outside the language group, all the clans banded together against that common enemy.

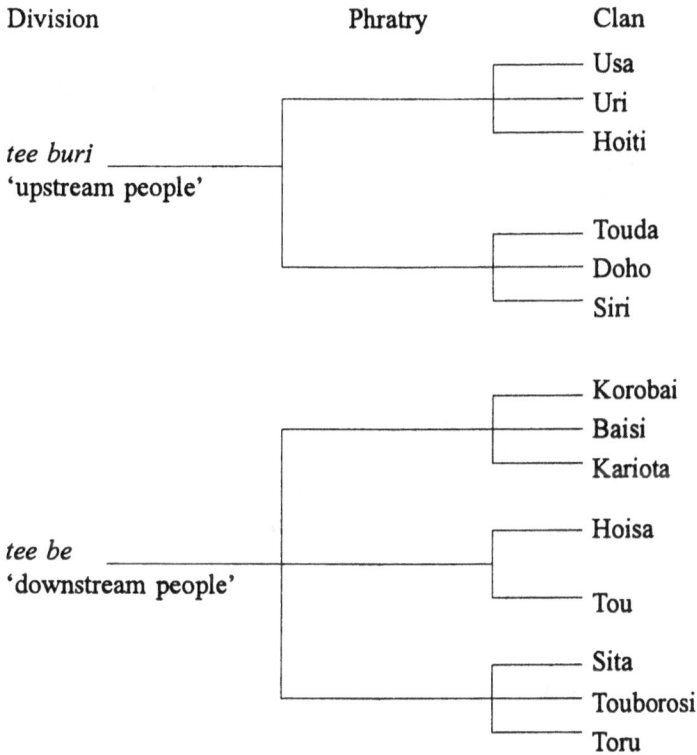

Division	Phratry	Clan
		Usa
		Uri
tee buri		Hoiti
'upstream people'		
		Touda
		Doho
		Siri
		Korobai
		Baisi
		Kariota
		Hoisa
tee be		
'downstream people'		Tou
		Sita
		Touborosi
		Toru

Fig. 4. Kordesi social structure

Clan

The unit I call clan is not exogamous, but is a land-holding unit whose members feel that they have descended from a common patrilineal ancestor. There is no Edopi word for clan, but a person can be identified as belonging to a certain clan by saying *tee hoisa* 'he is a Hoisa man'. Each clan has its own territory for living, gathering food, and hunting. All the men of the clan go hunting together, all the women go fishing together, and they share all the food gathered. Sharing is an important aspect of their life, however, even apart from clan connections. If anybody comes to the door during meal time, the Edopi always share their food with the visitors. Before the village was formed at Kordesi, the Edopi lived in longhouses on their land. Each clan had one longhouse for everybody except bachelors, who had a separate longhouse for sleeping. In the family house, all married women, older girls, and babies slept on one side of the longhouse; husbands and small children slept on the other side. Now, because of the influence of the Dani from the highlands, they have a small house in the village for each family as well as another house on their own land.

The name of the clan comes from the name of the land they control. If a man is adopted by a different clan when he is a baby, his original clan name is changed. There are fourteen clans which have at least one house at the village of Kordesi. There is no strong sense of a lineal principle that binds together individuals who belong to a certain clan. They simply use their rights to the land which is controlled by their clan. A man can go hunting on both his parent's and his wife's parent's land, but he cannot go to another clan's land unless someone from that clan (or who has rights to use that land) accompanies him. The Dauta, Siharu, Berita, and Tara clans have no surviving male clan members, so anyone can go to their traditional lands for sago and hunting because there is no one living who can claim ownership. Land rights are normally inherited from one's father.

Family

A nuclear family lives together in one house. The household usually consists of a husband, one or more wives, and their children. Occasionally, however, members of their extended family, such as a widowed mother or sister, son and his wife, or orphaned female relative may be added to the household. Boys begin to sleep at the men's house when they are around eight years old and continue sleeping there until marriage. Each family has two or more houses, one located in the village and the other on the land belonging to their clan. A family frequently travels on the river by canoe to get food from their land.

Kinship Terms

In this article, Edopi kinship terms are:

> defined by a generative approach which maps the primary and extended ranges of reference of each term over a field of genealogical relationships. The method is that proposed by Merrifield (1983 [a, b]) in which he presents four underlying principles useful to the analysis of kinship systems. They are: Filiation—the relation of parent (P) to child (C); Priority—the notion of temporal priority of alter to ego, elder (e) or younger (y); Affinity—the relation to a spouse (S); and Sex—the sex of alter, ego, or a linking kinsman, male (m) or female (f). Using these four principles and associated symbols, primary referential meanings can be defined by a 'PC string' for each kinship term. For example, the 'PC string' ePCm symbolizes parent's elder male child—elder brother.

> The extended range of a kinship term is generated from its primary range by the application of extension rules. Two extension rules are needed to generate the extended ranges of... [Edopi] kinship terms. The generational extension rule (G) extends reference collaterally to other kinsmen of the same generation.

> The second extension rule required for...[Edopi] is Merrifield's Extension Rule 1, which defines unlimited bidirectional extension, both lineal and collateral. This rule applies to the...[Edopi] grandkinsman terms. (Bateman 1983:196)

For more complete discussion of this system, interpretation of its symbolism, and further examples of its use, see Merrifield (1983a; 1983b).

Filial Kinship Terms

Edopi consanguineal terms are shown in figure 5 and can be divided into the following four categories: (1) grandkinsmen, (2) parent and child terms, (3) siblings, and (4) cross-cousin terms.

Grandkinsmen. All kinsmen more than one generation distant from ego are classified together under the single, reciprocal term *ai* 'grandkinsman'. Its primary referent is one's parent's parent or child's child irrespective of sex. As stated, it extends without limit to any known collateral or lineal kinsman beyond one generation of distance from ego (Rule 1).

Term	Primary Referent	Rough English Equivalent
1. *ai*	PP(1), CC(1)	grandkinsman
2. *awa*	Pm(G)	father
3. *ja*	Pf(G)	mother
4. *soi*	PfPCm(G)	mother's brother
5. *sao*	C(G)	child
6. *boi*	ePC(G)	elder sibling
7. *ida*	yPC(G)	younger sibling
8. *oita*	mPCf(G)	man's sister
9. *huru*	fPCm(G)	woman's brother
10. *urarei*	xPC(G)	cross-cousin

Fig. 5. Edopi filial kinship terms of reference

Parent and Child Terms. There are three terms for kinsmen of the first ascending generation in Edopi: *awa* 'father', *ja* 'mother', and *soi* 'mother's brother' (see figure 6). The term *awa* 'father' has the male parent as its primary referent, but it extends to all of father's kinsmen of his generation, irrespective of sex (Pm(G)). A father's brother is categorized with father, and father's sister is also called by the same term *awa*. The term *ja* 'mother' has the female parent as its primary referent, but it extends to any of her female or male kinsmen of her generation (Pf(G)). Parallel to father and his siblings, mother's sister and brother are called by the same term *ja* 'mother'. The term *soi* 'mother's brother' is an alternate term, but denotes only mother's male siblings, never her female siblings.

The term *sao* 'child' is the reciprocal to the three parent generation terms. Its primary referent is ego's child, irrespective of sex, and it extends to the child of any kinsman of ego's generation.

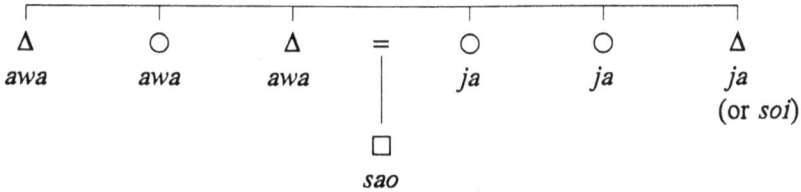

Fig. 6. Parent and child dyads

Siblings. In distinguishing the kinsmen of ego's generation, Edopi terminology follows the the Iroquois pattern of cousin terminology (Schusky 1972:21), equating parallel cousins with siblings but distinguishing cross-cousins. In sibling terms we find two sets of reciprocal terms, one determined by seniority and the second by sex.

The terms indicating seniority, *boi* 'elder sibling' and *ida* 'younger sibling', are defined respectively as ePC(G) and yPC(G). Their primary referents include any sibling of either sex who shares at least one parent with ego. As terms of reference they can be extended to any kinsmen of ego's generation (rule G), though cross-cousins are ordinarily referenced by a different term. In direct address, however, these two relative age terms are used only when ego addresses same sex siblings; when addressing opposite sex siblings, the opposite sex terms are used.

The relative seniority of alter and ego is indicated by using *boi* to designate a sibling born before ego, and *ida* to designate a sibling born after ego. In their extended usage, it is not the temporal birth order of ego and alter that is indicated by *boi* and *ida* but rather the order of birth of the original set of siblings in the genealogical chain that links ego to alter.

Figure 7 is based on data taken from a specific Edopi genealogy. It shows
the relationship between temporal seniority and conceptual seniority. The
numbers represent the actual order of birth.

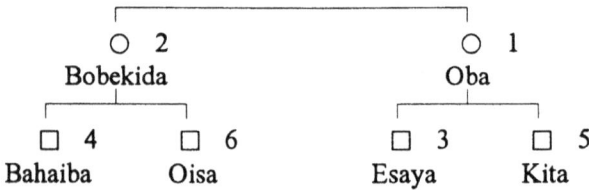

Fig. 7. Determining seniority

Thus, Bahaiba is *boi* 'elder sibling' to Oisa because he was born prior to
Oisa. But Bahaiba is *ida* 'younger sibling' to Esaya and also to Kita even
though Bahaiba was born prior to Kita, because Kita's mother, Oba, is *boi*
'elder sibling' to Bobekida, Bahaiba's mother. Thus, the choice of terms is
based on the relative age of ego's and alter's linking kinsmen.

The two terms which are used between siblings of the opposite sex are
used both for reference and in address. *oita* is a man's term for his sister and
huru is a woman's term for her brother. When seniority between siblings of
the opposite sex is in focus, the terms *boi* and *ida* are used for reference but
not in direct address. Instead, *huru* and *oita* are used in direct address
between siblings of the opposite sex.

Cross-cousin Terms. The term *urarei* 'cross-cousin' is reciprocal (see figure 8). It denotes a mother's brother's child or a father's sister's child, is
defined as xPC(G), and extends throughout ego's generation. The children of
ego's parent's same sex siblings (i.e., ego's parallel cousins) are classified
with his siblings.

O+   △+   △ = O   O−   △+

△   O   △+ △− O   △+ ▲ △− O   △+ △− O   △   O
4   4   1   1   3   1 EGO 2   3   2   2   3   4   4

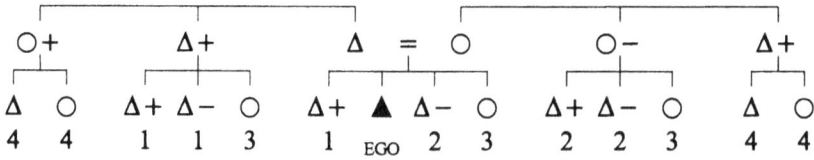

1. *boi*   2. *ida*   3. *oita*   4. *urarei*
+ and − symbols indicate greater or lesser chronological age

Fig. 8. Parallel cousin and cross-cousin

Affinal Kinship Terms

In Edopi, only five terms are used exclusively for affines, as shown in figure 9.

Term	Primary Referent	Rough English Equivalent
11. *teesi-awa*	SfP(G)	wife's parent
12. *sai*	SfPCm(G), PCfS(G)	man's brother-in-law
13. *tee-sao*	CfS(G)	daughter's husband
14. *tee*	Sm	husband
15. *si*	Sf	wife

Fig. 9. Edopi affinal terms of reference

Parent-in-law and Child-in-law. The term *teesi-awa* (lit. 'wife's father') is used both in address and as a term of reference for one's wife's parents. The reciprocal of *teesi-awa* is *tee-sao* 'the husband of my child'. A woman calls her parents-in-law *awa* 'father' and *ja* 'mother' and they call her *sao* 'child'.

Man's Brother-in-law. The term *sai* 'man's brother-in-law' is used reciprocally between male ego and his wife's brother. Thus, *sai* denotes either wife's brother or male ego's sister's husband.

Spouse. The term *tee* 'man' also denotes 'husband' while *si* 'woman' also denotes 'wife'.

The affinal kinship terms presented above are used after marriage, but they do not necessarily preclude use of the filial terms used prior to marriage. For example, if a man called his wife *oita* 'sister' before marriage, he may still call her *oita* even after marriage.

Other Affinal Terms. All other affinal kinsmen are referred to by the filial terms used prior to marriage. Figure 10 presents a specific example from an Edopi genealogy.

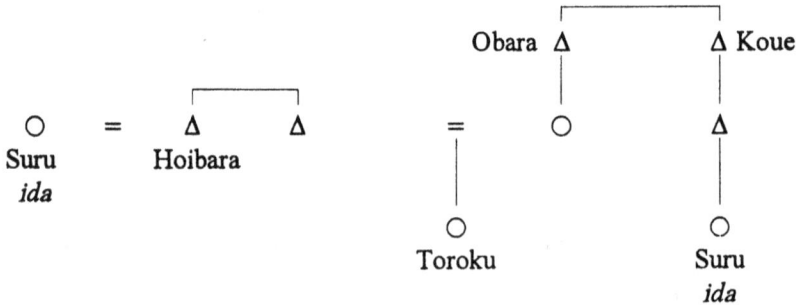

Fig. 10. Filial terms vs. affinal terms

Thus, Toroku calls Suru *ida* 'younger sibling' because Toroku's grandfather, Obara, was born prior to Koue who was Suru's grandfather. Later, however, when Suru married Hoibara, who is Toroku's father's brother, she still continues to use the same term of reference as she did before, that is, she still calls Suru *ida* 'younger sibling'.

Since the Edopi people are patrilineal, that perspective can be seen in the choice of kinship terms when two people are related in more than one way. Figure 11 presents such a case.

In figure 11, Tobias has two grandfathers *(ai)*, Bore and Bue, who each married one of his cross-cousins *(urarei)*, Ta and Hasa, his father's sister's daughters. He calls Kirikau (who is a daughter of Bore) *ja* 'mother', but he calls Oba (a daughter of Bue) *sao* 'child'. Because Bore is Tobias' maternal grandfather's brother, Bore is in his mother's kin group. Thus Bore is regarded as his grandfather. But Bue is Tobias' maternal grandmother's brother, so Bue is not in his mother's kin group. Therefore, his kin relationship with Oba is reckoned from Oba's mother, Hasa, who is his cross-cousin.

There are two varieties of marriage in Edopi culture. One involves a type of woman exchange while the other does not.

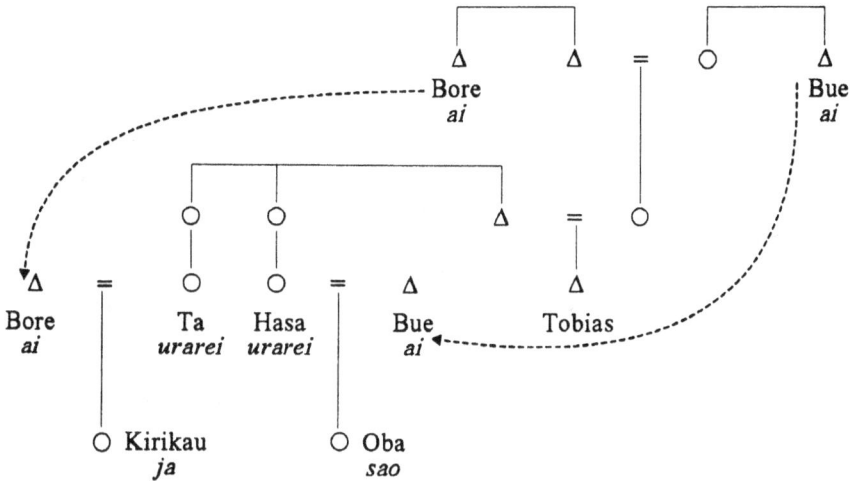

Fig. 11. Patrilineal vs. matrilineal relationship

Edopi Marriages

Woman-Exchange Marriage

To obtain a wife, a man may exchange anyone he calls sister *(oita)*, his own daughter *(sao)*, or one of his siblings' daughters (also *sao*), or sometimes even one of his cross-cousins *(urarei)*. Figure 12 shows two cases in which men exchanged kinswomen for wives. In the first case Hoira exchanged his own daughter, Hori, for Heya's sister, Aihi. As shown in the second example, Aurahere exchanged his sister, Tepu, for Hua's cross-cousin, Horu.

Nonexchange Marriage

If a girl's father sees a young man who he thinks would make a good son-in-law, he keeps him in mind as a prospective husband for his daughter. When his daughter becomes old enough to marry, he gives her to that man. If the man has no woman to exchange, he will be grateful for such an offer.

Nowadays, it is also possible for a man to approach a girl directly and ask her to marry him.

Age of Marriage

When a girl begins menstruation, she is regarded as old enough to marry. If a man wants to marry a girl who has not yet had her first menses, her mother would object that she is still too young to be married. Before a man can marry, on the other hand, he must be successful and skillful at hunting wild pigs, crocodiles, cassowaries, and birds, as well as be a good provider of sago and sago grubs. If he has proven to be capable in both these areas, it is agreed that he is old enough to have a wife.

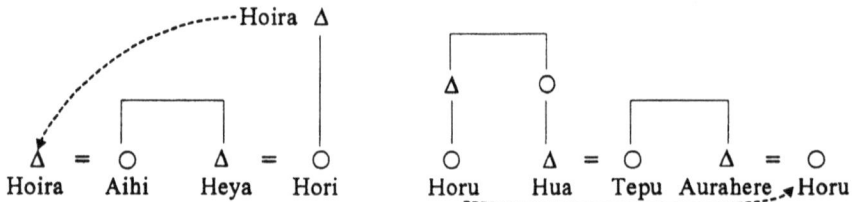

Fig. 12. Two examples of woman exchange marriage

Choosing a Wife

The Edopi say it is good to choose a woman from a clan whose territory is close to one's own (see table 1). Considering the fifty-nine marriages in Kordesi, in forty-eight marriages (about 82 percent) both spouses were from the same division (either upstream or downstream), while in only eleven marriages (about 18 percent) are the spouses from outside the division. Of the forty-eight intradivisional marriages, twelve involve spouses from the same clan.

WIFE'S CLAN

HUSBAND'S CLAN	UPSTREAM						DOWNSTREAM								OLG
	USA	URI	HT	TD	DH	SR	KOR	HS	TOU	BS	KRT	ST	TBS	TR	
U USA	–	1	2	1	–	1	–	1	–	1	–	–	–	1	–
P URI	3	1	1	–	2	1	–	–	–	–	–	–	–	–	–
S HT	–	1	–	–	–	1	–	–	–	–	–	–	–	–	–
T TD	–	–	–	4	–	2	–	1	–	–	–	–	–	–	1
R E DH	–	–	–	2	1	–	–	–	–	–	–	–	–	–	–
A M SR	–	–	–	3	–	4	–	–	1	–	–	–	–	–	–
D KOR	–	–	–	–	–	–	–	–	–	–	–	1	–	–	–
O HS	–	–	–	–	–	1	1	–	1	1	–	–	–	2	–
W N TOU	–	–	–	–	–	–	–	1	2	–	–	–	–	–	–
S BS	–	1	–	–	–	–	–	–	–	–	–	–	–	–	–
T R KRT	–	–	–	–	–	–	–	–	2	–	–	–	–	–	–
E ST	–	–	–	–	–	2	1	–	–	–	1	–	1	–	–
A TBS	–	–	–	–	–	1	–	1	–	–	1	–	–	1	–
M TR	–	–	–	–	–	–	–	–	–	–	–	–	–	–	–

USA	Usa	KOR	Korbai	TBS	Touborosi
URI	Uri	HS	Hoisa	TR	Toru
HT	Hoiti	TOU	Tou	OLG	Outside language
TD	Touda	BS	Baisi		group
DH	Doho	KRT	Kariota		
SR	Siri	ST	Sita		

Table 1. Edopi marriages patterns

The Edopi say that a man should avoid choosing a sister as his wife, though in Edopi all females in male ego's generation are called *oita* 'sister'. However, when referring to someone whom ego can marry, they mean that there is no traceable patrilineal connection. In figure 13, for example, Si and Esay are a married couple from the same clan and are also second cousins whose maternal grandfathers were brothers. However, in tracing their patrilineal connections they shared no known common ancestor; hence there was no reason why they could not marry.

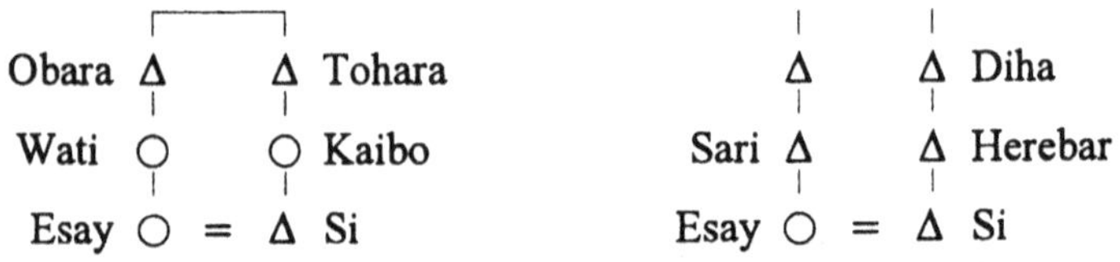

```
Obara Δ    Δ Tohara          Δ    Δ Diha
      |    |                  |    |
Wati  ○    ○ Kaibo      Sari Δ    Δ Herebar
      |    |                  |    |
Esay  ○ = Δ Si          Esay ○ = Δ Si
```

Fig. 13. Patrilineal concept in Edopi marriages

Bride Price

Traditionally, there was no bride price since the exchange of women was the only compensation deemed necessary. However, a man has always been expected to work for his father-in-law and to bring him game and sago. A parent-in-law has these expectations regardless of whether the marriage is an exchange or a nonexchange marriage. Recently the notion of bride price has been introduced to the Edopi by the Dani from the highlands. As the Edopi have instituted it, however, the bride's parents do not demand a fixed bride price. Rather, the man simply offers gifts to his parents-in-law to whatever extent he is able. Items such as cooking pots, kitchen knives, plates, machetes, fishing nets, clothes, and money are, of course, highly valued by prospective parents-in-law.

Residence Patterns

When a man chooses a wife from his own clan, the couple continues to live in the area controlled by the clan. However, if the wife is not from his clan, because of the heavy responsibilities of the husband to his wife's parents, the new couple typically moves back and forth between the husband's land and the wife's land, that is, they practice bilocal residence.

Polygyny

Taking more than one wife is widely practiced among the Edopi. People say if a man is so successful at hunting that he is able to kill many wild pigs, then he can have two wives.

The Levirate. If a man dies, one of his married brothers, either older or younger, may marry the widow. A brother who is still a bachelor cannot take his brother's widow.

Mother and Daughter as Wives. It is quite common in Edopi society for a mother and daughter to share the same husband. In all cases, it involves the second or third marriage of the mother. The typical scenario is that a man marries a widow who has a daughter, whom he treats as his stepchild. Later, however, when the daughter becomes old enough to marry, the stepfather may take her as his second wife.

Sororal Polygyny. It is a common practice among the Edopi people for a man to marry women who are sisters. If a father-in-law is happy with his son-in-law because he often brings him game, sago, and sago grubs, and works hard for him, then he may give his son-in-law another daughter. The Edopi say that in polygynous marriages, if a mother and daughter or two sisters share the same husband, there is less conflict between the two wives as opposed to other polygynous marriages in which the wives have no close blood relationship to each other. To get more of a longitudinal perspective on the incidence of polygyny among the Edopi, I have compared thirty-six marriages recorded in one of the genealogies I collected, with the data concerning the forty-eight marriages involving people now living in Kordesi. Based on these data, I see a changing ratio of polygynous to monogamous marriages. As shown in table 2, of the thirty-six marriages recorded in the genealogy, fifteen (around 42 percent) men had more than one wife. This number contrasts with the data from current marriages in Kordesi as presented in table 3, in which only ten out of forty-eight (about 21 percent) marriages are polygynous.

Status		Number
One wife		21
Two wives		15
sisters	5	
mother and daughter	4	
levirate	1	
others	5	
	Total	36

Table 2. Marriages from one genealogy
(collected at Kordesi)

Status		Number
One wife		38
Two wives		10
sisters	2	
mother and daughter	2	
levirate	2	
others	4	
	Total	48

Table 3. Present marriages in Kordesi

In the above samples there was an overlap of thirteen marriages which were included both in the marriages from the genealogy as well as in the current marriages in Kordesi. The trend toward monogamous marriage is highlighted further if only the nonoverlapping marriages are considered. Of the thirteen marriages which overlap, ten were monogamous and three were polygynous. These data mean that about 52 percent (twelve of twenty-three) of the nonoverlapping marriages in the genealogy involved polygyny, compared to only 20 percent (seven of thirty-five) of the "new" (nonoverlapping) marriages presently in Kordesi.

Division of Labor between Husband and Wife

Hunting, house building, cutting trees, and making canoes are men's jobs, while fishing, making fishing nets and string bags, and most gathering activities are women's jobs. When they travel by dugout canoe, women pole the canoe in the front, while men paddle the canoe at the back. The husband cuts a sago tree and pounds the sago to get the pulp out, then the woman processes the sago pulp. In Edopi metaphorical speech, the bow and arrow are symbolic of men, while a fishing net inevitably refers to women.

Marriage of Widows

The marriage of widows often causes fighting among the clans. This conflict is because the ideal is for a widow to stay single for the rest of her life as a sign of grief for the loss of her husband. However, if she wants to remarry she is supposed to wait for several years after her husband dies. If she marries too soon, her deceased husband's clan will take out their anger on her and her new husband. Nevertheless, remarriage is very common, as shown in table 4.

Status	Number
First marriage (Husband still living)	26
First marriage (Husband deceased, no remarriage)	2
Second marriage	23
Third marriage	4
Total	55

Table 4. Marital status of the women in Kordesi

Of the fifty-five women in Kordesi who have been married at least once, two have been divorced and twenty-seven have been widowed. Of the widows, only two have remained single and twenty-five have remarried at least once.

Summary

Membership in patrilineal land-based clans is a key element of Edopi social structure. Clans in turn are grouped together in phratries for mutual defense. Among the Edopi who operate out of the relatively new village of Kordesi, a binary division is recognized both in the village and in the territory where the clans' lands are located. These two groups, as well as the phratries within the groups, tend towards endogamy.

The Edopi practice polygyny, including levirate marriages, sororal polygyny, and marriages where co-wives are mother and daughter. Exchange of kinswomen (usually called "sister exchange") is the preferred method of obtaining a wife. Traditionally there was no bride price, but recently the custom of bride price was introduced by the Dani.

References

Bateman, Janet. 1983. Iau kinship and marriage. In William R. Merrifield, Marilyn Gregerson, and Daniel C. Ajamiseba (eds.), Gods, heroes, kinsmen: Ethnographic studies from Irian Jaya, Indonesia, 191–220. International Museum of Cultures Publication 17. Dallas: Cenderawasih University and The International Museum of Cultures.

Green, Ivor. 1986. Dou kinship terms. Irian: Bulletin of Irian Jaya 14:67–76.

Kim, Eui-Jung. 1988. Elopi names. Irian: Bulletin of Irian Jaya 16:114–132.

——— and Yun-Hwa Kim. 1989. Edopi phonology. ms.

Merrifield, William R. 1983a. On the formal analysis of kinship terminologies. In Frederick B. Agard, Gerald Kelly, Adam Makkai, and Valerie Becker Makkai (eds.), Essays in honor of Charles F. Hockett, 371–404. Leiden: E. J. Brill.

———. 1983b. Comments on kinship notation. In William R. Merrifield, Marilyn Gregerson, and Daniel C. Ajamiseba (eds.), Gods, heroes, kinsmen: Ethnographic studies from Irian Jaya, Indonesia, 177–88. International Museum of Cultures Publication 17. Dallas: Cenderawasih University and The International Museum of Cultures.

Schusky, Ernest L. 1972. Manual for kinship analysis. 2nd ed. New York: Holt, Rinehart and Winston.

Shaw, R. Daniel, ed. 1974. Kinship studies in Papua New Guinea. Ukarumpa, Papua New Guinea: Summer Institute of Linguistics.

Silzer, Peter and Heljä Heikkinen. 1984. Index of Irian Jaya languages. Irian: Bulletin of Irian Jaya 12.

Voorhoeve, C. L. 1975. Languages of Irian Jaya: Checklist. Preliminary classification, language maps, wordlists. Pacific Linguistics Series B 31.

Irarutu Kinship and Marriage

Michiko Matsumura

As with perhaps all people in Irian Jaya, kinship is very important to the Irarutu. Though the kin groups that I call clans do not function in many of the ways that clans do in other parts of Irian Jaya, they are part of each person's identity. The village is another important unit in the life of the individual. To people from another area, the individual also identifies himself by his village complex. Of particular interest in regard to kinship behavior is the special relationship between mother's brother and sister's oldest child. Several special ceremonies involving this dyad dramatize the significance of the relationship.[1]

The Irarutu

Irarutu is an Austronesian language spoken in an area north of Arguni Bay in Irian Jaya (see figure 1). Approximately 5,000 Irarutu people live in forty-four villages with some in the interior but the majority located along

[1]Information for this paper was collected in Tugarni village complex, which includes five Protestant villages, mostly during 1987 and 1989. This paper was written during an anthropology workshop led by Drs. Ken and Marilyn Gregerson in September and October of 1989. I appreciate their great help in making valuable suggestions and comments. I also wish to thank many Irarutu people who have helped me to collect information, especially Moses Syakema, Heret Werfete, and Aminadap Werfete.

221

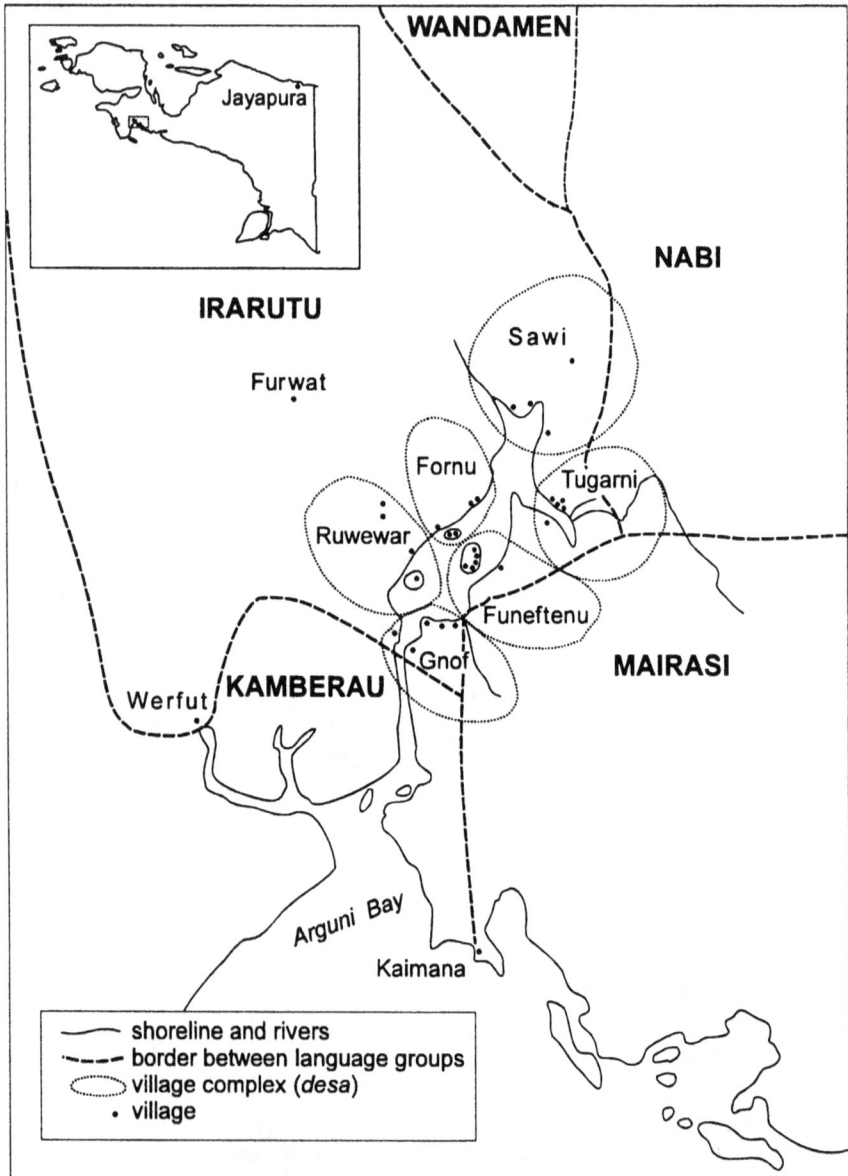

Fig. 1. Map of Irarutu villages in Arguni Bay

the coast. Food staples are sago, cassava, taro, and bananas. Leafy vegetables, papaya, lemon, pomelo, pineapple, coconut and various kinds of fish also provide a varied diet in the coastal area. For meat, the men occasionally hunt wild pigs or deer. Nutmeg and eucalyptus oil are harvested and sold as cash crops.

The traditional religion was animism, but earlier in this century the southern Irarutu villages became Islamic. Then around forty years ago a Christian evangelist came from Maluku to the Irarutu area. Following this contact, villages in the northern Arguni bay area became Protestant. In the far northern inland area there are some Roman Catholic villages.

Social Organization: Village and Clan

There are six groups of villages along the coast. Each group of villages I call a village complex. Irarutu people often use the names of these village complexes. Currently these names are recognized as names of *desa*, an Indonesian term which the government uses for a group of villages. The village complex names come from geographic features of the area, such as rivers, mountains, or islands. If asked who he is, an Irarutu would answer in reference to his village complex, saying for example, "I am a Tugarni man." (Tugarni was originally a name of the river, but is now used for the village complex.)

Each village complex includes four or five villages (see figure 2). Furthermore, in the Tugarni village complex, for example, each village has from two to four patriclans, as shown in table 1. The patriclans are not land holding groups nor are they exogamous, but all clan members consider that they have descended from a common ancestor and that their clan originated in a specific geographic area. Children customarily become part of their father's clan. However, exceptions are made in cases where the mother does not have any brothers to carry on the family name. In such cases the mother's family name is given to one of the sons. A woman keeps her father's family name even after her marriage.

Rights to land are passed from father to son. If there are two or more sons whose parents are still living, the oldest son, at marriage, looks for his own land on which to build a house for his new family. Subsequently, all but the youngest follow suit; only the last son remains with his parents after he has married. If, on the other hand, one of the parents has already died before the oldest son is married, he will continue to live in his parent's house after his marriage. The younger sons then seek their own land when they get married.

Village complex *(desa)*		Villages included	
Irarutu name	Indonesian name	Irarutu name	Indonesian name
Tugarni	Tugarni	Awaf	Afu-afu
		Busmafnu	Gusimawa
		Baid	Bayeda
		Mujan	Moyana
		Kakuruba	Kokoroba
Sawi	Sawi	Burgnurba	Burgerba
		Tifar	Tiwara
		Weswas	Weswasa
		Ergar	Eregara
Fornu	Furnusu	Wagit	Wangita
		Funia	Funiara
		Susunu	Susunu
		Sawatwer	Sawatawera
		Jafer	Jawera
Ruwewar	Ruwara	Wermnu	Warmenu
		Muger	Mangera
		Mudif	Mandiwa
		Jab	Jaba
Gnof	Genofa	Nagur	Nagura
		Seraruni	Seraran
		Ukiar	Ukiara
		Maisunu	Waromi
		Uris	Urisa
Funeften	Feternu	Gusu	Gusi
		Mufu	Mafuwa
		War	Waruwa
		Tugmaf	Tugumawa
		Abirwar	Ambirwara

Fig. 2. Irarutu villages in the Arguni

| | Village | | | | | |
Clan	Afu-afu	Gusimawa	Bayeda	Moyana	Kokoroba	Total
Syakema	16	0	0	0	0	16
Wayara	1	0	0	0	0	1
Sasefa	0	1	5	1	3	10
Refideso	0	14	0	0	1	15
Werfete	0	2	4	1	11	18
Bari	0	1	1	8	7	17
Nega	0	0	8	0	0	8
Total	17	18	18	10	22	85

Table 1. Household heads by clan in the Tugarni village complex

If land is not available near their parents' house, they look elsewhere in the village. Should one of the sons desire to build his house in a different village, he must get permission from the headmen of both villages.

Rights to use garden land are passed from father to oldest son. Other children may ask the oldest son to share the crops which their father planted.

Individuals may choose where they will plant their sago. If someone needs help to clear a new field, the headman of his village may enlist other village members to help him. Occasionally, all villagers work together to clear a big new field, after which each man takes one part of the area to plant his own sago. Clans do not control land used for sago groves.

Irarutu Kinship Terms

The Irarutu kinship system uses a combination of Iroquois and Hawaiian terminologies. In the first ascending generation, parallel and cross-kinsmen are distinguished in a bifurcate merging pattern, an Iroquois characteristic. In other generations kinship terms extend bilaterally distinguishing neither lineal kinsmen from collateral nor cross-kinsmen from parallel. In this sense the system is Hawaiian.

In this paper, Irarutu kinship terms are defined by a generative approach which maps the primary and extended ranges of reference of each term over a field of genealogical relationships. The method here is that proposed by Merrifield (1983a, b) in which he presents four underlying principles useful to the analysis of kinship systems. They are: Filiation—the relation of parent

(P) to child (C); Priority—the notion of temporal priority of alter to ego, elder (e) or younger (y); Affinity—the relation to a spouse (S); and Sex—the sex of alter, ego, or linking kinsman, male (m) or female (f). Using these four principles and associated symbols, primary referential meanings can be defined by a 'PC string' for each kinship term. For example, the 'PC string' ePCm symbolizes parent's elder male child—elder brother.

The extended range of a kinship term is generated from its primary range by the application of extension rules (Bateman 1983:196).

For further discussion of the symbolism, how it is used, and other examples of the use of this system, see Merrifield (1983a, b).

Three extension rules are needed to generate the extended ranges of Irarutu kinship terms:

1. The generational extension rule (G) extends reference collaterally to other kinsmen of the same generation.

2. The reciprocal extension rule (R) extends reference reciprocally. For example, the great-grandparent term is used for great-grandchild.

3. The affinal extension rule (S) extends reference to the affinal kinsmen. Affinal extensions may be designated by S- to indicate extension to the corresponding kinsman of a spouse, by -S to indicate extension to the spouse of a kinsman, or by S to imply both S- and -S.

When a kinship term itself does not determine sex or seniority, these distinctions can be made by the use of words which are not primarily kin terms. The term *sot* 'female' or the term *mran* 'male' is added to determine sex, while another set of terms is used to determine seniority: *bidi* 'elder' [lit. 'big'] and *kokon* 'younger' [lit. 'small'].

Since there is widely extended use of all consanguineal kinship terms, the term *jari* 'real' [lit. 'I own'] is added to any of these terms to denote unambiguously ego's consanguineal kinsman. On the other hand, *frfar* 'to rear' is added to indicate a stepkinsman.

Consanguineal Kinship Terms

Irarutu consanguineal kinship terms are shown in figures 3 and 4. These terms are presented in the first-person-singular possessive forms since they are inalienably possessed in Irarutu, as shown in the following set:

	atagfad	'my same sex elder sibling'	
	otabad	'your same sex elder sibling'	
	itafad	'his same sex elder sibling'	

	Term	Primary Referent	Rough English Equivalent
Grandkinsman terms	1. *aniyob*	PPPP, CCCC (R, G, S)	great-great-grandkinsman
	2. *awanus*	PPP, CCC (R, G, S)	great-grandkinsman
	3. *adat*	PP (G, S)	grandparent
	4. *agtat*	CC (G, S)	grandchild
Parent and child terms	5. *adie*	= Pm (G, -S)	father
	6. *aden*	= Pf (G, -S)	mother
	7. *amim*	xPm (G, -S)	uncle
	8. *afuf*	xPf (G, -S)	aunt
	9. *amo*	C (G, S-)	child
Sibling terms	10. *atagfad*	eaPCa (G, S-S)	same sex elder sibling
	11. *agfut*	yaPCa (G, S-S)	same sex younger sibling
	12. *aruig*	aPCb (G, S-S)	opposite sex sibling

Fig. 3. Irarutu consanguineal terms of reference

Grandkinsman Terms. There are four grandkinsman terms. Two of them, *awanus* and *aniyob,* are reciprocal (rule R) terms which denote either a senior grandkinsman or junior grandkinsman of the third or fourth generation, respectively, from ego. For example, *awanus* refers to both great-grandparent and great-grandchild. Another term *adat* is used for grandparent. However, this term is not reciprocal, *agtat* being used for grandchild. Each of these terms extends to all collateral kinsmen of their respective generations (by generation extension rule G) and to corresponding affinals (by affinal extension rule S), that is, to the spouses of grandkinsmen and to the grandkinsmen of spouse.

Parent and Child Terms. Four terms classify kinsmen of the first ascending generation: *adie* 'father', *aden* 'mother', *amim* 'uncle' (e.g., 'mother's brother'), and *afuf* 'aunt' (e.g., 'father's sister').

These terms further distinguish bifurcate categories, the first two terms referring to parallel kinsmen, and the other two to cross-kinsmen. Parallel and cross categories are defined, as in Seneca (Lounsbury 1964), by the sex of the

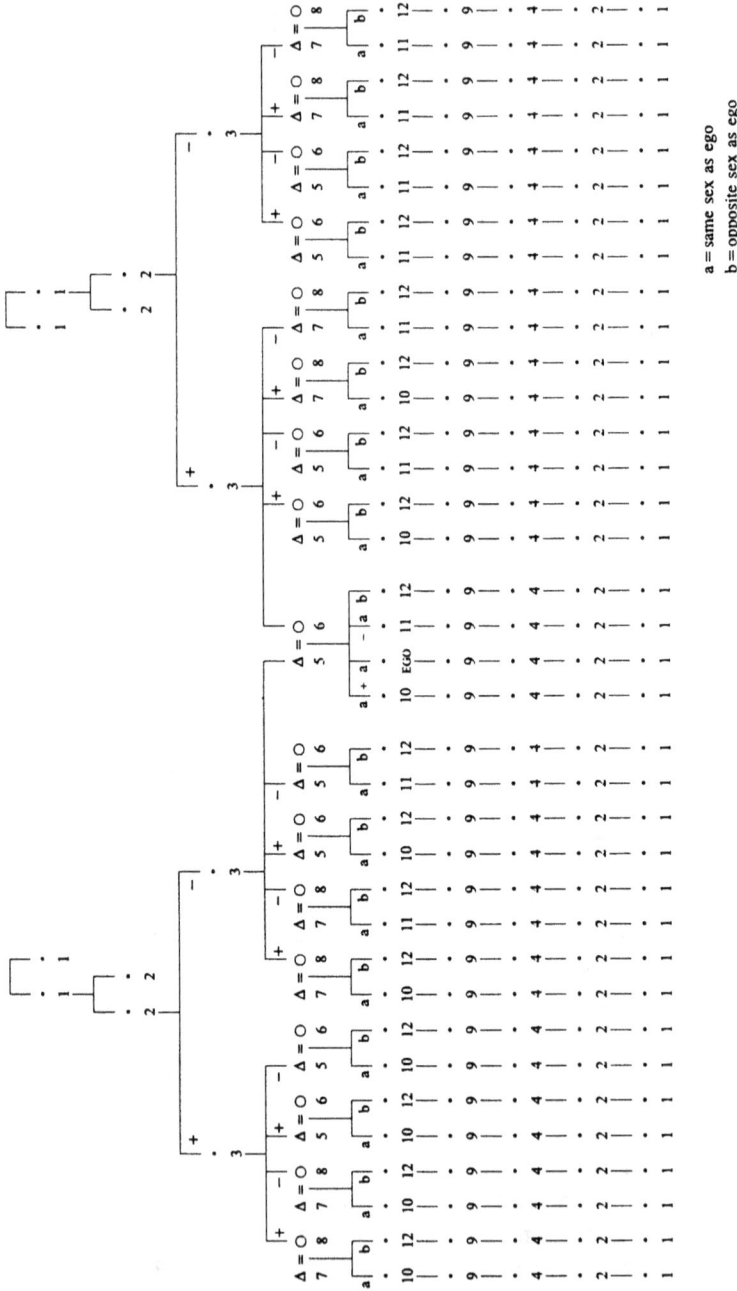

a = same sex as ego
b = opposite sex as ego

Fig. 4. Irarutu consanguineal kinship chart

relevant kinsmen of the first ascending generation. Within the genealogical chain that links ego to alter, if the sex of the two kinsmen of the first ascending generation is the same, they are parallel kinsmen; if their sex is different, they are cross-kinsmen. The sex of kinsmen of other generations is irrelevant for determining bifurcate categories.

All four terms extend to all collateral kinsmen of the parent generation (rule G). In order to specify the seniority of the collateral kinsman, *bidi* 'elder' or *kokon* 'younger' is often added.

Seniority is defined by the relative age of the pair of siblings who are the lineal kinsmen linking alter and ego, that is, the children of ego's and alter's nearest common ancestor. Any kinsmen descended from elder siblings of ego's lineal kinsman are called elder kinsman (see figure 5). Some who are referred to as elder are actually younger than ego.

Figure 5 illustrates how the system works. The double digit numbers represent actual ages. Thus, since A is older than B (ego's grandfather), E, who is thirty years of age, is called 'elder aunt' by ego, who is thirty-two. Also, since D is younger than C, her son G is called 'younger father' even though G is older than ego's real father.

The four parental terms extend to affinal kinsmen as well (rule -S). The term for mother *(aden)*, for instance, is extended to father's other wife and father's brother's wife. These terms cannot be extended to spouse's kinsmen in the corresponding generation.

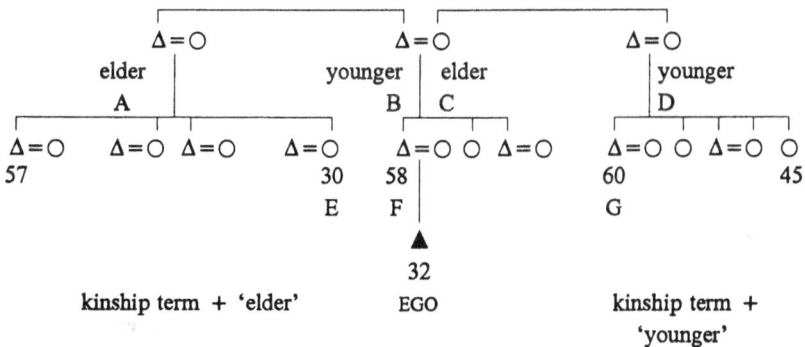

Fig. 5. Seniority terms and actual age

The term *amo* 'child' is the reciprocal of *aden, adie, amim,* and *afuf.* It indicates neither sex nor age and extends collaterally to any kinsman of the first descending generation (rule G). It also extends to stepchildren (rule S-). However, it does not extend to a child's spouse nor to the spouse of any other first descending generation kinsman.

Sibling Terms. There are three sibling terms. One is *aruig* which denotes ego's opposite sex sibling with no seniority indicated. The two terms used for same sex siblings distinguish seniority. One of these is *atagfad* 'same sex elder sibling' and the other is *agfut* 'same sex younger sibling'. If ego is male, all of his sisters are *aruig* while his older brother is *atagfad* and his younger brother is *agfut.*

These three terms extend collaterally in reference to any kinsman of ego's generation (rule G). Again, seniority in this generation is defined by the relative age of the pair of siblings who are the lineal kinsmen, linking ego and alter by being the children of ego's and alter's nearest common ancestor. These sibling terms are also extended (by rule S-S) to cosiblings-in-law (SPCS), that is, anyone married to ego's spouse's real siblings.

Affinal Kinship Terms

Figures 6 and 7 show Irarutu affinal kinship terms.

	Term	Primary Referent	Rough English Equivalent
Parent-in-law/	1. *agtamn*	SP (G, -S)	parent-in-law
child-in-law terms	2. *agetn*	CS (G, S-)	child-in-law
Sibling-in-law term	3. *arai (ataguf)*	SPC (R, G)	sibling-in-law
Spouse terms	4. *amran*	Sm	husband
	5. *asot*	Sf	wife

Fig. 6. Irarutu affinal terms of reference

Parent-in-law and Child-in-law Terms. Two terms are used, *agtamn* 'parent-in-law' and *agetn* 'child-in-law'. Both terms extend to collateral kinsmen of their respective generations (rule G). *agtamn* 'parent-in-law' further extends to persons who have married a kinsman of one's spouse on the parent generation (rule -S), e.g., a spouse's aunt's husband (SPPCSm). *agetn* 'child-in-law' also

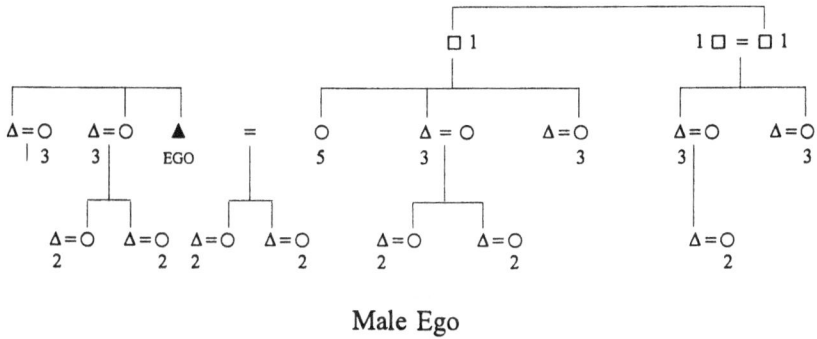

Male Ego

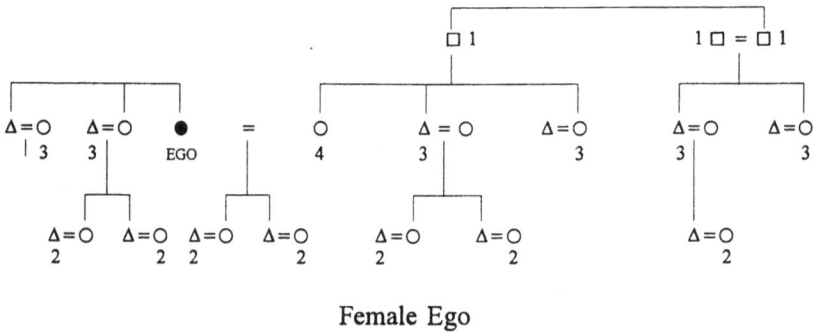

Female Ego

1. *agtamn*   3. *arai (ataguf)*   5. *asot*
2. *agetn*   4. *amran*

Fig. 7. Irarutu affinal system

extends to the spouse of spouse's child (rule S-), e.g., stepchild's wife (SCSf). These terms refer to both parallel and cross-kinsmen.

Sibling-in-law Terms. The term *arai* is used for any sibling-in-law, without distinction of either sex or seniority. This term extends collaterally (rule G) and reciprocally (rule R). *arai* is not extended to spouse's sibling's spouses. Instead, consanguineal sibling terms are used according to the person's sex and real age relative to ego. *arai* has a synonym, *ataguf.* No difference of use has been noted.[2]

---

[2]The neighboring Wandamen use the term *arai* for the first-person form of same sex sibling-in-law (Flaming 1983).

Spouse Terms. Words for man *(mran)* and woman *(sot)* are used with a
first person possessive marker *a-* to refer to husband and wife. These terms
are not extended to any other person. A man who has more than one wife
refers to them by adding the terms *fumta* 'first', *ntagr* 'next/second', or *mur*
'last' to *asot* 'my wife'. Cowives refer to each other as sisters, but often
continue to use the same term they used for each other before becoming
cowives.

In affinal relationships, as with cowives above, those who become related
affinally continue to refer to each other with the consanguineal kinship terms
they used before their affinal connection. For example, if ego's cousin
marries his uncle, ego continues to use the term *amim* 'uncle' even after he
becomes his brother-in-law.

However, when one marries his consanguineal kinsman, the consanguineal terms can no longer be used for spouse, child's spouse, or
parents-in-law. Instead, affinal terms are used to refer to each other. For
example, if a woman marries someone she calls *adie* 'father', she cannot use
that term anymore but must use the term *amran* 'husband'. If she had
previously called his parents *adat* 'grandparent', she must now use *agtamn*
'parent-in-law' to refer to them.

In Irarutu there are third person reference terms[3] for 'husband' and 'wife'
which are used with the spouse's name and with the third-person-possessive
affix, e.g., *Yacob iwabfin* 'Jacob's wife', *Yohana iwaman* 'Johanna's husband'. (I have also heard these terms used with second-person affixes as
terms of address.)

There is also a word *awag* that means 'spouse' with no distinction of sex.

Kinship Behavior

The basic ideal in Irarutu kinship relations is sharing material things and
helping each other. This ideal is in fact extended to everyone in one's
village. When, for example, a man shoots a wild pig, he shares the meat with
everyone in his village. He dare not divide it only with his kinsmen.

An Irarutu man once told me, "If someone saw me take a piece of meat
to someone else and I don't give him any, he will get upset. So only my
parents and someone who happens to be at my house can have the portions.

---

[3]Third-person terms of reference have been described in other languages of Irian Jaya
(Erickson 1976)

If I have more than what my family can eat, then I must share with everyone in my village, even though they only get small portions."

The work load is shared with other men whom ego calls brother—real or extended—who may not be in the same clan but who live in the same village. Thus, jobs such as building a house or a canoe, clearing a field, or making garden fences are often shared by all members of the village.

Taking care of children is the parent's responsibility. A father takes his sons along when he hunts pigs or deer. He teaches them how to use spears, how to make a canoe, how to pound sago, etc. Other men that a boy refers to as his 'father', 'uncle', or 'grandfather' occasionally teach him as well. However, there is no obligation for them to teach collateral relatives.

A mother teaches her daughters how to make a fire, how to cook, how to keep gardens, how to fish, how to weave baskets and mats, how to pound sago, etc.

Mother's Brother–Sister's Oldest Child. In Irarutu one particular dyad is associated with special rights and obligations, i.e., the relationship between mother's brother *(imim)* and sister's first-born child *(imo)*. This is not so much a reciprocal relationship but is more a ceremonial obligation for mother's brother.

When a first child is born, the mother's oldest brother prepares a feast. If the child is a boy, the feast is celebrated on the fifth day; if it is a girl, it is held one day earlier. A mother gives birth in a small temporary hut, where the mother and child will stay until this feast is almost over. The parents' relatives and their entire village come to the parents' regular house and eat together. They sing and dance all night. A little before dawn the child's uncle ceremonially ties a string on the child's wrists. Then the child is carried by the father's sister to the parents' house. The child's mother, grandmothers, and aunts join in the procession. When the child is brought into the house, the feast is over.

When the child reaches one or two months of age, the uncle prepares a second feast. Here again, there is feasting, singing, and dancing until dawn. On that morning the uncle cuts the string from the child's wrists and ties a string with two big antique beads around the child's neck.

When the child reaches one or two years of age, the uncle prepares a third feast. Again, the people feast, sing, and dance until dawn. On that morning the uncle cuts the string from the child's neck and a little hair from the child's forehead with a razor blade. Then he gives the child a piece of wild pork. Before this time wild pork has been taboo for both the child and mother to eat. At each of these three feasts the child's parents give a small gift to mother's brother to thank him for fulfilling this custom.

Traditionally, about one year after the third feast, the uncle prepares another feast. He does so with a pig he himself has raised. At the beginning of the celebration, the uncle paints the child's face with ashes. The child is first placed on the back of the pig and the uncle takes a sharp piece of wood and pierces the child's septum. Next he places a white plate on the head of the pig and breaks it with a hammer or a piece of heavy wood. An Irarutu says this act is a way of confessing for killing his own tame pig, but further study is needed to find out the reason for this practice. With the next blow he kills the pig, and the child is taken off the pig's back. People pour hot water over the pig, take the hair and skin off with shells, and then cook the animal. The uncle takes the child to a large stilt house which is used for various feasts. There the child's grandmothers dance to songs accompanied by drums. Holding long stalks of sugarcane in their hands, they pretend to spear pictures of food which are taboo for the child to eat. These taboo foods may include meat of pigs, crocodiles, cassowaries, large lizard, turtles, various species of fish, and certain kinds of sugarcane. As people eat the cooked pork and other food, the uncle gives a piece of pork to the child. This act is his initiation to eating the meat of tame pigs. Again there is singing and dancing until dawn. However, this ceremony is now seldom practiced.

These days a substitution for the ceremony is done just before the child's marriage, and for the guests' convenience it is held the day before the wedding ceremony. The uncle takes a sago stalk and merely measures the child's nose with it. The child's grandmothers dance as described above. Then as people eat, the uncle gives the child a piece of tabooed fish or tabooed sugarcane. This ceremony represents the termination of all food taboos. After the feast the child's father gives gifts again to the mother's brother. This time the gifts, though unrelated to the bride price transactions simultaneously in process, are constituted of the same sort of objects as the bride price.

The mother's brother–sister's child dyad is based on caring and trusting. The mother's brother takes care of the child in regard to matters such as food taboo, and his sister's child trusts him completely, even allowing his uncle to cut some of his hair (a favorite object for use in sorcery).

Marriage

The biggest event in an Irarutu's life is his wedding. More than at any other time his kinsmen are involved in preparing and celebrating this occasion.

The Irarutu say a person can marry anyone he wants to marry. The only restriction is against marrying someone with whom he can trace a consanguineal connection. One Irarutu told me that his daughter cannot marry anyone who shares a common ancestor up to the fourth ascending generation. He told me, however, that his daughter's child may marry his sibling's grandchild. He also has a classificatory sister who married a man whom she called "father." (Her fourth ascending lineal ancestor is her husband's third ascending lineal ancestor.) When asked if such a marriage is acceptable, the language associate said that it was "because both of them wanted to get married, even though they are a little too closely related." It should be noted that it is not unusual for a man to marry someone he calls *aruig* 'sister'.

A man is considered ready for marriage when he knows how to make a canoe and a house, to hunt wild pigs or deer, to spear fish, and to make a garden. A man usually gets married around twenty-three or twenty-four years of age, while a woman marries at about twenty years of age.

In choosing a wife, the Irarutu tell me that two important qualifications are that she should be an Irarutu and that she be an adherent of a major religion, i.e., Protestant, Roman Catholic, or Muslim, preferably of the same persuasion as the prospective groom. However, there are a few exceptions to these ideals.

Irarutu Marriage Patterns

Among the Irarutu it is customary for a man to find a wife for his son. To do so, he normally looks first in his own village, but if no suitable daughter-in-law is found there, he looks elsewhere in the wider village complex. If he fails there, he will look in other nearby village complexes. As a last resort he goes farther afield to even more distant Irarutu village complexes until he finds a suitable woman to be his daughter-in-law. The process may be diagrammed as in figure 8.

The search for a wife begins in the center of ego's world, his own village (1). If no suitable woman is found, the search continues in an ever widening circle, as shown in the diagram, 1→2→3→4. Though a few (only 3 percent in my sample) take wives from outside the language group, this practice is not the preferred arrangement.

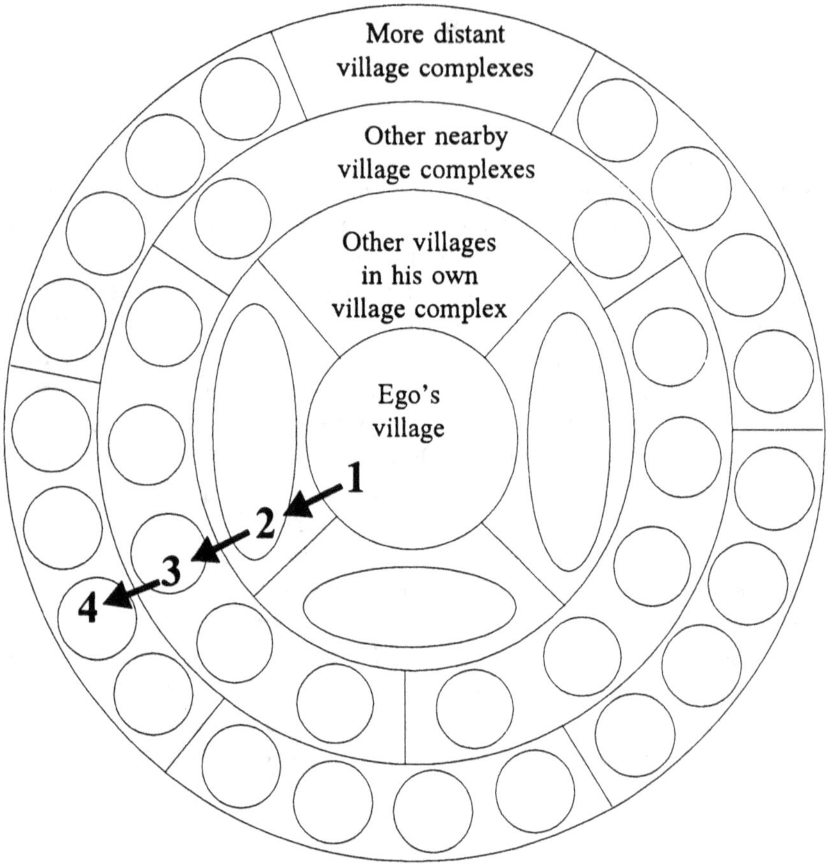

Figure 8. The process of finding a wife

Table 2 summarizes the distribution of marriages in the Tugarni village complex according to clan. Out of ninety-eight married men[4] in the five villages of the complex, sixteen men married women of their own clans. In each of the six clans which had nine or more members who were married men, the wives came from between five and eight other clans. These clans included the seven living in Tugarni village complex as well as the Wania

---

[4]Eight men have two wives and two men have three wives in the Tugarni village complex.

WIFE'S CLAN

HUSBAND'S CLAN	Syakema	Wayara	Sasefa	Refideso	Werfete	Bari	Nega	Wania	Other	Total
Syakema	4	0	2	1	2	2	2	3	1	17
Wayara	1	0	0	0	0	0	0	0	0	1
Sasefa	1	0	0	0	6	1	1	1	1	11
Refideso	3	1	1	4	2	2	1	1	1	16
Werfete	4	0	0	1	3	8	2	1	1	20
Bari	2	1	1	3	9	3	0	2	3	24
Nega	1	0	1	1	1	3	2	0	0	9
Total	16	2	5	10	23	19	8	8	7	98

Table 2. Marriage distribution by clan
in the Tugarni village complex

clan from Burgerba, the nearest village to Tugarni. The result is that each clan has affinal connections with most of the other clans in the area.

The data regarding marriages between men and women of different villages (see table 3) reveal that twenty-seven out of ninety-eight men in the Tugarni village complex took wives from their own villages. In addition, with only one exception, men from each of the five villages in the complex married women from each of the other four Tugarni villages as well as from the nearby village of Burgerba. (The only exception is that no man from Moyana took a wife from Bayeda.) The overall pattern therefore reveals strong affinal connections between all of the six villages as shown in table 3. Only four wives came from other Irarutu villages and three from other language groups.

Arranging a Marriage. The father of the prospective groom typically looks for a woman who has a good nature, listens to her parents, and is eager to help her parents, brothers, and sisters. After she gets married, it is hoped she will likewise take good care of her new family and listen to her husband and his parents.

Once the father finds a woman, he asks for his son's consent. If his son agrees, the father goes to the woman's father and asks for her, giving a small gift such as a pair of earrings. Then the father of the prospective bride asks his wife and daughter. If he gets their consent, he will inform the father of the prospective groom. If his daughter does not want to marry the man, she is allowed the privilege of refusing.

WIFE'S VILLAGE

HUSBAND'S VILLAGE	Afu-afu	Gusimawa	Bayeda	Moyana	Kokoroba	Burgerba	Other	Total
Afu-afu	5	2	4	1	1	4	1	18
Gusimawa	5	4	3	1	3	2	1	19
Bayeda	1	3	7	1	6	2	1	21
Moyana	2	5	0	2	3	2	0	14
Kokoroba	4	2	1	5	9	1	4	26
Total	17	16	15	10	22	11	7	98

Table 3. Marriage distribution by village
in the Tugarni village complex

Getting consent is important. Neither the bride nor the groom are forced to marry against their will. An Irarutu man expressed it this way, "If a father forces his son to get married, ignoring the son's desires, he will have trouble. Therefore he makes sure to get his son's consent."

Currently, some men find their wives by themselves without their father's help, but the other procedures are still followed.

When the groom's father gets the consent of the couple, he tells the headman of his village. Then the bride price is prepared. This payment, which is set by the bride's father, will be collected with the help of the groom's kinsmen and the people of his village, although the latter need not be from the same clan.

Bride Price

The bride price generally includes a few large antique plates, dozens of modern china dishes, a pair of gold earrings, a bracelet, and batik cloth. Sometimes money, a canoe, or an old cannon is included. We were told that the large antique plates and the old cannons were originally brought from Europe, the latter perhaps being of Portuguese origin. These two items constitute a very important part of bride price, as they do among the neighboring Mairasi (Peckham 1983:265). However, some of these items have by now been broken or sold for cash, making it difficult to require them in the bride price because of their current limited quantity.

In one case a man was asked to find a cannon and two large antique plates as well as other items. Unable to find them, he promised to procure them in the future and was allowed to marry. Four years later, he was still looking for them. It is possible, in fact, that he would need to substitute another payment, such as making a canoe or a new garden for his father-in-law. His brother said, "People used to give a large amount of bride price, but now it is getting less and less. Bride price gives a man a headache. For my daughter I might only ask for a canoe or a new garden."

In another case a man of the Werfete clan who married seven years ago gave three large antique plates, seven pairs of earrings, 10 dozen china dishes, 20,000 Rupiah cash, several pieces of cloth, clothing, and a large canoe for a bride price. Some of those who contributed are listed in figure 9, but so many people contributed items that he can no longer remember who contributed each of the less expensive items.

As figure 9 shows, not only the kinsmen of the groom's own clan but also kinsmen in other clans contributed items for the bride price. All of the contributors, however, were from his own village.

The bride price is received by the bride's father. He saves some for himself and the rest is distributed to his relatives and friends who helped him when he got married; more than half of the bride price goes to repay them for their help. People ask for their share until they are satisfied. Consequently, it is difficult to change the traditional bride price system rapidly.

Item	Contributed by	Clan
Large old plate	married real sister	Werfete
" " "	extended brother FBS	Werfete
" " "	himself	Werfete
Earrings (3pr.)	real father	Werfete
" (1pr.)	extended uncle FMBDH	Bali (non-Irarutu)
" (1pr.)	extended aunt FMFBSD	Wania
" (1pr.)	extended father FMZS	Nega
" (1pr.)	extended brother ?	Nega
Canoe	himself, extended brothers	

Fig. 9. Contributors of bride price

The Wedding Ceremony

The night before the actual wedding ceremony starts, the bride and the
groom celebrate with peers at their respective houses, singing and dancing
until the next morning. If the bride or the groom is a first-born child, then
he or she must have the "measuring nose" ceremony. It is held by his or her
mother's brother as discussed above.

The next morning all the women of the bride's village prepare food for the
feast. Many men help by gathering firewood and fetching water as well as
by hunting pigs or deer.

In the early afternoon they have a ceremony at church. Often a pastor is
invited from the closest village to give a short sermon and pronounce them
man and wife.

In the late afternoon, two of the groom's sisters take him to the bride's
house, each holding one of his hands, accompanied by his parents, relatives,
and all the rest of the villagers. They have a traditional marriage ceremony
there. The bride lights a cigarette and the groom and their sisters smoke from
the same cigarette. After the ceremony the groom takes the bride to the large
temporary structure that he, with the help of his brothers and friends, built
especially for the occasion. The groom and the bride sit on a small stage
decorated with coconut leaves and batik cloth at one end of the house. Then
the guests come into the house.

Usually the headman of the village complex and the headmen from both
the groom's and the bride's villages offer words of advice to the young
couple. Guests who have come from distant villages often get a chance to
give advice too. Then a meal of rice and meat is served to everyone. Sweet
tea, fried bananas, and sometimes cake are served for the dessert.

After the meal all the guests shake hands with the groom and the bride.
Then they dance to music and/or drums, the bride and groom joining the
dance. Most guests stay until dawn.

The next morning the bride and groom both return with their parents to
their respective houses. Then the groom brings the bride price to the large
temporary structure. There the bride's father receives it, and if any items
which he asked as bride price are missing, he asks the groom to bring them
quickly. If the groom does not have the items, he promises to give the items
later.

The bride's father then shares the bride price with his relatives and friends
who helped him when he got married. Some of them in fact insist on getting
back the same item as the one they gave at some prior exchange. But often

substitutions are made because the entire amount of the bride price is increasing.

After all these events the bride is escorted to the groom's parents' house by her parents, brothers, and sisters. If the bride's house is on the other side of the bay, the groom stays at her parent's house for three or four days. Then he returns to his parent's house with his new wife.

Conclusion

Almost all Irarutu village members are related to each other through lineal or affinal connections. Even though there are a number of clans in each village, everyone is considered a close part of the group. Irarutu people consider the village unit to be a framework for their behavior. In their basic concept of kinship relationships, sharing and helping is very important.

References

Bateman, Janet. 1983. Iau kinship and marriage. In Merrifield, Gregerson, and Ajamiseba, 191–220.

Erickson, Carol. 1976. Isirawa kinship and exchange marriage. Irian: Bulletin of Irian Jaya 5(1):22–44.

Flaming, Rachel. 1983. Wandamen kinship terminology. In Merrifield, Gregerson, and Ajamiseba, 244–53.

Lounsbury, Floyd G. 1964. The structural analysis of kinship semantics. In Horace G. Lunt (ed.), Proceedings of the Ninth International Congress of Linguists, Cambridge, Mass., 27–31 August, 1962, 1073–93. The Hague: Mouton.

Merrifield, William R. 1983a. On the formal analysis of kinship terminologies. In Frederick B. Agard, Gerald Kelly, Adam Makkai, and Valerie Becker Makkai (eds.), Essays in honor of Charles F. Hockett, 371–404. Leiden: E. J. Brill.

———. 1983b. Comments on kinship notation. In Merrifield, Gregerson, and Ajamiseba, 177–88.

————, Marilyn Gregerson, and Daniel C. Ajamiseba, eds. 1983. Gods, heroes, kinsmen: Ethnographic studies from Irian Jaya, Indonesia. International Museum of Cultures Publication 17. Dallas: Cenderawasih University and The International Museum of Cultures.

Peckham, Nancy. 1983. Mairasi kinship and marriage. In Merrifield, Gregerson, and Ajamiseba, 254–70.

www.ingramcontent.com/pod-product-compliance
Lightning Source LLC
Chambersburg PA
CBHW050421280326
41932CB00013BA/1941